PASS IT ON

This book is meant to be passed on.
Sign and share with support.

*You can do it all,
not at the same time,
and not alone.*

Praise for *Carry Strong*

"I wish I had *Carry Strong* as a companion when I first entered my life phase of mothering. Yet it still resonates with me and should be read by everyone who is a caretaker. Kramer anchors her research in profoundly personal stories and comes up with a glorious road map for navigating work and parenthood. A must read."
—Eve Rodsky, author of *Fair Play* and *Find Your Unicorn Space*

"Navigating the stages of pregnancy and balancing a career while pregnant can be daunting. Stephanie tackles all the ups and downs by sharing the moving personal experiences from a breadth of individuals, as well as her own motherhood journey and the career balancing act that came along with it."
—Katherine Schwarzenegger Pratt, author of *The Gift of Forgiveness* and creator, BDA Baby™

"A deeply relevant and inspirational guide to navigating one of the most uncertain periods of a woman's career—and coming out the other side feeling stronger and more confident than ever."
—Arianna Huffington, founder and CEO, Thrive Global

"*Carry Strong* flips the script on pregnancy at work from secretive and stressful to an opportunity for growth. Covering everything from fertility struggles and loss to the invisible and visible phases of pregnancy, it's packed with vulnerable stories and strategies to help set boundaries, focus, navigate tough conversations, and create the career and family that is right for you."
—Leslie Schrock, author of *Bumpin'* and *Fertility Rules*

"Embracing the best of both worlds begins in pregnancy. In this empowering and encouraging book, Stephanie shares how real, ambitious women have navigated the journey toward birth and working parenthood, and emerged stronger on the other side."
—Laura Vanderkam, author of *I Know How She Does It*

"I plan to give *Carry Strong* to every woman I know who is pregnant or considering becoming so. By reframing both working pregnancy and working motherhood as opportunities to also grow and deepen our professional lives, Stephanie has done a great service. Magnificent!"
—Sally Helgesen, author, *How Women Rise* and *Rising Together*

"*Carry Strong* is an important reflection of real women and real life and real stories—an authentic reference for the most exciting and anxious time in a woman's life."

—Libby Wadle, CEO, J.Crew and Madewell

"In *Carry Strong*, Stephanie Kramer normalizes the challenges that so many women face in the workplace, from considering a pregnancy through being a working mother. Kramer offers a refreshing perspective based on research and anecdotes on how we can harness the power of motherhood to achieve personal and professional success."

—Sarah Oreck, MD MS, reproductive psychiatrist

"*Carry Strong* is the missing link between books that celebrate the new feminism and bemoan the challenges that mothers, particularly those of us in the paid workforce, still face. If we normalize, document, and celebrate every stage of parenthood, including pre-conception planning, then caregiving will become better supported in our society."

—Leslie Forde, CEO and founder, Mom's Hierarchy of Needs

"Stephanie has forged a new path for women in the workplace, who often grapple with pregnancy, fertility struggles, and loss privately. Rooted in research and loaded with compelling stories, *Carry Strong* should be required reading for the future of work."

—Claudia Reuter, author of *Yes, You Can Do This!* and host of *The 43 Percent* podcast

"*Carry Strong* is creating a balanced conversation and important progress for Gen Z around pregnancy and work, ourselves included."

—Lola McAllister and Pilar McDonald, cofounders, Project Matriarchs

"*Carry Strong* is the right mix of inspiration and perspiration that will change the way we look at pregnancy and work as concurrent to our careers. It gives words and tools for something we don't talk about—with heart."

—Joan Kuhl, author of *Dig Your Heels In*

"This is the book I wish I would have had when I was pregnant with my daughter. I'll be adding it to every baby shower gift from now on! There is a wealth of books about motherhood, but Stephanie's focuses on the critical intersection of the workplace and new motherhood. Our identities as mothers and as professionals get so mixed up during this time and Stephanie guides us through, names the feelings and phases, and shares the stories of women who have gotten through the 'messy middle' of blending those identities."

—Aya Kanai, head of editorial and creative, Google Shopping

"*Carry Strong* is an important and necessary reimagining of pre-conception, pregnancy, and work, drawing on robust research and compelling personal stories. Stephanie's narrative-centered approach amplifies the voices of those who have gone through it to help create a powerful blueprint for others."

—Kimberly Seals Allers, author of
The Big Letdown and founder, Irth App

"*Carry Strong* is a must-read for women seeking to balance the rewards and challenges of pregnancy alongside their developing careers. Stephanie Kramer inspires readers to unlock their potential at this pivotal moment in their personal and professional lives with a truly empowered approach."

—Keith Ferrazzi, author of *Competing in the New World of Work*
and *Never Eat Alone*, founder and CEO of Ferrazzi Greenlight

"*Carry Strong* is a powerful and thoughtful dive into navigating the complex situations women face in pregnancy for their careers. Full of authenticity, Stephanie's stories and research will help women everywhere shape the future of the workplace and break down the barriers for these critical conversations."

—Dr. Marshall Goldsmith, executive coach and
author of *The Earned Life*, *Triggers*, and
What Got You Here Won't Get You There

PENGUIN LIFE

CARRY STRONG

Stephanie Kramer is a beauty industry executive. She teaches management communication for the graduate business program at the Fashion Institute of Technology and serves on the program's Industry Advisory Board. Stephanie has two young children.

CARRY STRONG

AN **EMPOWERED** APPROACH TO

NAVIGATING **PREGNANCY**

AND WORK

STEPHANIE KRAMER

life

PENGUIN BOOKS

An imprint of Penguin Random House LLC
penguinrandomhouse.com

A Penguin Life Book

ISBN 9780143137283 (paperback)
ISBN 9780593511244 (ebook)

Printed in the United States of America
1st Printing

Set in Macklin Text
Designed by Sabrina Bowers

To Sue and Cooper

In honor of working mothers with pride and gratitude.

To William and James

Becoming your mother empowered me so others could be too.

Contents

PART II
The Five Carry Strong Phases

Author's Note

I WANT YOU TO KNOW that while I use the terms "woman" or "working mother" throughout the book, the research I conducted was with self-identifying women or gender nonconforming individuals. I also recognize that all mothers work, whether or not they work outside their homes. My hope is eventually to no longer need the "working mother" title at all, that it will be just part of who you are. We don't often call dads "working fathers" unless we're talking about "working parents" and what affects both partners. But for now, I find it helpful to delineate "working mother" as the term the women I interviewed often use to talk about themselves as a group.

Notably, this book is focused on support for non–primarily manual-labor-intensive roles and centered on the physical pregnancy of female-identifying birthing persons. There are stories included of other ways women became working mothers, and this book may be helpful to those who will not undertake physical pregnancy by choice or by necessity. Yet literature and resources related to, for example, adoption and surrogacy are unique and require their own dedicated space.

Lastly, this is not the only book you should read while you are pregnant. Practical medical advice, specific legal regulations, guidance on exercise and diet, and preparations for labor and your newborn are paramount. The most important thing through all of this? Your health and the health of your baby. I am hopeful that *Carry Strong* will be a resource to support you in this journey and guide one facet of it: pregnancy and work.

Introduction

PREGNANCY *IS* WORK, but as you build your career while you grow your family, it is more than a milestone. It is monumental. The importance of this journey is something to recognize, to normalize, and to celebrate. Now is the time to unburden your confidence, broaden your perspective, and unlock your potential for the journey to working motherhood, to Carry Strong and create your future.

Long before you consider how to tell your boss you're pregnant, the intersection of pregnancy and work is powerful. This is a unique moment of remarkable capability and vulnerability, but it is also the reality of the "fertility gap," before you even think about it—and the moment you do. You or your colleagues could be pregnant at work for years without giving birth, or could be pregnant before you even considered the possibility of an impact to your career. This intersection may mean retroplanning a promotion conversation with your body temperature, secretly taking your fertility injections on a work trip in dry ice that melts over the Atlantic, or searching "Am I having a miscarriage?" from the office bathroom and scrolling for the conclusion of a long-archived message board thread.

Pregnancy and work may also look like successfully interviewing for two and exhaling your baby bump after a long day of sucking it in—both done with pride. It can mean you become an entrepreneur and a mother in the same year. It can feel not only like the weight of pregnancy bias, but also like the additional layered burden of racial inequity. It may mean you choose the ideal health care or a better salary over work that you love, postponing getting pregnant because of your responsibilities during a global crisis, or announcing your pregnancy with two weeks to go because of a pandemic.

The physical pregnancy of your child may represent 2 percent of your career, but the impact and profundity are far greater. Pregnancy is a time of private crucible moments, which often happen in a crucial (and critical) public window. At their best, they are empowering. At their worst, they are overwhelming and isolating, but one thing is for certain—they are going to happen. These moments can change your professional course or, at the minimum, the way you approach your work. And yet today support may be buried in one of the ten thousands of "pregnancy and work" online searches a month. Or, if shared beyond your private thoughts, support often emerges one-on-one, behind closed doors. We don't talk about it, but it's time we do and with enthusiasm.

While we are aware of the real and perceived challenges of pregnancy—and that pregnancy itself is just one facet of motherhood that can hold us back in the workplace—it is never positioned as an opportunity, rather than an obstacle to be overcome with our ambition. But it should be. Your journey to motherhood is not something to "get through," or a time to keep your fingers crossed that "it won't throw everything off." Each moment carries weight individually and cumulatively as a pivotal part of your career.

It's time to flip the script and Carry Strong.

Carry Strong seeks to change the narrative around pregnancy and work, considering both the very real challenges *and* opportunities, unburdening today's women, who often unconsciously plan their careers around their fertility. What to expect? A new way to navigate your childbearing years at work with a pragmatic and optimistic perspective on a cultural constant. You may have heard the saying "Just because you carry something well, doesn't mean it isn't heavy." This book encourages you to carry your someday bumps with a positive tilt, even if your hands are on your lower back. But most importantly, in sharing a balanced approach packed with tangible tools and lived experiences, it seeks to propel you forward on your personal journey. The objective: to not only *normalize* pregnancy and work, but to celebrate motherhood as *concurrent* to our careers.

In September 2020, I conducted a survey of 400 women who worked full time for the entirety of their pregnancies. This was the first of four comprehensive quantitative research studies encompassing 1,350 individuals, which fueled my quest to rethink pregnancy and work. One of the highlights: of the women who experienced any reported change in their work life during pregnancy, 69 percent said their confidence increased and 80 percent of those women said they worked harder—a direct correlation of confidence and effort.[1]

In addition, I also conducted more than two hundred qualitative interviews of a unique collective of contributors, many of whom are women I admire, utilizing a consistent set of questions based around their own stories of pregnancy and work. Their stories bring to life the data in core themes you will see throughout the book, but most of all they fuel the pages with motivating, self-reflective, and deeply humanizing moments. Some women shared that "mommy brain," often a shorthand for mental fog, lack of focus, and exhaustion, can be a gift. They reported that their altered consciousness unleashed reserves of creativity, "crazy superhero strength," and a newfound purpose in life (and work). Even in the darkest and most dire stories of pregnancy and work, women reflected on themselves as "badasses" or "warriors." In response to the question "In hindsight, who would you like to thank for support during this time?" one creative director definitively responded, "Myself." This change in confidence and conviction during pregnancy at work, along with significantly noted decisiveness, proactivity, and empathy, are commonly attributed to characteristics that set successful leaders of all genders apart.[2]

Throughout my research for this book, I also heard of specific moments of self-doubt from otherwise incredibly self-assured women. Others discovered a newfound courage in the unknown, a release from the illusion of control, and even a "catharsis" of their previously untapped potential. In this unique time in your life, there may be surprising moments of weakness as well as unprecedented strength, something that can be unlocked within you—something that gives you prevailing clarity as you both change and stay very much who you are. There is drive, courage, and compassion in becoming a working mother. My hope is that, for you, *Carry Strong* will encourage this power when you need it, or at the minimum will keep you in neutral, but most of all will help you recognize that this is not business as usual.

Normalizing and navigating pregnancy at work is about you, but it's also about the big picture. Windsor Hanger Western, cofounder, president, and publisher of Her Campus Media, shares, "Today 57 percent of bachelor's degrees are being awarded to women and women outnumber men earning master's and doctoral degrees, and yet when you look at the S&P 500, only 6 percent of CEOs are women. We're making progress but still have a long way to go when it comes to attaining gender balance and pay equity." Pregnancy is a key point of attrition in the workplace for women. What if, before, during, and after baby, there was a focus on your retention, one that could create a positive ripple effect beyond your pregnancy for the rest of your career and for the pipeline of women around you?

Today women represent half of the workforce.[3] More than 60 percent of women work during pregnancy. That number was just 17 percent in the early 1960s."[4] This number grows to 87 percent for women who have a bachelor's degree or higher.[5] Overall, 82 percent of female workers pregnant with their first child continued to work until they were within one month of their due date. There are 35 million working mothers in the United States. By 2026, 80 percent of millennials will be parents.[6] Being pregnant at work is a very normal experience, yet demands a fresh perspective and a closer look, especially now.

In the first year of the COVID-19 pandemic, more than 2.3 million women in the United States left the labor force.[7] While we are making gains, we are still recovering three years later from the loss of jobs by women.[8] One of the highlighted factors: the ongoing impact of caregiving, including a starting point, pregnancy. In parallel, we have all just experienced the greatest evolution of the way we work in the past hundred years—a paradigm shift. The pandemic jolted us to take a closer look at employee expectations for employers and for ourselves—including how we want to spend our time and energy *beyond* work, and with our families. By benefiting (and demanded by) all genders, the inclusive adaptation of new flexibility models can help destigmatize alternative ways of work. The added benefit: a heightened visibility on unpaid labor. Notably, the United States remains the only industrialized country without paid family leave.[9]

Every moment counts, and now is the time. It is imperative to have engaged pregnant women and returning mothers in our workforce. You represent an opportunity to equalize the gender wage gap, support pipeline attrition, and grow the economy. If a woman works full time during pregnancy, there is an increased likelihood of her returning to work after birth, and of that return being sooner than if she did not work full time throughout her entire pregnancy.[10] Working mothers are more productive than nonmothers who work and, over the course of their career, outperform their counterparts.[11] There are hurdles to anticipate, recognize, and eliminate, but there are also tremendous rewards and results. The key point—awareness with optimism, not an alternate reality. I recognize that throughout your pregnancy this book may only be the tip of the iceberg or something to throw when it all seems too much, but we all have a role to play.

MY STORY

I am the mother of two young sons. With a lot of hard work and plenty of good fortune, I am an executive of a large beauty organization and an adjunct professor in a master's degree program. Both William and James were conceived and born while I was working in dream jobs full time, in supportive companies with incredible leaders. In fact, during my road to my second pregnancy and through it, I even had an awesome executive coach. I recognize my privilege and that this experience was extremely rare and therefore must be used as an opportunity to help others, because it shouldn't be.

While in hindsight and at ten thousand feet I realize I navigated my career through this the crucial window with grace and fortitude, it didn't always feel that way. I had moments when I felt afraid, stuck, anxious, but also fueled, thoughtful, and ambitious—often within the same hour. I was conflicted before, during, and after my pregnancy about something that is both normal and miraculous, having a baby, and what that would do to my career. If *I* felt this way with my resources and environment, then I knew I needed to do something about it for others—and it needed to be significant in order to move the needle.

While I have memories of mixing potions in my bathroom at a young age and winning the science fair for a project called "Skin Science," foreshadowing my career aspirations, my first memories of wanting to become a mother came a bit later. I vividly remember being very nervous about someday being able to breastfeed, because I was teased about my flat chest in middle school, when the letters on my cheerleading uniform fell low on my stomach until my mom resewed my jumper. (Cut to my engorged cantaloupes after William was born—painful, but vindicated.)

In high school anatomy, I considered what type of doctor I could be and still have "reasonable" work hours, leaving time for a family. I certainly thought about becoming a working mother when I chose my major, chemistry. Still, in 2021, one out of two college women made this consideration when picking their major.[12]

Personally, I was even more conscious of the "ticking clock" in my belly ten years later, the year I completed graduate school and got married, I also made a career move from one company to another. I did this because it was an incredible opportunity, but also because I felt I had a window to get all my ducks in a row and establish myself in a new job before we would try to get pregnant sometime after our first anniversary.

One week before this date, I almost lost my husband to extreme hyponatremia suffered after an Ironman race. As his wife, I was thrust into the unthinkable act of permitting him to be intubated in the emergency room as he seized despite being unconscious. I was sat down by the head of a large New York hospital and asked about my religion so they could be prepared to give last rites, "should they be necessary." They also asked me if we had children or if I was pregnant. I remember where I was sitting, and even which direction I was looking, when I answered no, and was told, "It's a good thing that you don't."

That same week, my boss and my boss's boss were on vacation. I was reporting directly to our president. The gracious expectation had been to use the moment to shine as a relatively new employee, but after two days (which would become more than two weeks) of keeping my head down and barely holding on while my husband was in critical condition, I walked into her office and revealed to her what was happening, the air in my chest held captive. With a calm, reassuring strength, she said, "Go."

With many thanks to the tremendous team of medical professionals and a community of support, my husband made a miraculous recovery and gingerly walked out of the hospital with only my help. Our relationship bond accelerated, but our pregnancy timeline was put on pause, cautiously waiting for my husband to be cleared by his physicians. I remember a mixed undercurrent of worry creeping into my mind when someone asked, "When are you going to have kids?" because I realized how much it was something we wanted, not just a milestone or expected next step. I kept my head down at work, focusing on what I could control and grateful for developing relationships with mentors, advocates, and friends. Motherhood ebbed into our work conversations, observed through them as a positive possibility, and that reinforced our desire. Another year later, I was finally pregnant. We were elated.

Despite the magnitude of what we had just experienced, I remember trying to time my pregnancy just right to "only miss" a quieter time at work, scratching retrotiming dates in my notebook when someone would share something on our horizon. Though getting pregnant took much longer than expected, it serendipitously happened in one of those windows. I walked across the street to my office building with my hand on my nonexistent belly. I carefully made discreet markers on my calendar to anticipate when to share news before midyear reviews were finalized. I poured out drinks in the bathroom at happy hour and couldn't have enjoyed it more: a precious secret. At thirty-one, this was all I knew about how to navigate pregnancy and work.

Our pregnancy was our light at the end of the tunnel, but I kept it to myself. In fact, the only other person who knew I was pregnant besides my husband was the cashier at the Upper West Side Barnes & Noble who rang up my pregnancy books. I hid them in that drawer in our apartment where you hide things. God forbid someone saw them. I had an app loaded on my phone that described the size of my baby as a fruit, and our "little blueberry" was ready for its first appointment, snuck in on a Friday afternoon. We took a photo outside the doctor's office. I wore a dress.

The appointment did not go as planned. The uncomfortable ultrasound showed a slow blip of our baby's heartbeat with a minuscule likelihood to continue. I remember my disbelief. For weeks at work thereafter, I distinctly remember not carrying any extra weight to set up for meetings, making extra trips. I skipped events with guilt and was extra consumed with my thoughts. It all felt so tenuous. At the end of my first trimester, I suffered a miscarriage that started while I was at my desk. I remember the inevitability I felt after so much hope. Darting between the bathroom and staring at my monitor (but not reading anything), I grabbed my laptop and went to tell my boss I was ill. Later, she told me I had been white as a ghost.

In the time that followed, work felt reliable and a way to feel normal and capable again. But it also felt like I was suppressing my reality, and in most instances, just going through the motions—or ready to be triggered. At a company Halloween party where everyone brought their kids, I had to leave and sobbed on a street corner. I confided to two colleague-friends when I came back inside with puffy eyes. They supported me in that moment. They supported me months later when I finally shared the happy news that I was pregnant again, at a whopping twenty-four weeks. They still do today.

I now recognize that I hid both of my pregnancies for way too long at work. I was protecting my privacy, especially after loss, and I was also worried about what it would signal to those around me. I had a lot of pride, too much I felt I needed to accomplish, and a lot of guilt. My expectations were incredibly high for myself, which is a common theme for pregnant women at work—and women everywhere.

I remember thinking that I would feel like Beyoncé in that moment when I would finally share *my* news. I would wear a tight shirt into the office and show people my bump, radiating joy. While it was, in fact, a huge relief, I also had a total panic. Along with the celebration around me (because it could not have been a happier place to be pregnant), I also received questions about my due date and what that would mean for travel, big projects, and my team members. These were normal questions, not intended to provoke me. I had thought about all those things, but not about how it would make me feel when I was asked for answers. Fear, uncertainty, and pressure crept into my confident joy. I hadn't realized how much I was carrying. What we all carry.

One thing to know about me and my career is that I credit my growth to being willing to say yes to any menial task or challenging project, and to exceed expectations if I just work harder. I wanted to be an ambassadress of "leaning in." At work, I hadn't yet learned how it felt to have to say no, not because I wanted to, but because I had to. So, with my feelings of pure happiness at being pregnant, and the release of not hiding it, I also felt this weight of the inevitable nos I would have to give and what that meant for my career. It was, excuse my language, a mindfuck. I told my mom that night to stop telling people I was pregnant because I didn't want any more questions.

I have those tough visual moments from my pregnancy ingrained in my brain, but I also have some that were radiant. Moments when sadness and fear swung the other way and I decided to "own it" and embrace my pregnancy at work. I remember giving a communication presentation to interns at thirty-eight weeks, teetering in heels and calling out that fact to them: "This is the last thing I'm doing at work before I have my baby, and I'm so glad it's with all of you."

That night I sent an email to my future second child (versus the sweet, detailed journal I wrote with my first son), capturing all that we had done together already and how much I couldn't wait to do *with* him. I felt brave and bold *while* I was scared and hesitant—recognizing that strength was liberating and galvanizing. I started to recognize that my pregnancy at work had pushed me to learn perspective and balance with my own ambition in a way that was not constraining but propelling.

But I was still wrapping my head around it. Even when I returned to work, I shared often about "pumping" in the "wellness room," hoping I'd help normalize it for the team, yet I pumped on high and ran back to my meetings lightheaded, hoping not to miss anything. I love my job and I know what it's like to have people make you feel embarrassed about that. I knew that I was a rare example of someone who was working full time, sincerely happy in their job, and staying "on track" on their career—crushing it, even. I felt a tremendous amount of pressure to show up as that person every day, and I still do—but now I consider that pressure more of a responsibility and an opportunity as an authentic leader to demonstrate capability, as well as boundaries and the willingness to fail.

My own experiences were a catalyst for me to rethink pregnancy and work in a bigger way. With a heightened state of focus, I realized how each step of the journey before, during, and just after pregnancy matters—not just while you have a big belly, not just the maternity leave—and how much it would continue to matter for working women. Now I know that my own experience as a pregnant and then working mother has made me want to be a better employee, teammate, and leader. I also know that my experience at work has made me a better mom. My hope in sharing my own story is that you can consider this moment an opportunity to feel this way too.

As a mentor and advocate for someday mothers, pregnant women, and new parents at work, I have helped individuals navigate good and not-so-good bosses, teams, and situations. One of the biggest pieces of advice I share with them is to acknowledge that if something is a big deal to them, it is. For that reason, for different pregnant teammates, I have been a vocal cheerleader and a privacy bouncer. When I have an opportunity to share an anecdote or advice that I think could help just one pregnant or "hopefully someday" mother in the audience of a panel discussion or podcast, I try to weave it in, but I also recognize that I am just one person. In fact, I hesitated to share much of *myself* in *Carry Strong*. While I did do *some* things right, with all the support around me, I also did many things wrong, which has encouraged me to seek out incredible expert resources I wish I'd known existed.

I also know that while I can relate to others' pregnancies with empathy, none are exactly the same, and there are many life experiences that I can only appreciate with respect, acknowledging that they are influencing every moment of their pregnancy or the road to get there, that I have no business saying anything but "I'm here for whatever you need," with as much specificity as possible. I sought out women with a broad range of experiences and backgrounds to give their stories space and recognition, and with a collective deep appreciation of all women's unique, yet connected, journeys.

In 2020, I saw women like Mandi Tuhro, FNP-C, an ICU RN, breastfeeding her newborn son in her mask and scrubs during the first peak of the pandemic. She looked physically exhausted, mentally drained, yet undefeated—so damn strong. I decided to go beyond my own experience to find out how to help others in a way that would be about them, versus about what I knew. I started small focus groups to inform and formulate the preliminary questionnaire for my first study. I began the interviews. It snowballed. I have been propelled by the groundswell of energy around this topic. I occasionally fist pump from my keyboard late at night or very early in the morning, or in the times when I have written this book in the margins of my working-mom day, because I am so motivated by what women have shared of their private lives and their immediate willingness to be a part of this living project.

Carry Strong will guide you in two parts. In part I, I will introduce to you to the Carry Strong Principles. These five big-picture pillars based on the core themes of my research—perspective, balance, community, communication, and identity—will reframe what you know about pregnancy and work and create a solid foundation so that you can confidently navigate your own individual pregnancy experience.

Next, in part II, you will apply the principles as I take you through the five common, but previously undefined, phases of a Carry Strong pregnancy. The relationship between work and pregnancy goes beyond trimesters delineated by weeks. In fact, it begins before your pregnancy starts. For half of women who worked full time while they were pregnant, its impact started with their journey to motherhood. They shared that conception, not only pregnancy, had an impact on work.[13] This is a big deal and demands unique support, as well as the support needed throughout your pregnancy and after your baby is born.

The five phases of a *Carry Strong* pregnancy are pre-preconception, or Before Trying to Conceive (BTTC); Trying to Conceive (TTC); from the period of privacy when a woman finds out she's pregnant, which I call The Hush, into The Push, the window of modern nesting, after she shares her news; and, of course, Anticipating the Great Return (or Not) after the birth of her child. You will find that each phase is distinct but connected.

Throughout both parts of *Carry Strong* there are personal reflections, advice, and statistics. When you read a story, remember that while you may relate deeply or feel far away from an experience that you read about, each is an opportunity for reflection, growth, and progress. Every expert included uniquely shares their own story, in a human way giving their advice context, but most importantly telling us what was right for them. Keep in mind too that sometimes statistics can make you frustrated because you feel an expectation to align with the common experience. Take off the burden of expectation. *Carry Strong* is about defying expectations, not creating new ones.

In both part I and part II consider this book *your* coach—one to make you feel less alone, that has empathy for what you are going through, and, with respect, gives *you* space to find your own way. As you will see, I encourage you to take a moment at the end of each chapter to reflect with guiding questions, particularly if something you read felt especially energizing, centering, or perplexing. These questions are just for you, an opportunity to rethink pregnancy and work, to Carry Strong in your journey to working motherhood and through it with confidence and comfort.

Carry Strong is not about powering through your pregnancy at work. It is about being pregnant at work, powerful.

QUESTIONS FOR REFLECTION

Why am I reading *Carry Strong*?

What are my expectations of myself as I read it?

Is there someone I want to share my experience with as I read it? *Carry Strong* is a book you can keep to yourself, but you may find you it helpful to invite your partner or a trusted mentor, perhaps a member of your "board of directors" (more on that in chapter 3), to share in all you're taking in.

Carry Strong Stories

EUNICE CHO, CEO OF PAIRE

*One of the biggest hesitations I had about starting a family was
how that might change my relationship to work. I am a business
owner of a fashion company, and that had always been my baby.
When I was considering starting a family, I'd already been at it
for a good three to four years, and I didn't want to be sidetracked
by motherhood. My reaction to the thought of having someone
who would become my number one priority was always, "I don't
have time for that." But my husband and I decided to go forward
because we figured there would never be a good time, and we had
to consider our age.*

*As it happens, I got pregnant while I was raising my first
round of outside funding for my business. My pregnancy came
up unexpectedly but also casually in a phone call with my lead
investor—also a woman, also a mom—when we had still not finalized the term sheet. I wasn't hiding my pregnancy, but I also had
no prior plans of actively bringing it up, because I didn't want my
narrative to be at all about my impending motherhood. At the
same time, I had known, well before I was pregnant, that I felt kin-
ship with this investor because she had explained, at our first
meeting months before, how motherhood had changed the trajectory of her career in a meaningful and positive way. She congrat-
ulated me genuinely when I shared the news, and we went right
back to talking business. The deal went through as planned.*

*That phone call was a great sign, and I felt very empowered
and optimistic, whereas before I had been worried. Once I had
my baby, I realized that I actually became much more productive
and effective as a businesswoman. Before, my work was so all-*

*encompassing that I had trouble getting out of my tunnel vision;
or I was frequently at risk of becoming too emotional. I am the
last person to have expected myself to say this, but motherhood
has been very grounding, and it has made me so much happier
with my work at the same time.*

PAULA FARIS, JOURNALIST, AUTHOR, FOUNDER OF CARRY MEDIA™

*Throughout history, women have worked. Whether as the first
professional beer brewers, who were all women, or the Old Testa-
ment's Proverbs 31 description of a noble wife who "sets about her
work vigorously," she "considers a field and buys it; out of her
earnings she plants a vineyard." History is clear—women work.
Yet American culture and religion have done a great job distort-
ing this fact. Which is essentially the birth of mom guilt. Doesn't
a good mom stay home with her kids? However, if you step back,
the global notion of motherhood and work is much different.
Globally, moms take a great deal of pride in contributing to the
home, of putting food on the table, of hard work. And guess what?
They don't really have a choice not to work. Mom guilt doesn't
exist at the level it does here in America. Our research at CARRY
Media™ has shown that the majority of moms these days are
working to help provide. Let's celebrate those moms who are contributing not just as providers, but in procreating and further-
ing society. Without us, society ceases to exist. We should be
celebrated, not scrutinized. But we first must embrace there's no
one like us—no one who can get the job done as efficiently, effectively, or compassionately. And those skills are learned only
through motherhood.*

ERICA KESWIN, BESTSELLING AUTHOR, SPEAKER, AND WORKPLACE STRATEGIST

A letter to my daughters:

> *Dear J and C,*
>
> *When I think about motherhood and career for you, I see so many opportunities. I didn't have the ability to bring my human to work, or at least I didn't feel like I could—sneaking out of my office for mid-day IVF appointments and taking a two week "vacation" after a miscarriage. Or, after you were finally born, having a senior woman say to me, "You can work from home one day a week, but shhhh don't tell anyone and don't make it Friday so no one notices."*
>
> *Given all the technology to enable WFA (work from anywhere), the universal desire for flexibility, and the focus on holistic workplace support, I hope motherhood can be a "possibility and positive" for your career versus a punishment. It has been one of the biggest gifts in my life and I would never change a thing.*
>
> *Love,*
> *Mom*

JOHNETTE REED, DIGITAL EXPERT

I felt enormous pressure to keep it hidden until I couldn't anymore. Keeping my pregnancy a secret made simple tasks like doctor's appointments feel so hard. I've always felt the pressures of being a Black woman in majority spaces. This is the pressure to be better than good in hopes of proving that I, in fact, belong. Pregnancy heightened this pressure for me specifically for two reasons: I was Black, and I didn't want to be seen as incompetent. The pressure to keep up while going through the most transformative process of my life was taxing. I remember thinking, "They can't think I'm not good at my job." The truth is I wanted so badly to slow down, rest, and ponder what life would be like with our new little one. Unfortunately, there was little time for those thoughts.

My final trimester was filled with business travel and the urgency of pivoting content in a pandemic. In the days following my delivery I realized just how fast I had been moving. I wondered how I had let my job dictate so much of my self-worth. As I prepare to return to work I crave boundaries and balance. It's no longer about the pressure to prove I'm superwoman. Now it's about finding the balance to enjoy my work and show up for my family.

ANNIE CAVALLO, CREATIVE DIRECTOR

I only wish I had my post-pregnancy confidence in myself earlier in my career when I really needed it the most. Being a mother changed my respect, my priorities, and my love for myself and in a way that positively affected my career choices and tolerances. If I choose to give you my dedicated time away from my children, you better believe that I won't be wasting it feeling undervalued, underpaid, or underutilized.

PART I

The Five Carry Strong Principles

CHAPTER 1

Perspective

*Reframing Your Reality
with a Paradigm Shift*

FIVE DAYS AFTER I had my son James, he had to return to the hospital for the second time since he was born to be treated overnight. I had to keep myself awake in the hospital to use a breast pump to fill tiny bottles to feed him through the incubator vent, so I was reading *The New York Times* on my phone. I distinctly remember throwing my arms in the air when I read the article "Reframing 'Mommy Brain'" by Dr. Alexandra Sacks.

In the article, Dr. Sacks, a reproductive psychiatrist and the coauthor of *What No One Tells You*, writes, "There is no convincing scientific evidence that pregnancy causes an overall decline in cognitive performance or memory." She also speaks to the proven neuroplasticity of the pregnant woman's brain and the fact that "many women experience 'mommy brain' as a deficiency . . . if we look at the changes without judgment we may find that they confer advantages."[1]

So here I was, in a pretty dire place. My fragile son's five days meant I was only five days postpartum. I was alone, unable to hold him, and spontaneously crying due both to my hormones and to watching my tiny baby in miniature protective goggles under blue light, yet as I read, I was uplifted. Uplifted not just for me, but for all moms and someday mothers by the idea of positively and factually reframing the common (mis)conception of "mommy brain." This was tangible proof that we are not at a disadvantage by becoming moms. In fact, it was recognition that motherhood can be an asset. Until then, while I knew that motherhood *and* my career were important to me, and I had fantastic examples of women who had done both successfully [and now in hindsight clearly believe that motherhood has become a boost to all facets of my life], I still had only ever thought of it as a risk.

This chapter will help you understand why you too might feel this way, and recognize that some of the biggest pressures women feel regarding pregnancy and work are time, money, and perception. We will break each of these pressures down, identify the truths from the myths, and consider them from all sides to normalize pregnancy at work by making them more neutral forces than threats. The goal is to help you realize what might be holding you back before you even get started, and to give you a new mindset about pregnancy and work. Embracing perspective is about unlocking your potential, but first you need to begin the conscious unburdening of what you may be unaware you are carrying, including what you've been told (if anything at all).

THE UNBURDENING

Ninety-two percent of college-age women without children believe that motherhood will have an impact on their career.[2] You probably have realized that the number should be 100 percent. The relationship between work and motherhood is real and essential. And there is nothing wrong with that. Your inherent duality (and further, multidimensionality) can be your ultimate motivation and source of clarity, or, on some days, seem nearly impossible to reconcile. However, today the scale is heavily tipped to the negative side when we talk about the impact of pregnancy and motherhood on a woman's career. Headlines like "Pregnancy Is Still a Career Killer" continue to dominate women's brain space before they even start to try to become pregnant in the 2020s, even though the article with that title is ten years old.[3]

When I asked that same group of college-age women without children if there was a gender advantage when it comes to career, 79 percent said gender does affect career success and 68 percent said men had an advantage over women.[4] There were two themes in subsequent interviews—"bias" and "babies," and with regard to pregnancy and work they are often intertwined. When I dug deeper on the latter the response was often a consistent "That's all I've ever heard."

Amanda, who is twenty-two and recently graduated with her MBA, shared, "I was told, early in my career, that motherhood would be pivotal to my career. If I chose not to bear children, my peers will assume that I am a subpar, 'heartless' woman; and several peers reiterated that women who choose not to have children are harsh and cruel. I was also told not to have children young, or I'd be viewed as immature—but not too late, unless I wanted to be tired and passed over for promotions. . . . I felt overwhelmed and worried that I may not achieve the career and life experience of becoming a mother at the same time."

Jaime Bartolett, an actor in New York, shared, "It's ingrained in my brain to think, 'If I want to take time off to get pregnant/be a mother, I am weak and will miss out on opportunities that those who choose not to be mothers will receive.'"

On the contrary, an anonymous contributor said, "I have never heard a male peer asked, 'What are you going to do about work after the baby is born?' when they hear that their partner is expecting."

The reality is that today these headlines and underlying biases have a disproportionate negative impact on women versus men and, in fact, will affect women regardless of whether they have children. Women are judged by the fact that they *could* have babies, which *could* affect their performance (which you'll see is not true), and the effect of this misconception takes hold in the workplace long before they become pregnant. If bias continues to exist against women at work until they are significantly past the age where pregnancy is likely, the possibility of a pregnancy will always hang over us as a risk.

In addition, when women are successful in their careers *and* are pregnant, or later when they have children, they feel that they are met with shock, surprise, and phrases like "I'm impressed." My sarcastic favorite is "actually," as in, "She is pregnant and *actually* pretty good at presenting her case." This was well noted particularly by women of color. One contributor to my research told me, "I was paraded out as an example . . . 'Look at her triumph' . . . I was just doing what today should be normal. . . . What I really wanted recognition of in that moment was the work of my team who, by the way, each have additional dimensions to who they are too."

This has got to stop. We need to change the way we talk about pregnancy and work. Today it's negative or not at all. A currently pregnant contributor, Nathalie Han, reflected, "It's mind-blowing that no one talks about [pregnancy and work] and yet it is just as real as when you see those two lines on the stick." This is not a taboo topic, it's table stakes to supporting working women. Microaggressions regarding expectations don't just affect those who must endure them in the moment, they create an environment that perpetuates dismissive thinking. The playing field needs to level—from pre-pregnancy through parenthood for all genders. Another contributor, Kathy Kennedy, DrPH, MA, the executive director of Regional Institute for Health and Environmental Leadership (RIHEL) and clinical professor at the University of Colorado, shared with me a statement that has guided me in this book: "There shouldn't be something unnatural about work and pregnancy." And yet today the words we use when we talk about pregnancy and work are antiquated and dismissive. This is true even in the field of obstetrics itself, where we don't just need a different way to talk about pregnancy and work, we need a new vocabulary.

Caitlin Bump, MD, MS, is a Georgetown-educated women's health expert who is passionate about the holistic wellness of her patients. She has extensive training in integrative medicine, acupuncture, and more than a decade of experience as an ob/gyn. Dr. Bump specializes in patient-centered care surrounding pregnancy, from preconception to postpartum, and is sought globally for her expertise. She shares:

While in medical school we memorize fifteen to eighteen thousand new terms to speak "medicalese" fluently, but few of us are focused on how these words and this language come across and feel to patients. I certainly wasn't—until my third year of medical school on my first clinical rotation, in Obstetrics and Gynecology, when I came across the term "EDC— Estimated Date of Confinement." for a woman's due date. Confinement?! *What a horrible description and image. Then, and now as a board-certified ob/gyn, I use EDD—estimated date of delivery, or simply due date. There are many medical terms that, with only a little bit of thought and consideration (or personal experience), we can acknowledge need to be changed. "Confinement" is distressing. "Miscarriage," not technically a medical term but so commonly used, assigns fault and blame. The word "deliver" can be disempowering to the mother who has just done the incredibly hard work of birthing her child. And applying for "disability" after having a baby is downright inaccurate. And these are just a few words, in just one specialty.*

I fondly remember one contributor telling me proudly about when she was applying for maternity leave "disability." She held up the paperwork with a smile and said, "I'm sorry, I think this is the wrong form," very aware that it was the right one. The irony of her child-bearing "superpower" ability labeled this way was not lost on her.

Remember that you don't need anyone's permission to have a career and be a mother. Nearly nine out of ten working women like you will become mothers during their careers, and it doesn't need to feel like preparing for battle, a secret rite of passage, or a minefield of awkward conversations. The aim of this chapter is to get you into a headspace where you can see the pressures that face you as a future working mother, consider them with balanced views and a fresh perspective, and press reset to question what you have been told, including what you've told yourself.

Actress and producer Alysia Reiner reflected on what she wished she would have known before she got pregnant and wants other women to know: "I wish I had a big sign that said, 'Allow.' You are allowed to have it all. Allow it all in. It is your right to do both. Don't let anyone tell you otherwise." Alysia felt torn over what motherhood might do to her career, but with a community built on high trust and no judgment, "nothing has made me feel more powerful or creative."

Abigail Dunne-Moses is the director of Global Equity, Diversity, and Inclusion at the Center for Creative Leadership in North Carolina. She is also a mother of five. In the 1990s, she was pregnant at age thirty-five, and she shares her journey to motherhood to illustrate her powerful insight—to consider what we are carrying with intentionality.

I was a breadwinner, businesswoman, traveler, and mother. I traveled across the nation with my baby wrapped in Nigerian fabric so I could carry my briefcase in the one hand and push my suitcase and the stroller in the other. I had to care for my whole family. And I did. My third child was welcome but unplanned. The prospect was daunting—how was I going to manage my career and manage my home? My professional reputation lifted me up. My lack of confidence dragged me down. My boss lifted me up with the opportunities that he was preserving for me. My friends dragged me down: "Look what you did to yourself!" My mind was terrified at what I considered a poor choice—to get pregnant again. My pastor lifted me up by saying, "Get excited!" My internal conversations dragged me down.

The pregnancy was my best. No vomiting, no Braxton-Hicks, no cravings. I had all that I wanted, career and my baby. The joy that lifted me finally turned into the reality . . . My choices and my adaptation demonstrated who I am, but I know it was also how I was made to feel like an anomaly. . . . I was lifted up by my network at work and at home. Those who pushed me down became irrelevant. Because of this support I could carry strong physically, emotionally, and spiritually.

This was thirty years ago but feels like it could have been four. It's time to recognize what is dragging you down in your journey to motherhood and lift it up and off your shoulders—or at least intentionally know what's on them. Gaining perspective is something both freeing and grounding that you can experience today, no matter what phase of pregnancy and work you are in. Right now there is probably a lot on your mind, but there are three considerations with multiple dimensions that are likely on the list regarding pregnancy and work: time, money, and perception.

TIME

For many women, one of the biggest pressures to navigate when it comes to planning our pregnancies and our careers is time. We can feel limited by it, or like there's not enough of it, or that it'll never be the "right" time to have a baby. But if we shift how we approach time and release ourselves from its grasp, we can begin to manage our time as a working mother with more awareness and less stress. Let's start by examining one of the most tangible factors of time with regard to pregnancy—our biology.

When I graduated college and got engaged, I felt like one of those wind-up egg timers, the kind that clicks and basically is impossible to manually unwind. If you try to rush or stop the timer, it feels like you are going to break it—until there is a loud "ding"! The combination of my ambitions at work (which were within my reach if I just kept going) and knowing that I wanted to have children made me feel spring-loaded—a fear of there not being time to do both. The compounding factor, ironically, was my cringeworthy "biological clock." Time was ticking, or so I thought.

We can't talk about a woman's biological clock without addressing the reality of the "gender fertility gap," the less cringeworthy way to think about why time impacts women's journey to parenthood significantly more than it affects men. Dr. Bump explains, "Those who are born with ovaries are born with a fixed number of oocytes (approximately one to two million), so we don't produce new eggs after birth. The number of eggs (quantity) and the quality of the eggs declines with age. By puberty, approximately two hundred thousand to four hundred thousand eggs remain. Of these, three to four hundred will be ovulated monthly over a person's reproductive lifetime." On the contrary, men make new sperm every sixty to seventy days for the duration of their life. While this may not be "new news," it gives perspective to why, beyond physical implications, women feel the weight of time sooner and men may not feel it at all. Notably, while male fertility is a factor in 30 percent of infertility cases (which affect one in six couples), age is the most influential factor in female fertility—which leads to "the window."

Dr. Bump describes a woman's fertility in this way: "Fertility starts to decline as we age. It starts gradually in the early thirties, around age thirty-two, and more quickly declines starting at age thirty-seven. After age forty-three, very few people conceive spontaneously." The incidence of pregnancy loss (we will spend time talking about its impact on work in part II) increases from 10 percent at age thirty to 40 percent at forty.

The median age of all employees in the United States was 42.5 in 2020.[5] The average age of first-time mothers in the U.S. is 24. For women with a college degree, it is 30.[6] If you line that information up with the biological "window," it's no wonder we feel a crunch. But the truth is, there isn't a magic formula for making the most of your career and your childbearing years. There's only what works for you, and what you make happen—with awareness of a lot of variability with regard to fertility and particularly age to consider.

Another time consideration you might make when navigating pregnancy at work is how long it will take to get pregnant. Dr. Bump tells us, "Timing of pregnancy, when desired (and planned for), is an incredibly personal choice. It does, however, require some forethought depending on each person's situation and history. Approximately 80 percent of couples conceive within the first six months and 85 percent within the first twelve months. This, however, can be affected by medical conditions, such as polycystic ovarian syndrome (PCOS), thyroid dysfunction, obesity, and endocrine disruptors. Most physicians recommend discontinuing birth control six months before trying to conceive. This gives people time for their regular cycle to return. . . . Keep in mind to discontinue birth control only when you are ready to conceive if it happens—because it can happen in that first cycle, but also that, on the other end of the spectrum, some people need a longer time, up to two years, to optimize their health."

Overall, physicians, including Dr. Bump, remind us to think about how our individual bodies, risk factors, and those of our partner (or not) affect our timeline to get pregnant both when we are ready to try and actively trying to conceive. I encourage you to do your own research and speak with your physician as soon as you are ready—the sooner the better. This means get comfortable with being uncomfortable in advocating for yourself including with regard to your fertility. Recognize that this is why for many women getting pregnant can feel like a full-time job on top of their . . . well, full-time job. Take it as information and one step at a time, while you maintain perspective on the big picture.

Niomi is a special education teacher, one of the 3.5 million U.S. school educators, 76 percent of whom are women.[7] The mother of two shared her experience of timing her pregnancy:

> If you time your pregnancy just right, you can have your full pay and benefits during the summer. If not, then you are only going to have six or eight weeks depending on how you deliver. With my second child, after a loss, we were fortunate, and it happened in this narrow window. I gave birth in June. Because of the timing I didn't have to take my maternity leave and I directly told my boss, "I'm giving birth this weekend, I'll be in the hospital Friday, Saturday, and I'll be back on Monday" to finish the school year. I was entitled to my leave by law, which I deserved, but adding even a few weeks I would have been a teacher starting in October instead of September, not the best look. For me, and so many other teachers, it wasn't just about the summer timing and time with my son—which is what it should be, and maybe what you would expect—it was also about the expectation of when I would return, and security for what I needed for my family. . . . I got my bachelor's degree when I had my daughter, then my master's, and then my son was born. I have felt so capable, powerful in what I have achieved . . . strong, and I have support around me, but that uncertainty was real.

Her advice: "Don't compare yourself to anyone else. Don't worry what the world thinks of you, it's what your kids think of you, and you think of them. With so much uncertainty in pregnancy, enjoy your baby. That's the moment. That's the time. You're juggling, especially with the second one, but you don't get that time back—even if it isn't in June."

Obstetricians, one of the highest percentages of female physician specialties, second only to pediatrics,[8] deliver on average more than a hundred babies a year. Dr. Monica Washington, a mother of two, said:

Pregnancy IS my work. It's what I do. It's what I know. So I just knew that when it came time to plan my own pregnancy, my plan would fall into place. I would track my cycles, I would determine the day I ovulated, I would have intercourse at the appropriate time, and then I would get pregnant. I had a plan and I needed for the plan to happen at the time I had allotted. Because just like the rest of my life, pregnancy was supposed to happen at just the right time in the window I had picked.

Monica wanted to get pregnant and deliver as a third-year ob/gyn resident so she could have the longest maternity leave allowed, only six weeks, and still graduate on time. The problem was, it wasn't happening.

After more than a year, one day while doing my reproductive endocrinology and infertility rotation, my attending asked, "Do you want children?" I broke down and told her my story. We secretly started the workup for infertility and set up an appointment for my husband and me to come in for a consultation. And guess when I found out I was pregnant? The night before that consultation! I delivered at thirty-seven weeks after breaking my water on the way to work in my fourth year of residency. I breastfed my baby and I made it work—thankful every day for my amazing husband, colleagues, and community around me. I graduated on time, and I was pregnant again at graduation. Pregnancy kept my mind focused; it gave me empathy for my future patients while I learned to care for them in other ways, and I enjoyed how strong it made me feel as a woman.

Her advice about time:

While it is important to think about what makes the time the "right" time for you, know that even when you think you have the answers and have done all the research, there will always be a curveball thrown your way. You have gotten to this phase in your career by being a badass and fighting for what you want. Pregnancy is no different. Sometimes we must recognize that there are alternative routes, timelines, and ways to think about what we can and cannot control. Take care of yourself and embrace that motherhood is part of what you want and you need to give it time and attention. If you are having difficulty getting pregnant, know that other methods are out there and can be explored and have been proven to be successful.

Like many women I have interviewed, Niomi and Monica felt the force of time—the timeline of biology and fertility, the drive to achieve, and the search for the right time to accomplish both on their own terms. Today, many women indicate that their decision to wait to have children is very much driven by career expectations that they put on themselves. They believe that if you want to reach a top position, it is better to wait until you are "well-established" in your career.[9] That's why often when I talk to women about fertility and expanding the window, the first thing they bring up as a tangible topic is egg freezing.

While egg freezing, covered in chapter 6 regarding the impact on work, is an important consideration that has had more visibility in recent years, it is important to think about it beyond just extending your fertility window. There are lots of reasons to freeze your eggs, including health concerns before or during the pregnancy process and wanting to find the right partner of any gender for your family. One contributor to my research expressed, "I actually feel freer than my straight friends and their timelines. I already know that to have children with or without a partner someday I'll use IVF, and that I'm going to freeze my eggs soon." She also shared that the major financial services company she was working at upon graduation openly talked about its egg-freezing coverage when recruiting their junior trainees—and that was very significant in her decision. This is important because when companies talk about egg-freezing coverage as a career benefit, they need to do it in a balanced way that acknowledges all the reasons why a woman may freeze her eggs. Otherwise, it can perpetuate that women *have to* wait to have children. For companies and individuals, egg freezing isn't only something to delay motherhood, it's to prioritize it with your career and the rest of your life.

Especially as more women than ever are in the workforce and waiting longer than ever to have children, it's time to reframe how we think about time. Instead of thinking about your timing as a narrow window, think of it as a door, one of those big sliding doors, the ones that you need to personally push with some effort (i.e., awareness and planning) to open.

This leads us to the second dimension of time to consider with a new perspective. My first newlywed year before my husband and I were ready to try for a baby, I visited my friend Louisa in the UK. I had her daughter on my lap, and we were discussing my ambitions to get promoted before we prioritized pregnancy. She told me something that stuck with me: "You know you have about forty years ahead of you to work, right? But only ten to have your kids? How many levels up are there, anyway?"

Like many of us, I used to think that career and pregnancy were two different entities, and that one would end when the other began, even though I had never even considered stopping working when I had kids. I hadn't thought of them as concurrent. I knew I wanted to be a mom. I also knew how ambitious I was in my career. The fact that Louisa gave me permission to do both, but also gave me perspective, was incredibly helpful. It was also very much in my mind when I didn't get pregnant for three more years, restrained by other variables that were not in my control, like my career was.

Elana Meyers Taylor is an Olympic and world champion bobsledder and mother whose powerful story and advice is in the conclusion. Elana knew when she was nine that she wanted to be an Olympian. I asked her when she knew she wanted to be a mother, and she said from an even younger age, but that it wasn't until she saw Noelle Pikus-Pace, skeleton Olympian, travel to competitions with her two young children that she recognized that one dream wouldn't stop when the other began. "She made it work, as a mother in a demanding sport who won an Olympic medal—and I knew as long as I had the talent, effort, and the support of my husband—my biggest fan—I could be a mom-athlete and make it happen."

Your due date is only a finite deadline for having a baby, not for everything in your life. Joanna Coles, CEO of Northern Star Acquisition Companies, executive producer of *The Bold Type*, and former chief content officer of Hearst Magazines, changed jobs both times she was pregnant. She shared with me, "It was always framed, 'How are you going to manage . . . it's going to be exhausting, you have to give a lot up . . .' Yet, you gain in almost all ways . . . (so) this is just not true."

There is an opportunity to reinforce a positive concurrent experience. Zoe Wechsler, cofounder of the *Am I Embarrassing You?* podcast and daughter of fellow contributor Dr. Amy Wechsler, shared how, because of her mother, she never questioned this fact: "I have memories about my friends' moms being able to come on every single class trip in elementary school and thinking that their moms must not have to work that day. Seeing my mom juggle two medical degrees and two kids and her own practice while always being present for me at every turn shows me that I can pursue any career and have the kids I've always wanted to have."

Whether you want to reach a certain level in your company, complete a certain course, or are still defining what type of career you want in the first place, motherhood to women can at first seem like a constraint to achievement. Instead, shift your perspective and you may even think of it as a boost. Some of the women that I mentor come to me and ask how to get promoted with urgency. After discussing their merits and rationale, I reset their temporal expectations. I tell them, no one is going to look at your résumé and say, "Oh, I see here that you were in this role now for two point eight years and not two," or "Interesting that you took two lateral moves in a row," or even "I see here that you took more than the usual amount of time for grad school." But I also tell them that if timing matters to them and that's what's motivating them at work, they need to be transparent with their boss or organization. There is nothing wrong with wanting to be promoted when merited, whether it is about scope of role, title, or money, but there is also nothing wrong with it taking a different amount of time than it took a peer, or an altogether different direction. Notably, some careers have clear time delineations, so these natural points are realistically going to happen. But these are *your* timelines.

This sets up the ultimate time question: when is the right time to get pregnant? Sara Daly-Padron has over twenty years of experience as a Human Capital practitioner, is the founder of SDP Advisors, an executive coaching and consulting firm, a lecturer at Columbia University, and a Maven health-care platform adviser, with a focus on life-change transitions and career. In anticipation of starting a family, many women ask Sara, "When is the right time?" She answers, "From an employer's perspective, there's never a perfect time. So instead, focus on what timing is right for *you*."

Instead of playing Jenga to assure your pregnancy doesn't conflict with your career, change your mindset from "There is never the right time" or "It needs to be the perfect time" to "It's never the wrong time." Just like that, you're flipping the script. Even when you are in a time-dependent or seasonal role, from academia and accounting to hospitality or retail, there is only so much control you have over when you get pregnant. Many women reflected on this retro-timing only to share that it is essentially impossible. At the end of the day, remember that this is about you. This isn't about your job, your company, or your school. This baby isn't part of their narrative; it's part of yours.

Lastly, will you have time? To have children? To have a career? To spend time with your kids and be fully present? The answer is yes. The difficult thing about time is that it's finite. But what you do with it is not. Sometimes you'll have a lot more time than you think and sometimes a lot less, but you will *make* time, because you want to, and that desire is reflected in the choices you make and in what you prioritize. I recently saw a quote from author and professor Adam Grant that gave me particular pause in appreciation: "Sacrificing health and family for work is not an expression of loyalty. It's a sign of poor priorities. Dedication is not what you give up for your job. It's what you give to your job."

As you add your new important priority of motherhood, your schedule (i.e., how you use your time) may have to change, but while you look at what you're adding also think about what you can move, subtract, downgrade, or delegate. You can in fact create "time" using your strengths and the strengths of others and compensating them for their energy so you can use yours in the best way possible for your job, your family, and you. It's also important to recognize that energy too, although not limited by hours in the day, cannot be discounted as infinite.

Anna Kaiser, celebrity trainer and creator of Anna Kaiser Studios, told me, "Today, with two kids it's hard to break away (and often I just can't imagine leaving them in the morning!), but I remember how much better I'm going to feel when I get to the studio—better for myself and better for them, physically and mentally. That is even more of a priority now than before I had children. I used to take that time for granted. Your priorities change when you become a mom, your day-to-day schedule changes. The hours you have at work become more precious."

Kate Elsworth, singer-songwriter and cofounder of Lunar Disco, adds the perspective of the shift of time throughout the phases of motherhood in her story of a surprise pregnancy and its impact on her unique schedule:

> *I make music with my partner around the world—we met making music, and after four years together as a duo, Lunar Disco, I unexpectedly got pregnant right before our summer tour. Tours can be hectic, going to clubs, energetic electronic music at all hours. One weekend I found out we had a three-day gig on a cruise through the Mediterranean, leaving the next day, but I wasn't feeling great—I was pregnant. I cried when I first found out, I really thought I was just late. At the time, I was living in Paris, and my French is terrible, but I bought a test and it was clear that I was pregnant. How was I going to do it? I knew I wanted to have kids, but I was just thinking about the next three months on tour, and the next three days. Together with my partner we digested it and I was like, "I can do this." On the cruise, I had to watch horrible re-runs on television below deck between sets. I wanted to do anything to be protected and safe. Yet after that I reset, and I ended up DJing until I was eight months pregnant. I switched to a lot of day gigs, not late at night, and made choices. People were really understanding, and I felt powerful. I remember a big festival in Morocco. I had a big bump and people were re-spectful, gave me a lot of space, and literally I got put on a ped-estal, which was awesome. Shortly thereafter, I stopped working and had a traumatic birth—quite a few things went wrong, but then two months later I went back to the day gigs, just two hours at a time, and when Lily was six months old, we went back on tour as a family.*

Your time does not define you; you define *your* time. Although we can't change the tangible time of our age, how long it takes to get pregnant, or the amount of time we spend being physically preg-nant, with awareness and perspective we can decide what's most important to us along the way. Same goes for answering "Will I have time?" If something is important to you, you will make time. Will it require thoughtful prioritization more days than not, yes, but it's not impossible, and not a net loss. Balance, communication, and community that you will find in *Carry Strong* help to create energy to propel you forward, not hold you back. Lastly, remember that time does not stop. Give yourself information but also grace with your timelines, and think about the other variables that can be creating rigidity, like societal expectations or goals to hit. Truly think about the concurrent nature of your entire pregnancy journey to your career—before, during, and after.

MONEY

The financial impact of pregnancy is another one of the biggest contributing factors to viewing pregnancy as a risk to a woman's career, with the United States' (and global) gender wage gap in mind. In fact, it can be a responsible reason for why more women are waiting longer to have children. Not only do you have to consider the costs of maternity leave, but also the costs of having and caring for a baby. There are few scenarios where the aphorism "time is money" holds truer than if you work hourly or are paying someone hourly to care for your children. In these cases, juggling parenthood and work can feel like doing mental math gymnastics. You might rationalize whether work is worth the long-term benefits of nurturing a career, even if it means paying exorbitant childcare costs and having financial struggles in the present. You may think about it as an individual, or as a household of multiple incomes.

In addition, there is the impact of perception that impacts women's financial earning, otherwise known as the "motherhood penalty" versus the "fatherhood bonus." Employers view motherhood as a "signal of lower levels of commitment and professional competence." Working fathers, on the other hand, may be viewed as having "increased work commitment and stability, and typically earn 15% more than men without children."[10]

Jennifer Barrett, head of content at Fidelity Investments, former chief education officer at Acorns, *Forbes* contributor, and author of *Think Like a Breadwinner,* explains that "new fathers may get more assignments and opportunities for advancement under the assumption that they'll work harder and be even more dedicated because they're the breadwinner for a family now. But that's not the case anymore for millions of families. Increasingly, women are the main breadwinners for the household. So this is a particularly pernicious assumption that not only hurts women, but the families they may be supporting." In fact, my first study shows that 38 percent of the women were the household breadwinners, and 20 percent contributed equally. So, it's safe to say that the gendered "breadwinner" assumption is 58 percent wrong.[11]

You should also consider changing your perspective about finances overall, especially now—and make it a priority. Jennifer continues: "The prescription most women get is to get a career—or a job—get married and save a little for a rainy day and for retirement. And that is not enough to truly support the lives so many of us want. There are so many potential goals we may have for that period that require financial planning—from buying a home to starting a family or a business. It also diminishes our financial capabilities and our potential aspirations. The questions to ask now are: What do *I* want in my life? And what are the money and career choices I need to make to support that? That is thinking like a breadwinner. Then regardless of whether you get married, or whether you earn more or less than a partner, you will have the confidence to know that you can provide the life you want."

For many of the women I spoke to in my research, pregnancy and early motherhood turned on a switch from providing for themselves for now to providing for their families for the future. I also saw this reflected in the data. Working pregnant women are twice as likely to work harder if they changed their effort at work during pregnancy. As one of the participants, Sarah Steele, wrote, "I could quite literally feel, with each kick, what I was working for. While I have always enjoyed pursuing a career, it was life changing to know that I was working in pursuit of being able to provide for my future family. That made the longer and more taxing days feel more rewarding than draining."

Future and current moms are motivated. By shifting our perspective to forward thinking, there is a positive ripple effect for our dependents; even if we are making less today, our motherhood pays forward. In the United States, "daughters of working mothers earned 23 percent more than daughters of stay-at-home mothers . . . (and) sons raised by working mothers were significantly more likely to have a wife who worked . . . and spent additional time caring for their family."[12]

Contributor Gabriela Alvarez was faced with an incredibly difficult situation when the father of her child passed away when she was eleven weeks pregnant. She also has an eight-year-old son whose father lives far away and is unfortunately financially absent. She shares her powerful motivation as a single mother:

Everything I do is for my family. Before he passed, my boyfriend had taken on the role of head of our household with all the love in the world, and I was blessed to quit my job and finally have time to start training for a career in real estate and not just live paycheck to paycheck. Now I must get back on my feet as quickly as possible. Being pregnant and looking for a job that pays more than minimum wage is very difficult. Jobs that are quick and decent pay are usually those for which pregnant women aren't very welcome, such as bartending or the restaurant business. I've decided to start a career in mortgages, and with the help of close friends, I've been able to find a job that looks promising and welcomes us pregnant women. I see it as the beginning of a new career, and now six months

pregnant I must act fast. I use my children as the motor of my
life, which gives me reassurance that everything is going to be
all right. As a mother, life broadens, and failure is not an
option.... I want my daughter to be fearless and open-minded.
To know that she can do it all. She can be an amazing mother
and professional. At the end of it all, life is about perspective,
and the last thing I want is for her to feel limited as a working
mother.

PERCEPTION

More than one hundred years ago, the Supreme Court upheld limiting
working hours for women because their reproductive potential was
vital to "the strength and vigor of the race."[13] Midcentury, if a woman
didn't leave her job when she got married, she was discharged when
she became pregnant.[14] In 1974, the Supreme Court stated that discrimination against pregnant women was not a form of sex discrimination because women could choose whether to become pregnant.
The late justice Ruth Bader Ginsburg fought the decision, and the
Pregnancy Discrimination Act "made it illegal for employers to treat
pregnant women any differently from other temporarily disabled
people."[15] Unfortunately there are still a lot of damaging perceptions
about a woman's ability to perform at work while pregnant. Discrimination, including "benevolent discrimination," is still a major reality.
In the past ten years, nearly forty thousand pregnancy discrimination cases have been filed with the U.S. Equal Employment Opportunity Commission.[16]

As I worked on this book, I wanted to know where we stand today
in the perceptions of working individuals, parents, nonparents, and
by gender. I conducted a fourth study, this time of 650 people, in May
2021. More than half of participants said that parents on their team
were an "asset." Specifically, "Their experience as a parent is an asset
that adds or contributes to our success." What's even more incredible

is that only 5 percent across the board said parenthood is a risk to the success of the workplace. While it should be negligible, this statistic needs to make some headlines instead of the ones that consider parents as risks.

Today, employers do not talk about their pregnant or someday pregnant employees as invaluable.[17] But here's why they should. First, working while pregnant is better for your mental health.[18] This fact means that there is a positive impact on overall employee health. Second, along with the significant boost in women's confidence while they were pregnant that correlated with an increase in self-perceived work ethic, working while pregnant directly correlates with a higher likelihood to return to work (i.e., retention).[19] Third, if you are engaged and retained during pregnancy, this momentum can carry you to the next phase of your career upon your return, with a positive effect on future performance and advancement opportunities.

In fact, there is the possibility you could outperform your peers. A contributor was newly and privately pregnant and had just been offered a new role. It was a competitive and exciting offer, involving hiring a new team and a lot of change management at a high-profile medical tech company. She would be taking on a new leadership position and be the only woman on the leadership team. She took a day after receiving the offer from her new boss in writing to get back to him. She shared that she had "just" found out she was pregnant, and at the same time cited the paper "Parenthood and Productivity of Highly Skilled Labor: Evidence from the Groves of Academe" to reassure him when she accepted. This study of ten thousand economists conducted by the Federal Reserve Bank of St. Louis outlines that not only does pregnancy pose no detriment to productivity, but in fact, working mothers outperformed their peers without children.[20] You can't argue with that.

This is all good news! But it comes with a potential risk. You may have heard that often working mothers feel like they need to "work like they don't have kids and mom like they don't have a job." This can start at pregnancy. You do not need to "outperform" to keep up at work or to anticipate changes in perception. The truth is, there are a lot of unknowns that can have an impact on your performance, so maintaining your current effort should be the goal—and is quite impressive in itself. I was shocked and frankly embarrassed when I read resources to guide pregnant women that said, "Make sure you demonstrate your value to your team." You have nothing to prove, and in fact the most important part of your pregnancy has nothing to do with your performance for a few months, and more to do with the fact that the way you feel now will affect your return post-baby for years.

The tipping point to change negative assumptions to these positive ones without creating new burdens in the process (i.e., not burning yourself out while also pregnant) is complex, but it starts with recognition of perception and its many layers. Perception can be challenged through shared experiences, facts, and societal evolution, but it doesn't mean that it isn't a heavy burden to carry when it is experienced.

A neuroscientist and mother of two remembers being told while pursuing her PhD that she was "not committed to science" when she revealed she had a child and was considering a second. The fact that she had a child already certainly hadn't stopped her getting into the prestigious program in the first place.

Writer and actress Jill Kargman's story in part II is about being an in-demand freelance writer with a cool and edgy MTV crowd and her secret three-month bump who stopped getting calls to write for the same spots at seven months pregnant. She remembered, "There were jaws on the floor." The only change—their perception, because of her physical change.

There is also a very real perception of pregnancy that is intertwined with racial stereotypes and expectations. Kimberly Seals Allers is an award-winning journalist, author, and maternal and infant health strategist who founded the Irth app ("as in Birth, but we dropped the B for bias"), the number one Yelp-like platform for the pregnancy and new-motherhood journey made by and for people of color. Kimberly is also a mother of two who remembers hiding the fact that she was unmarried and pregnant with her first child to her cohort of master's degree colleagues. Not only did she feel she needed to demonstrate that she belonged with them in the prestigious program as the only Black woman of the group for "the benefit of all Black people," but she could not let them "view me as a stereotype." In addition to this pressure, Kimberly reflected on the weight of all that she was carrying:

> *You are carrying the burden of a working person, in this case also as a student, while carrying the burden of a pregnant person, while carrying the very real fear of what we know about Black women's birth outcomes. Black women are three to four times more likely to die during or after childbirth, across socioeconomics, regardless of education and class. . . . This is a triple burden. And it is exhausting.*

Public awareness of this triple burden is essential. These unique social stressors may contribute to your health or the health of your baby, for example, resulting in preterm labor or low birth weight, and they certainly affect your mindset. It may cloud your joy and deter your confidence—a disconnect from the picture we have in our minds of the radiant pregnant woman, including at work. My first study's results regarding confidence demonstrate that while overall 34 percent of women had an increase in confidence (69 percent of those who experienced a change) versus a 15 percent decrease, for women of color they are significantly different: 16 percent increased, 22 percent decreased.[21]

So what can we do? First, these stories need to be heard. Changing the narrative is about communication and engaging your community, two of the principles you will read about shortly. As an advocate, Kimberly often shares her journey with other women, encouraging others to do the same. This is what Irth is inherently about: shared experience scaled by a digital platform that goes beyond "sister circles" yet has the same proximity for impact. Through collective experiences, reviews become meaningful data to empower you to take charge of your health and safety and to better inform doctor and hospital practices. Specific tools like Irth are powerful and necessary.

In addition, representation in work organizations is crucial, with specific efforts regarding diversity, equity, and inclusion for working women and pregnancy. This includes recognition of the realities of the triple burden—the interconnectedness of health outcomes and how you are treated at work during your pregnancy. You need to see women like you, and you need to feel supported in your own choices as a mother. Kimberly shares, "She needs more societal affirmation. And that 'society' can also be the workplace culture. How is the culture affirming? How do other women in this culture at work affirm other ways of mothering?"

This also means affirming that not everyone's pregnancy is the same. Kimberly put it so clearly: "The length of time—nearly forty weeks—could be the same, but not her experience during them. And the nature of that experience is impacting what is happening at the end of it."

To come full circle with the beginning of this chapter, there is one more dynamic of perception to be aware of throughout your pregnancy: Beyond what society thinks or what those around your work really think, it's what you think they may think that can be most draining. For many women, the personal fear of perception is often greater than the fear of the ticking clock or the financial impact of pregnancy.

Katie, a CFO contributor, reflected on her experience during pregnancy at work:

I remember right after I got back from my honeymoon, people at work were asking me when we were going to have children. I always thought I'd have trouble getting pregnant given my

fifteen-year history with an eating disorder, but I wasn't
quite prepared for what I'd have to go through to get pregnant.
Almost every other morning I'd find myself at the doctor hav-
ing an ultrasound and lab work, only to get disappointing
news from the nurse's call later that day at work. When I did
find out I was pregnant after multiple rounds of IVF, I vividly
remember leaving several large meetings in our conference
room to go be sick in the bathroom. I had spent the last year
hiding my infertility problems by going to my appointments
at six forty-five a.m. so I could make it in without anyone
knowing, and now I was puking in the bathroom with paper-
thin walls where everyone could hear.

I was so nervous about staying pregnant and didn't want
anyone to know until I was sure. Not to mention how this
would affect my career. Sure, people ask when you are going to
get pregnant, but when you do, they start talking. Would they
continue to respect me and take me seriously or would they
write me off as a lost cause to motherhood?

There were so many emotions and fears during my early
pregnancy that occupied my thoughts when I should have
been thinking about how happy I was about the family that I
was starting with my husband. Once people found out, I was
relieved but also trying to prove myself repeatedly so that I
wouldn't lose credibility or become an afterthought when I
went on maternity leave. . . . Looking back, I feel strong, proud,
and resilient. I wish I hadn't been so concerned about what
others thought at the time. It was my business, not theirs.

Just a few decades ago, the nuclear family was defined by the bread-
winning, career-driven father and the domestic goddess and caregiver mother. Over time, we were encouraged to push forward, to
break glass ceilings and to be conscious of sticky floors. And we
needed that push, but climbing the ladder isn't the only route to

"owning it." When you add the weight of responsibility to both work and your family, plus so much ambiguity to navigate, it really is a lot. No wonder women can feel off-balance. The best way to center? Evaluate what's right for you—not for work, not for those around you, but you.

Think about time, money, perception, and anything else holding you back as you navigate pregnancy at work from all sides, with perspective. Break them down and evaluate whether there is a way to think about them differently. Reflect on your own perceptions to take the first step toward awareness, lifting off self-doubt that might hold you back. Think about what you are capable of and embrace what you can look forward to as you change and stay very much who you are. Remember, perspective is powerful—one of the greatest gifts of motherhood.

I'll leave you at the end of this first chapter with a powerful reflection by LaShăda DiCosmo, founder of 1 Cove. "I am and have been a young mom, a bonus mom, an unmarried mom, a working mom, a married mom, and now an adoptive mom. All those titles have one word in common that matters to me and, more importantly, matters to my children."

QUESTIONS FOR REFLECTION

What makes your perspective unique? What are blind spots that you want to see?

Have you ever thought of the pregnant woman on your team as an invaluable asset? What about just neutral?

Before you read the next chapter on balance, think about how you know when you have it and when you don't.

Carry Strong Stories

ANONYMOUS

When I was in my surgical training as a resident in California, I was in the recovery area putting in orders for a patient I had just operated on. Two male attendings from a different specialty were chatting. One told the other that their program had just matched more women than men, and that he hoped they would make injectable long-term birth control mandatory because what would happen if they got pregnant at the same time? The second attending laughed and said, "Good point".

I interjected and asked how many of their male residents had children and how many of their current female residents had children. Almost all the male residents were married with kids, and none of the female residents were. Additionally, I said that as a female surgical resident myself, training to become the best surgeon possible was my number one priority. If I thought that I could do that and become a mother at the same time then I know that my program would support me, and they should think the same. What would they do if their male residents were diagnosed with cancer or major depression or decided to leave medicine? Their program should have plans for what to do when residents need a medical leave and not be worried about female residents getting pregnant....

But during their conversation my immediate thought was good point. I mean, what would they do with multiple residents out at the same time? I felt guilty for thinking like them. The fact that their first thought was "Oh no, we've got to protect these women from getting pregnant" still boils my blood. Here these amazing women who had matched at a top-three program were being penalized for children and pregnancies they didn't even have.

JESSICA MAY, FOUNDER OF JUST GO NUDE™, NUTRIENT DENSE LIFESTYLIST

My husband and I were together for five years, married for two. He was ready to have kids; on the other hand, I felt like it wasn't time yet because I still hadn't found my voice. I was an aspiring actress living in New York. I didn't feel ready to dedicate my life to a child without accomplishing my success first.

Until surprise! I got pregnant. I had such a mix of emotions— excited/grateful/blessed, while nervous/uncertain/guilty. I knew I wanted this baby, although it wasn't when I wanted. So I devoted myself to learning as much as possible. The biggest lesson I learned was how toxic and undernourished my lifestyle was. I'm talking everything from food to furniture. That was a big aha moment, and I could not stop myself from digging deeper. I never felt a passion so resolute in my life. I remember after my son was born the drive and determination only became stronger. Instead of taking naps with him all I wanted to do was get up and work.

There was a moment one night when I was working in the kitchen while pumping after I put my son to sleep, and I realized that the day my son was born, I was born. When I finally let go of the former IDEA of me, I BECAME me. I found my passion and purpose. Now I'm a health coach who focuses on a nutrient-dense, nontoxic lifestyle. I now have two kids and feel as though my life is just beginning. . . . Giving birth to my little humans connected me to my ultimate strength and confidence, which rippled into every aspect of my life. I'm a better coach because I'm a parent and I'm a better parent because I'm a coach.

AYA KANAI, HEAD OF EDITORIAL AND
CREATIVE, GOOGLE SHOPPING

I was working in the fashion industry for the better part of the past twenty years of my life and a lot of the time I was the fashion director at various publications including Cosmopolitan, *Women's Health, and* Nylon. *One of the key elements of being a fashion director in terms of "getting the job done" is styling celebrity photo shoots, which are usually for the cover of the magazine. Of course, this is an important image to get right—right for the celebrity, and to ensure it represents the aesthetic of the brand for its readers.*

When I was five months pregnant and worked at Cosmopolitan, *I flew to LA from New York. I wasn't worried traveling, but I was tired, my whole body was tired—as a pregnant woman you are often putting your body through something that is already exhausting, going through the airport, the flight rigamarole . . . and you're pregnant, so I wasn't sure what to expect from the shoot.*

I was on the set with Mandy Moore, who is perhaps one of the most lovely, lovely human beings, and ended up having a wonderful day. It was especially wonderful because she was so excited about the baby, was asking me a million questions; most of them I had no idea what the answer was, but it felt so good because I could tell she was genuinely feeling my joy with me.

Another special memory of that day was that the photographer, my friend Eric Ray Davidson, did portraits of me on the set in the downtime. He knew it was a moment to capture. So while I remember that it was an extremely exhausting trip, and I should not have taken a red-eye home, I also have a memory I can share with my daughter, made special by the group of people on set with me going through a major moment for my career and for my life.

I had my daughter when I was forty, and I often think about who she will know me as when she is a teenager or in her early twenties figuring out her own career. My career has certainly changed a lot over the years, and I have watched my own mother as a working mom my entire life. She is still working in her late seventies. She can't give it up, she just loves to work. I'm not saying that I'm going to be working when I am seventy, but I do want my daughter to be aware of what choices she has, including the joy of work, while also showing the other side. I want her to know what I am doing when I am not with her, and that Mommy was happy to be working instead of just that "I'm sad to be leaving you" or "Work is hard, but I have to do it." I think that's important for children to have that positive perspective from a young age so they can form what they want for themselves.

CARRIE KERPEN, CEO OF LIKEABLE MEDIA, AUTHOR OF *WORK IT: SECRETS FOR SUCCESS FROM THE BOLDEST WOMEN IN BUSINESS*

I was pregnant with my third baby and was on a call with a client. I was leaning back in my rolling chair and the chair fell to the floor. In that split second I panicked. I was considered "advanced maternal age." I'm on this important call, I was very pregnant, and I am suddenly on the floor. I was the definition of every work-life balance challenge I ever had in my life. I quickly assessed, "Okay, I'm here. Here's what I'm going to do." I didn't tell the client, I finished the call more quickly than I usually would, very professionally let everyone know I was okay in my (glass) office, then I promptly got on the train and went to the hospital, where I was evaluated and fine.

When I had my first baby, I left and started my own business to control my own time, but here with my third I'm a business owner on the floor with a client on the call. Now I felt fine, but it was the quintessential work-life moment. In hindsight, I would have done the exact same thing and would have told myself to stop judging myself. Whatever is right for you is right at that moment. I don't think there was any expert that could have told me what to do.

CHAPTER 2

Balance

Deciding to Have It All,
Not at the Same Time

MY SECOND NAME, Mae, comes from my great-grandmother, Mae Lameroux Cupps, who was born in 1888 and had ninety-eight grandchildren and great-grandchildren. She had her ninth child, my grandmother, Betty June Cupps, when she was forty-five, and her eldest daughter had a baby girl a month later. Mae had graduated from Duff's Professional School, so when her husband died at age fifty-nine, she volunteered to work as the chair of the Women's League, which reviewed films for family ratings. In this role, she went on a trip to visit Paramount Studios in California. Betty, who today is still a force for good at ninety, was not happy about her mom leaving her for work, and still reminds us of it. The only thing that did make it better for Betty were the signed photographs of celebrities like Ronald Reagan that now are in my mother's apartment.

Betty worked as a secretary until she was "in the family way" with her first child. As my grandmother told me, "They didn't say the word 'pregnant' back then, that was too medical and personal."

While Betty did return to work after her children were grown, my grandfather Bill, who is now ninety-two, bent steel bars for forty-two years at a factory in Pittsburgh to support his family. He was instilled with a powerful work ethic and enduring sense of responsibility from his own mother, who had only finished eighth grade before working at a linen company.

The push and pull of work and motherhood, driven both by paycheck and sense of purpose, is a long-standing yet ever-evolving relationship. Fortunately, today women have more personal control and visible options than they did in the early 1900s. However, there is a lesson we can glean from both working women and men from the past: a reminder that your job is working for you and your future family, not the other way around. Trying to get pregnant, being pregnant, and certainly your newborn baby jumps up the priority list, but there is no reason to feel guilt, shame, or fear about keeping career at the top of it too.

You can do it all, not at the same time.

Let's take the first part of the statement—you *can* do it all. This doesn't mean you *have* to do it all or that you *should* do it all. It does not mean that your all is someone else's all. But, for what you want on your list, you can.

Now the second part—not at the same time. So many women stress about how we're going to get it all done, or worse, what we're going to have to give up. This chapter is about creating realistic balance. This includes learning a new way to navigate work-life balance with grace called work-life fluidity, assessing your current state at work through a traffic light so you know where you are and where you want to go in this time of change, and establishing priorities and boundaries to do so in a way that is motivating and sustainable.

WORK-LIFE FLUIDITY

According to my third study, "work-life balance" is a term that 84 percent of people with and without children use, and it is quite polarizing.[1] To be honest, I don't really like this term. Don't get me wrong, the number of times you'll see the word "balance" in this book is high. I like balanced views to make my decisions, to have a balanced diet somewhere between green juice and donuts, and I even run in New Balances. But work-life balance needs a reframe, especially in this important time in your life with a lot of shifting priorities.

Think about when you have been off-balance or have tried hard to be balanced physically. Even if you can do a perfect handstand, balance takes practice. If you have ever tried to change into heels on a city sidewalk without holding on to a wall, you get it. Balance takes a lot of effort.

Now I want you to visualize a seesaw. Imagine that two people are trying to balance with their legs off the ground perfectly. It is nearly impossible, and not nearly as fun as bouncing up and down. If that seesaw has "work" on one end and "life" on the other, and your expectation is to keep those legs off the ground in an uncomfortable and unrealistic position, the balance is tenuous. Plus, you are giving a hell of a lot of credit to "work" to measure up to everything else that is "life." But there is a positive in delineating them—it means you can have boundaries between the two.

Personally, in reflecting on "work-life balance," I found a way to think about it that sets me free. Instead of a work-life-balance seesaw with "work" on one end and "life" on the other, imagine a sliding scale. The idea is that different roles take priority at different times; the concept that instead of a balance, on a seesaw, I was sliding along in my day from different dimensions of priority in the same plane. For example, it could be a full day or even a week when I could slide in the direction of my job, prioritizing it one day, or even one week, and devote my energy and focus to that area of my life. That doesn't mean that I am out of balance. It just means that on that day, I am consciously sliding in that direction. Other times, I can slide in different directions within the hour—I am going to take this call with focus for one minute, but then I am 100 percent finding a Band-Aid or making a Play-Doh snake. While it's not ideal to get out of "the flow" of work when you're in it, it also means that there are moments when you can slide your energy, output, and responsibility where it's needed. The other things don't disappear; they are there, waiting for you to slide into them with intentionality. I loved it when discussing work-life balance with Ali Levine, host of the podcast *Everything with Ali Levine* and mother of three, she asked, "How do you make the ebbs and flows work?"

I call this "work-life fluidity," and I prefer it to "work-life harmony," "work-life integration," or several other attempts to name this concept, because they don't account for movement. They still are seeking something constant. The idea of fluidity allows us to recognize that work and motherhood, though incredibly important, are only two of our many dimensions. Imaging the sliding scale instead of the seesaw releases us from the expectation that we can be in two places (or more) at once. It allows us to focus our efforts on the task at hand, to choose what's important, and to not constantly be disappointed about the lack of balance. Instead, we can recognize that we're where we need to be right now. When I asked Dr. Hina Choudhary, a contributor to my research, what she admires in strong working mothers, she captures her sentiment perfectly: "They are fully present for what matters most."

Embracing work-life fluidity is also about real flexibility. Figuring this out now means that you put less pressure on yourself as you're about to add another variable of pregnancy and ultimately motherhood, and it also gives you a way to make your energy work for you. Remember you have the power to maneuver time, not the amount of it in the day, but the way you use it, including how you free it up, and recognizing where your energy has value.

A few weeks ago, I was working late at night, and a colleague, also a working mother, pinged me. "Mother's hours," she wrote. I pinged back, "Mother's hours." While the tone of that "mother's hours" could have been read with a sigh, the relief I feel to have those hours has been a game changer. Instead of thinking about these late nights as "working once they go to sleep," I think about it as having the type of energy they need from me when they are awake, but also having my quiet flow of emails I enjoy at night without any distraction, family, work, or otherwise. Later I thought that the other people I saw by their little green icon at that time doing the same thing—signing off a little earlier, staying up a little later with some sunlight hours in between—weren't all mothers. While the warning flags of our "always on" life are real because of hybrid work, and I encourage you to cali-brate your efficiency, there is also a possibility of freedom we can all appreciate.

For me work-life fluidity was a mindset shift to remove frustra-tion where my energy wasn't. I have boundaries, but because it's a sliding scale from work to life, those margins where life and work col-lide are graceful. Instead of being frustrated that I'm working late at night, I enjoy it because I enjoy my time-focused evenings with my boys (or getting a workout in) even more. I still have a traditional schedule dictated by the demands of my job, but in the margins, the ones that I define and actively create, I set myself up for more balance than I had when I was constantly chasing it.

I encourage you to recognize that what you need in different mo-ments, and even on different days, might change. My schedule is dif-ferent now than when my sons were younger, and I'm sure it will continue to evolve as they get older. It's different when I am writing a book, teaching for the semester, or training for a half-marathon on top of my day job. But I organize and assess them, along with who and what I need for support—and how the kitchen might just have to stay a mess, in service of "achieving it all," just not all at once.

Recently I was in a meeting regarding the future of the workplace, one with more flexibility. One of the key topics being debated was whether in a hybrid environment people would have more balance or less. One participant reflected, in a semi-Newtonian statement, "Mo-tion is a series of unbalanced movements." Unbalance is what keeps us going, creating complexity to navigate, but also growth. This leads us to the next consideration for you to find *your* balance: accessing where you are and where you want to go, and making sure that, even like the seesaw, there is motion—that you aren't stuck.

THE TRAFFIC LIGHT

The women that I have heard from regarding all things work and life share a common theme—the need for simplicity, to see through the clutter and distill what they really want. As you think about your journey to motherhood or, frankly, whenever you want to assess your career moves, visualize a traffic light to help frame where you are right now in your career and think about where you want to go.

Green Light

Are you in the zone? Do you feel like you are learning at work? Are you happy with your tasks and responsibilities? Do you get energy from the people you work with and what you are creating or changing? Do you feel motivated and stretched in your role?

If you answered yes to most of these questions, your light is green. This is awesome! Embrace this time at work. Don't be afraid that it's going to go away or change when you are pregnant or become a mother. Instead, try to understand why you feel this way—is it the people, is it the topic of interest, is it because you are comfortable or positively uncomfortable? How can you find that sentiment, both throughout your pregnancy and in anticipation of your return—or especially in your return? Who and how can you share your great green energy with? Both for them and for you to keep it going.

The women I've spoken to who have a green light might worry that their future family changes may affect the "go!" of their green, but it can also mean that work is in such a good place that it may smooth any unease in another part of life that might feel unstable.

This is a good place to be when you're thinking about big life changes, even though inherently it means that you're staying the course. Those green vibes can propel you if you need the positive boost throughout your pregnancy.

Some of the best advice that I've received for assessing my career has come from Maureen Chiquet, former CEO of Chanel, speaker, author of *Beyond the Label: Women, Leadership, and Success on Our Own Terms*, and mother of two. Maureen helped me to find and keep my green light when I was thinking about a career move. While weighing the pros and cons between staying at my current job and leaving, she told me, "Make three columns. One is what you know you are good at contributing, where you add value, and where you feel most energized. Two is what you want to learn that will continue to grow you in your career. The third is what you need for your life right now."

I realized that all three, especially that third column, pointed to staying at the job I had. There are two lessons in this. First, sometimes this third column is about what keeps you in the green light: family, including financial impact and/or flexibility. There is *nothing* wrong with having that third column. It's not third because it's last in the decision-making order, or because we don't talk about it. Keep in mind the temporary nature of "what I need for my life right now," no matter how long or short that "temporary" is. Secondly, sometimes staying green ironically is not going anywhere, just staying in the flow.

Yellow Light

Are you comfortable with where you are in your career but starting to think about what's next? Do you have space or bandwidth to try something new? Is there someone you may want to talk to about your current role, or about what they do? Do you feel "stuck" at work in some way, and does that make you feel anxious or unsettled?

If the answer is yes, you might have a yellow light. This isn't a bad thing, but it is a warning as you start thinking about getting pregnant. Try to remember the last time you had a green light. Were you cruising along, and something suddenly changed? Or did you outgrow the stage you were in? Is there someone that's sucking up your energy, or something that you might take off your plate? Do you need to add back something that gave you a green light, or stretch a bit to get that feeling of connecting to others? Do you need help from people, including a mentor or your community, or their resources? If you've been at a yellow light for a while, it might be time to explore something new.

I have found that women who have a yellow light at work and are in any phase of pregnancy are really assessing this time at work hard, including trying to get pregnant, and work. Should they stick it out with what they are doing now because they are or hope to be pregnant soon? Do they need to push to use their pregnancy as an opportunity to shift their priorities, or even use their maternity leave to make a slight or drastic career move?

It's important to figure out the "why" of your yellow light to know how the intersection of pregnancy and work will impact it. In addition, it can be important to assess now to set yourself up for a green light during and after pregnancy. For example, if you are feeling stuck, examine why. Are you bored? Do you feel like you aren't getting anywhere either alone or in a team? If it's because you are underutilized, what's the right way to make an impact now in a clearly defined way?

Red Light

When people come to me about making a career change, I usually ask them, "Is this a rescue mission, a 'get me the f out of here,' or an 'I'm having a crappy day'?" (It usually also comes with "Do you want advice, do you want to vent, or you want me to personally do something about it?") Red is a slim band for most of us. If you are at a red light for too long it looks like, "I really dislike what I'm doing every day and every minute of it is making me less motivated and more willing to sacrifice what can make me green just not to be red." It stinks, but you also know it when you feel it.

Red is a big deal, a deal breaker for your career and for finding the energy to both "do it all" and enjoy it. In fact, some women talked about that red-light stress as having an impact on their ability to get pregnant. That is clearly a big red stop sign. If you're at a red light, don't stay there mentally or physically. How can you get yourself into a yellow light, even if you have restrictions that don't allow you to make a big move? For example, if you just got pregnant, you have a big project you want to finish, or you're on track for a new role, you can push to just get through it, but you can also identify where you can get some green vibes to make it bearable and know that red is temporary. You need a plan.

PUSH, PAUSE, PIVOT

Now that you've identified whether you're breezing by, cautiously crossing, or sitting at the intersection at work, what should your next move be? While the traffic light can be used at any juncture in your career, I have found in my research that for pregnancy and work it comes down to three options: push, pause, or pivot. These are deliberate choices that you can make in this specific window of time. You can do one or all three at different stages of your pregnancy and into working motherhood.

Push

While I dedicate chapter 9 to the phase in your pregnancy called The Push, when your pregnancy is public and you are heading toward the finite deadline of your due date, a "push" could be happening at any time throughout your pregnancy-at-work journey. More than a clever play on childbirth, there is specific, recognizable exertion often observed during pregnancy because what you do, including at work, can feel like it matters even more than usual because your life literally is about to change.

For this reason, during pregnancy many women decide it's the right time to push to catch the green light, move past a yellow light, or get out from behind a red light. It can be a very conscious moment to decide to "go for it." Your perspective and needs right now, when considering your future baby, might just encourage you to give it a push. Don't think that it's strange to want to push when you're pregnant. Instead, know that you are capable, but also recognize when enough is enough.

An anonymous contributor shared the following story about her decision to push pre-baby and during pregnancy, and ultimately for her future family:

> We found out we were pregnant two days before leaving for a vacation to Vietnam, two weeks before I had planned to give notice, and two months before I was hoping to start a new job. I had been on the road over thirty weekends that past year, worked tirelessly to build my client network, and been promoted to manage education programs for our novel technology segment of our med-tech business. I didn't feel pregnant, but the plus sign was there. The switch from my usually calculated behavior at client dinners, four cups of coffee, and rush through airline scanners was about to significantly change my productivity at work.
>
> While keeping my secret, I asked my old boss, my future boss, and senior friends at work (all were men) for advice. They said, "Don't leave, stay where there are better benefits. You won't get your FMLA if you start somewhere new. There never is a good time for this, just suck it up and get a good

nanny. Don't tell anyone till you show. How are you going to keep traveling? Who will pick up your slack? You could still lose it, it's early to start making decisions. . . ."

At twenty-six weeks, we found out from a scan that my little baby boy had a congenital heart defect. What a roller-coaster. Work drama didn't go away, but baby drama was added on top.

I was planning with the NICU team for birth when a re-cruiter reached out to me on LinkedIn with my dream job at a start-up company. They were based in Europe. I decided to go for it. I did Zoom calls (head up), which got me to the final interview, which I timed a few weeks after my due date. After thirty-six hours of labor and delivery, my son was here, and I wouldn't let him out of my sight until three weeks later, when I was off to Paris under the guise of maternity leave, pumping in the airplane bathroom and around my interviews. I didn't realize the whirlwind it was, and while the whole time I felt like a failure, I look back now and I see my successes. . . . Don't be afraid that you can't do your job as well as you could before: YOU GET BETTER.

Pause

If you feel the desire to push at work and feel good mentally and phys-ically, go for it, but don't let that overshadow priority number one: the health of you and your baby. Momentum is essential, but you also need to know when enough is enough. Deciding to pause—which can mean anything from literally eliminating any nonessentials from your to-do list to moving to a temporary "cruise control" in your ca-reer to coming to a full stop—is an option.

In the grand scheme of things, you have a lot more time to work than to be pregnant and have a newborn. Remember that the bizarre, dated advice about "proving your value" and overcompensating for other people's perceptions is bullshit. Yes, you have a responsibility at work, to the role you are paid for, to your colleagues, and to your goals that you want to achieve both for yourself and your organization, and if you cannot meet those needs then you need to have a real and balanced conversation with your team. But you don't have to overdeliver. Slowing down can allow you to be more present in your pregnancy, and it can also be truly essential to protect it.

Maureen Chiquet remembers the guilt of pushing herself when she was pregnant:

As women, we're already working twice as hard because we have something to prove. There is a feeling that you have to work hard; it's not even about what you produce, it's about the impression of you trying hard to succeed. I'm going to show everyone—I'm going to power through my pregnancy. I was in a positive and supportive environment. It was my desire to push. To do it despite the pregnancy. In hindsight I wouldn't have waited for my doctor to tell me to stop. I knew it intellectually, but I needed perspective and to better know my own body.

Old Navy was born in 1992 and Mimi was born in 1996. Old Navy was at the most explosive stage of growth; we were working day and night. There were no limits to the pace and hours we were putting in. We were chasing the business. It was booming. I was vice president of the Women's Division with a lot of changing managerial responsibilities; I was also pregnant. Mimi was my second child, and my first daughter, Pauline, was only two. Fortunately, my boss, Jenny Ming, who was president of Old Navy, and Nancy Green, who was a vice president of merchandising, were positive role models of women leaders who had children, and they handled it differently. Nancy, who had young children, was good at leaving the office on time and showing up for her family. Jenny's kids were a bit older and so she didn't have to rush home in the same way. Jenny is a machine; she would work a full day, bake cookies, and bring them back for us, unflustered. She just had the capacity and the right partner. I too had the right partner at home and these women as reference points, and the company, which at that point was full of energetic thirtysomethings, was a positive environment. It was exciting to be there. And I was in it.

When I was pregnant, I thought my body could perform in the same way. I exercised at a level I probably shouldn't have; I was a little impervious to anything and everything. I worked as hard as I wanted to. I went to the doctor, and during the sonogram he very matter-of-factly stated that I was very low on amniotic fluid. That I would have to come in every week for an ultrasound. That I could go on bed rest. That I needed to drink lots of water, stay off my feet, and get more rest, or I would put my baby at risk. Three weeks later, at one of the check-ins, I was told that I needed to have the baby that night.

I remember one of my first thoughts was, "What do I tell my boss, Jenny?" Then that I was going to miss a meeting with Gap, Inc. CEO Mickey Drexler, and I hadn't reviewed the plans yet. But this wasn't about me.

At this point in my life, I didn't have a relationship to my body that told me this was a big thing happening, something bigger than my capabilities, that I couldn't overcome. You know it intellectually, but personally knowing when to stop is a far different thing. If I had to do it over again, I would have been more cautious and aware that I put her at risk. I would have put it into perspective—instead of to push and achieve at work despite the pregnancy, to make decisions because of it.

During pregnancy, a lot of us might be tempted to push in our careers when we should be pausing. The only timeline that matters is yours and your baby's, and in fact, pushing now against yours doesn't guarantee success later—you can't force it. Personally, there are moments I remember leaning in so hard at work that as a pregnant person I felt more off-balance than what my belly and back were causing, but also so worried about sitting back that I couldn't physically or metaphorically get out of my chair, in the same way it got harder to tie my shoes.

In one of those moments when I was pushing (when I should have been pausing) during my pregnancy and feeling overwhelmed, I took a step back and asked for help. I wasn't pushing because I had something that I wanted to do for me or for my future family, but because I didn't want to let anyone down. But I didn't need to carry it all. Cortney Cahill, executive coach and senior consultant, helped me to communicate my needs to my team. Instead of assuming that people understood that I was being over-organized for their benefit, she suggested that I explain my motivations so my team didn't think I was just being controlling, but ultimately to set them up for success (without me) and to do it for themselves.

In that vein, coaching also helped me shift my focus to those around me. Instead of gunning for myself in a narrow window where work needed to be priority two, I also started thinking about the projects that my two direct reports would take over for me when I was out, and how I could set them up for success. In other words, my pause became their push.

Pivot

There are times when pregnancy creates a shift in perspective. You might realize you want more financial stability, better health insurance (or a better healthy lifestyle), or the right community around you. But to achieve those things, you must make a career change. While having a baby is a big change and making another one at this time can be challenging, the decisions you make now *will* impact not just you but your future family.

Alli Kasirer, the founder and CEO of Robyn, a dynamic maternal health platform, and Amanda Cole, the founder and CEO of Yummy Mummy, the expert retailer for all things breastfeeding, made significant pivots in their careers and as a result improved the intersection of pregnancy and work for all of us. Their stories show us that pregnancy can create powerful crucible experiences that can fuel the next step in your career.

Alli:

I was a recently promoted at a large investment bank and was working on the trading floor; everything was going well. I was excited about the future and being a female leader at the firm someday. But then the challenges of getting pregnant flipped my world upside down.

It was traumatic. Physically I felt poked and prodded, and emotionally it was jarring and felt too out of control. We were young and it was unexpected. I think like the millennial workforce "Lean In" generation, I always thought I would be able to have work-life balance; I would make it happen when I had a family. Experiencing the force of that balance while trying to conceive was never in my purview, I never anticipated it, and it took me by surprise.

I garnered support, but I needed more. I had a fertility doctor and a reproductive psychologist and then made a tough decision to take a sabbatical. It's just what I had to do. It didn't feel feasible that I could do both. My hours were six a.m. to six p.m., and I traveled one to two times a week across the country—that was the job. It was sales, it was being in front of CFOs and treasurers. This was before Zoom. No one was having teleconferences. We didn't realize how much time we could have saved and not felt as strained. The logistics were challenging, but it was also that so much of my ego and persona was being a Wall Street person, and it was hard to put my health and wellness, this personal experience, first.

The whole thing was a shock to my system.

I have always been the type of person who puts myself all-in. I've always wanted to break glass ceilings. I studied engineering at Penn, I was on Wall Street, and at each hurdle I just did it. It wasn't until this time that I wasn't able to show up as my full self. It was just work until then.

Very few people knew at work. I chose a few that needed to be brought in regarding my leave, but I was self-conscious about the decision. I didn't openly talk about it, and I regret that now. If you think about being a leader at an organization, you need to be someone who can show up as your full self. I could have been more of a force for change, but it wasn't in my personal journey yet. Nobody knew why I was taking this time off.

I was fortunate that my company had great insurance and most of my IVF was covered, but I still remember being in the filing cabinet room at work and crying over insurance coverage as a pivotal moment. Had I activated my plan properly? Had I gone through all those hoops? I was in there because there wasn't anywhere else to go; my desk was in an open plan office and the conference room walls were glass.

I became passionate about wellness. It was my own experience that showed me the opportunity. I took my skills and my intuition to help others. I had a mission: I wanted to give women the power in tools, resources, and experts to support their journeys so that they would not have to be alone. I started sharing my story publicly, and then we became a platform, and we added expert providers. That's how it got started, and I didn't look back.

I launched my company, Robyn, the same month that I had my twins in 2017. Today, Robyn connects aspiring, expecting, and new parents to parental wellness providers, resources, and classes for their unique path to parenthood.

Only 2 percent of venture funding goes to female founders, and in 2019, when my third son was born, I secured it for the business. I had three under three, was a solo female founder, and got funding. We also moved across the country from New York to Los Angeles. I went from a low in 2018, after tough postpartum with my twins, to a super-high high. Throughout it all, I realized that you have to learn to let go a little bit. That first loss of control was a lesson in the impermanence of everything. Letting go and, in hindsight, sharing more would have resulted in even more growth. Growth I am now grateful for and want to help other women find in this important time in their lives—for their whole selves. Mothering yourself is the first step to becoming a mother for your children.

Amanda:

My preparations for having a baby—and being a working mom who could "have it all"—began on the day I contemplated attending business school. I was not yet pregnant and had just recently married, but business school would give me leverage, I thought, to fulfill my dream of having a rewarding career while still being a very present and accessible mother.

In business school, I majored in marketing, the career choice for business school students who prioritized work-life balance. I even wrote my ethics class thesis paper on how I would achieve the exalted "work-life balance" state, hoping that by writing it on paper it would become a self-fulfilling prophecy.

In keeping with this theme, for my post-business school job, I applied only to companies listed on the Working Mother list of best places to work. And I felt hopeful that the sixty-to-ninety-minute commute to my new job would all pay off once I had children and a flexible, understanding corporate culture.

But many people working in marketing at large consumer packaged goods companies are young and female with pregnancy on the near-term horizon and with work-life balance in mind. So, after two years of killing myself to prove myself, working twelve-hour days (not including the commute), I probably should have prepared myself for a different response when I asked my boss if I could work from home one day a week or work four days a week at 80 percent pay. The powers that be were blunt: Everyone working in marketing is a young thirtysomething soon-to-be pregnant female. If they made accommodations for me, they would need to make accommodations for everyone. It would have "a domino effect."

In that one very moment, it felt like the past four years—from preparing for business school to registering for marketing classes to scrolling through that best places to work list—crumbled to dust. It was crushing and demoralizing and left me, now five months pregnant with no career path in sight, gripped with fear that I would be left with two options I did not want: keeping a job that would separate me from my newborn baby fourteen hours a day or hanging up any prospects of a career to become a stay-at-home mom.

Thankfully, I followed a different path entirely. I did end up quitting my job, but not to stop working. Instead, I took my newfound freedom to start a business, Yummy Mummy, which is now one of the largest breast pump providers in the country and a nationally recognized brand to breastfeeding moms. And I haven't looked back since. While not easy and certainly demanding, this decision gave me the opportunity to find my own work-life balance, one that is fulfilling on both a personal and professional level. A lot has changed for working women since that fateful day twelve years ago when I mustered up the courage to ask my supervisors to help me achieve work-life balance. And I'm rooting for all the women who are mustering

up the courage for a similar ask today. The answer may leave
them with a painful and scary and (sometimes) agonizing de-
cision, but it will be the right choice, if only for that moment
in time.

PRIORITIES AND BOUNDARIES

When making decisions throughout your pregnancy, the concepts of
the traffic light and push, pause, or pivot can help you identify where
you are and where you want to go. But you also need two more things,
along with a healthy dose of organization, to guide you toward achieving work-life fluidity: priorities and boundaries.

When faced with a decision, ask yourself, "Will it matter today?"
Then ask, "Will it matter tomorrow?" and "Will it matter in a week . . .
month . . . nine months, a year?" and so on. The idea here is to evaluate a decision according to its effect over time. It also reinforces the
"impermanence" Alli shares, meaning that these moments can be incredibly positive or negative, but all are temporary. There is also the
scale of impact to consider. My mom calls it the "Ah! A bug!" test.
What is the appropriate reaction to seeing a ladybug on your water
bottle, versus watching a giant insect carrying off one of your children? Calibration when the stakes are high, like in pregnancy, can be
hard but necessary.

Dr. Margaret (Molly) McNairy poignantly illustrates this idea
along with recognition of the non linear nature of our priorities.

Pregnancy and work—it's a lot to juggle. With work and chil-
dren it can feel like it all comes undone in an instant or you
have the momentum to keep going forward, but it doesn't have
to be all or nothing. I have found the key is knowing that balls
will drop; just make sure that you let the plastic balls rather
than the glass balls drop. What I mean by that is that preg-
nancy, maternity leave, family obligations, and your mental

health are all glass balls, and you must hold those close and not let them drop. Work challenges are most always plastic balls, and you can pick them back up. Second, you can't have it all at the same time, but careers come in fits and spurts; I don't think they are linear. When you can, put your foot on the gas and work as hard as possible for a season. Then when you have a baby, take your foot off the gas for a season and go at a slower speed. Success ultimately is about recognizing when you are in each gear.

The project, the meeting, the trip, even a semester that you may choose to prioritize will be long forgotten in months or years, but the body and child you need to nurture and protect will be with you always. Facing decision fatigue? Every time that happens to me, even begrudgingly, I think about how grateful I am to have options. Again, it's about perspective. Work is not always going to win out on the work-life balance seesaw; sometimes it will be a distant third or fourth place.

An anonymous contributor is a global sourcing and supply chain executive in the food industry. She has traveled the world in search of fruit, vegetables, and more that are in all our grocery stores. She was breastfeeding her first child when she discovered a lump in her breast. The pain and fears of a clogged duct that just wouldn't go away with the cabbage leaves or warm showers resulted in calls to lactation consultants and eventually her OB. What she discovered was that it wasn't a horrible case of mastitis. It was cancer.

When her son was four months old, she began chemotherapy. Exhausted yet resilient, the new mother continued working until it was no longer feasible, then took a medical leave. A few months later, she returned to work and there was a "crisis." It was a shortage of cauliflower, which we all know is now a bizarrely popular vegetable. Exhausted from beating cancer postpartum, and now working full time traveling to source tropical foods so we all can eat pineapple during a blizzard, she said, "They can eat broccoli."

This story alone is a powerful lesson in priorities, which concludes with a very happy ending and next-level perspective. When she was going through her treatments, she had her eggs frozen should she decide that she and her partner would try for another baby after she was cancer-free, but they agreed that a second child would be risky. The chances of her becoming pregnant without them was miniscule. Months passed and she wasn't feeling well, so she visited her oncologist and later her OB to confirm early menopause. Just to be safe, she also did an ultrasound. As she looked at the screen with her OB, they saw two strong flashes beating side by side. She was eight weeks pregnant with twins.

Revisiting perspective can guide what really matters to shape our priorities, and although thinking about them can feel big and heavy, you can also break them down by using something light. Make a list of your top priorities. Then take a stack of ten sticky notes—you cannot exceed ten—and write one priority on each. Put them in two piles, a Yes and a No pile. "Yes" means they are 100 percent nonnegotiable priorities. "No" means you hesitated, and this priority is not mandatory. Once you sort the Yes and No piles, put them in order. You can reshuffle them—both the Yes and No notes and their order of priority. You can even cross one off and write something new, but you can't just keep adding to the pile, and you still must do the sorting. You can't have two number ones.

Taking time to set priorities is key to managing your productivity *and* your stress, especially right now. With each priority, think about the time and impact of what needs to be done and when, what can be delegated, and what needs as much dedication and effort as you can give, or conversely what needs to be given a "good enough" effort. This notion of finding the sweet spot of time, effort, and impact will allow you to unlock and downshift a perfectionist mindset in parallel to evaluating how much you can take on in a particular moment versus always. This is something that will come in handy as a new working mom.

This also means that if you're at a green light at work and you're pushing, you might have a bigger stack of priorities in the Yes pile than in the No pile, but how many are feasible? Ask yourself if they are leading toward a bigger picture. Or are they just a lot of Yeses? Sometimes there might be Yeses that you'll kick yourself for and maybe a No that you'll regret, but aligning on these priorities will make those moments less frequent and then you can give them more energy.

On the other hand, if you're at a yellow or red and need to pause, pull back on that Yes stack and focus just on what matters in this moment. Women at work are much more likely to volunteer for non-promotable tasks, and it doesn't mean that it's not good to put in the extra effort, but you do not need to always step up—especially right now in your pregnancy.

The Nos are just as important as the Yeses, especially when it comes to taking care of ourselves. "No" is a powerful word, and one that you need to get used to. "No" gives us ownership and the power to create boundaries. While many contributors commented that pregnancy was one of the first times in their lives that they felt boundaries were put into place for them, consider the boundaries you have been making already pre-baby. This includes a range from how long you work to where you work and with whom you work—and how much you share with them.

The most important thing to know about boundaries is that you don't need anyone else's permission to have them. Kate Gold, a real estate investor and former digital media executive, captures this important distinction: "Be conscious of how often you say 'I'm sorry' in the workplace. Use it when you need to, of course, but remind yourself that you do not need to apologize for being a mom or taking time to attend to your family commitments. You can show that you are a team player by having compassion for others when they have commitments, by being accessible within boundaries you have set, by being solutions oriented, and by having a positive attitude." It's up to *you* to decide when your boundaries need to change based on your priorities, or whether they need to be firm or flexible.

Libby Wadle, CEO of the J.Crew Group and mother of two, shares an important point that illustrates how blurred lines can actually empower us to embrace our priorities concurrently: "'Work-life balance' is part of the script you are given as women . . . but I involve my kids— we talk about everything at the dinner table, I bring them on store visits, I bring the two together instead of having stress about keeping the two apart." Personally, I have found that the more I share that I have multiple priorities (but remember, not in the same order), with my family *and* work, the more I feel like I'm showing up in both places as my whole self.

Pregnant women I interviewed often reflected that for the first time they must be more selfless by being *selfish*. Mandi Tuhro, whom we met in the introduction, shared, "Give what you can where you can—but don't think you can give it all to everyone else without giving the most to yourself." This includes setting boundaries so *your* priorities stay in line and you don't end up sacrificing one for another. As Christy Turlington Burns, founder of Every Mother Counts, shared with me, "The one instruction you hear on the plane that we all remember, 'Put on your air mask before you help those around you,' being pregnant and hearing that reminded me how important it is to take care of yourself as a mother—and not just when you're on a plane."

Poppy Harlow, CNN anchor and mother of two, reflected on priority decision making in two ways—the importance of "slowing down, which won't slow *you* down" and assessing the powerful value of yes and no.

"I passed out anchoring CNN on live TV when I was pregnant with my first child and it reminded me to slow down," she told me. "But that 'slow down' was more than a lesson about the priority of my health, it was permission, because slower doesn't mean doing less at work. Slowing down doesn't mean doing worse. Motherhood has taught me how to prioritize and cut out things that weren't needed in the first place—and ultimately made me better at my job." She continued, "My friend Kara Swisher [a renowned journalist and *New York Times* writer focused on technology], taught me the power of no. What's important is that saying no allows you to say yes when it matters."

One of the biggest fears that women have regarding the impact of motherhood on their career is that they will have to say no . . . a lot. Poppy shares:

> *You do not have to default to no when you have children. I remember I was pregnant with my second child, my son, Luca, I got an email from Columbia University, where I went to college, and was asked to interview Supreme Court Justice Ruth Bader Ginsburg for their first annual She Opened the Door, Columbia University Women's Conference. That evening, I said to my husband, you won't believe this, I can't believe I have to say no.*
>
> *The interview was February twelfth, Luca was due the twelfth, but then my due date was moved up to the fifth. I just thought I had to say no. My husband said, "You can't say no, this is what you will tell our kids about—and what am I, chopped liver? I can take care of our baby son." A lot went through my mind—I have my husband, I have a pump, and I have formula, and it's in the same city—I should . . . I want to . . . so I did it. I rented a large skirt from Rent the Runway.*
>
> *That interview changed my life in so many ways, transformed and completely inspired me. I called my husband after and he said, "Take your time, I'm at a wine bar with Sienna and Luca." After some surprise, I realized I also could say yes to a glass of wine and toasted the fact that I interviewed the iconic Supreme Court Justice Ginsburg . . . while I was wearing essentially a diaper—just days after giving birth.*

Do you know what Justice Ginsburg said in that interview in response to a question from Poppy about what she sacrificed? "The question is often said as a statement, 'Women can't have it all.' My response to that is, 'I *have* had it all in my long life, but not necessarily at one time.'"

Balance, like standing on one leg, is uncomfortable, but you have three choices: you can practice hard and get used to it; you can forget about it and constantly wobble; or you can switch legs, sometimes stand on two feet and give yourself a break. Balance is temporary, but everything is temporary—the good, the bad, the sweet moments with your kids, or the wins with your teams—so take a moment and recognize the reality of balance. Consider a more fluid approach. Assess it with the traffic light, and the push, pause, pivot choices. Establish boundaries and priorities, but most of all ground yourself on what you want and what you need to make it happen, including who you will need around you. As you move to the third principle, consider: You can do it all, not at the same time—and not alone.

QUESTIONS FOR REFLECTION

Are you at a green, yellow, or red light at work? Why? Is that something you want to keep or change before, during, or after pregnancy?

Do the sticky-note exercise yourself. Start with five to ten. Write your big-picture priorities for this month. Put them in order. What are the boundaries that you want to have right now?

What are you most worried about regarding work-life fluidity during pregnancy? Keep breaking it down until it's something manageable. For example, you don't want to miss work or being with your baby. Break it down even further—what specifically do you not want to miss?

Carry Strong Stories

JOAN KUHL, AUTHOR OF *DIG YOUR HEELS IN*, FOUNDER OF STAY TO LEAD

After working for fourteen years at a global corporation in the pharmaceutical industry, I launched a research, training, and consulting company and wrote three books. My schedule was extremely inconsistent as I was traveling across the country and around the world for client and speaking engagements. So it was in the bathroom of a Midwest hotel that I both confessed and cultivated my intentions for working motherhood to a client counterpart and fortunate trusted confidante.

This was my second pregnancy, so I wasn't new to the endless juggles and demands of working motherhood. In fact, I was minutes from going on stage at a conference to share the findings of a global research study focused on the enablers and barriers encountered by women in the workplace that impact her engagement and advancement. I blurted out that I was pregnant, overwhelmed, and emotional about everything we uncovered in the deeply resonant data. At the time I was so hyperfocused on spotlighting and supporting the women working for my client that I didn't make any space to think about what I wanted, what I needed, or what I deserved.

Her compassionate response made me feel seen, heard, and valued. I knew that from that day forward I would not only report the research but do something about the findings, because all women deserve to rise and thrive in all dimensions of their lives. We experience such intense pressure across all our roles in work and life. How can we meet unrealistic expectations to be the perfect mother, daughter, manager, colleague, friend, neighbor, vol-

unteer, and the many other roles we play? I wish I could have seen in that moment, without any more accolades or accomplishments, that I was "enough." That we all are. The reflections that were inspired by that moment in the bathroom influence my determination to help other women truly see their value and go after what they deserve.

ALYSIA REINER, ACTRESS AND PRODUCER

Once we decided we wanted to get pregnant, I was fortunate that I got pregnant naturally. I had morning sickness for twenty weeks and was nervous to share because of fear of miscarriage . . . so we just kept waiting. I was working on two jobs and thought I was hiding my pregnancy very well at both, but then on the set of The Starter Wife, I saw Spanx in my dressing room. I panicked and thought, "They know." I found out shortly thereafter that everyone in the cast, and probably everyone in LA, had Spanx in their dressing room.

I had also gotten a job doing Shakespeare in the Park playing Rosalind in As You Like It. I was fortunate that one of my best friends, Purva Bedi, auditioned, and got the role, to be Celia, who is Rosalind's best friend in the play. I had met my husband doing Shakespeare and I had her with me, so it felt right. She was such a gift when I was not telling anyone else through all the rehearsals. It kept me at ease. I didn't share until opening night of the play. I think the costumer started to get a hint when I said, "Make sure the pants are really low." Rosalind goes from being a woman to a man to a woman again, and wearing a corset was tough!

I was so afraid of what motherhood would do to my career, what they would think, and honestly it had no negative ramifications.

However, going back to work right after having my daughter and breastfeeding on set, I did realize that the business I am in is

*not set up for women to succeed today. While there are women
figuring it out and advocating for them, like TIME'S UP, where I
am on the global advisory board, the more we can share the
better—before, during, and after we experience it.*

*For example, I was a big breastfeeding advocate, not that ev-
eryone should breastfeed, but they should have the opportunity if
they want to. You don't want to be the "weird or difficult one," and
you need support. And again, you need that one friend (or more).
In my case I did a lot of research on breastfeeding, had a lactation
consultant ready, and had a great friend who was a mother of
four to teach me. I was ready because I had tools to succeed thanks
to my community. . . . It really is about community. At home and
at work, you need to feel valued. Having friends who could guide
me with their answers and made me feel their "I've got you" with
high trust and no judgment. That's what we must give women.
and sometimes support comes from unexpected sources, men,
and women. One of my "I've got your back" heroes didn't have
kids, and I felt so taken care of. And one of my daughter's god-
moms is a friend I met over the past couple of years, not yet married, single, and they are so close. Be willing to look in unexpected
places—and be open to being that unexpected source for others.*

TRISH NUGENT, ADVERTISING, MARKETING, AND PUBLIC RELATIONS AGENCY SENIOR LEADER

*I lost my second son, Baxton, at three weeks old. His death was
unexpected, and every moment of that traumatic day haunted
me. When I returned to the office, I was operating through profound grief. My colleagues were patient with me, and work moved
forward, but my world felt like it had stopped spinning.*

Six months after my loss, I was called across the country to kick off a new client project. These meetings would demand sharp thinking and a bit of charisma—neither of which I felt especially ready to offer. Days before my departure, I learned I was pregnant once more. This was welcome news, but it was a foundation-shaking revelation too. My new pregnancy felt fragile and undeserved, and it was hard to leave the sanctuary of my family. I pushed through the early nausea and a blend of heartache and happiness for the meetings that followed.

There was a moment on the trip that I'll never forget: As I entered my hotel room, relieved for a break between appointments, I found a baby's crib arranged by my bedside. Intended for another guest, it had mistakenly delivered it to my room. The scene embodied all that I had lost and all for which I hoped. An unexpected laugh emerged from my throat; the error was too ironic. Of course, I wanted to crumble at the sight of that crib, but I knew this would derail my day. So I quickly had it removed and transitioned to the next meeting on my agenda. Carrying grief, hope, and a career in tandem is complex work. Now I recognize the resilience that working motherhood demands, especially when we're feeling our most vulnerable. Often out of view is the intense effort we're investing to navigate pregnancy, parenting, and all the joy and sorrow it can bring.

When I reflect on this story, I feel grateful for the perspective—and healing—that time allows. In the thick of my grief, the mountain felt insurmountable. I didn't know if my former self would ever reemerge. I wish I'd known then that healing would come. There is still heartbreak and plenty of tears, of course. But there is a lot of joy to find in the four years since my son's death. We can feel strong and broken at the same time. Entrust your truth to worthy colleagues and let them prop you up when needed. The right community will do it gladly.

AMY SLOAN, BEAUTY INDUSTRY EXECUTIVE

My journey to motherhood was unique and extraordinary. Definitely not what I thought it would be when it came time to start a family. I approached family building like I approached everything in my life—work hard, put in the effort, and you will get results. At the start it seemed to just happen; I got pregnant right away, but it unfortunately ended in miscarriage. Fast forward four-plus years, we were faced with many roadblocks and challenges I never could have imagined, but with a lot of resilience, unrelenting hope, and a small circle of encouragement we persevered, welcoming a beautiful baby boy via gestational carrier.

Throughout the arduous journey, I chose not to share with many people, mainly because I could not face the explanations and questions. I felt no one could understand what I was going through, so I kept all our wins and losses to just within my family unit of my husband, mother, and sister, along with three women at work. These work relationships were critical for both my personal and professional success.

For one year we tried multiple embryo transfers, with the last one making it to a heartbeat but failing at week eight. During this year, I continued to push professionally, building a team and driving business to ensure I could be elevated to the next level when the time was right. What came with this drive and pushing was a keen skill of compartmentalizing; navigating everyday complexities all the while with no one aware of this incredibly steep hill I was climbing. But I had this small circle of encouragement, cheerleaders really, that would come to turn into rock-solid bonds that go way beyond the office. Without these relationships, I am not sure I'd have made it through. They not only provided me the space to take on each hurdle and small win but allowed me the physical and mental flexibility I needed, especially when our final chapter revealed I was not able to carry our child and we embarked into an incredible partnership with our friend/ gestational carrier and her family to bring our child into this world.

Nine months later we welcomed a beautiful baby boy, a true miracle. The bonds I formed with these women at work will be forever. While I would not change my journey for anything—it was meant to be—what I know now is I would have shared the journey with others earlier, because as I was entering the light there were some in my orbit who were just beginning their journey, and I see now that I can support them just by telling them about my experience. Life is funny, and everything truly does happen for a reason.

CHAPTER 3

Community

Choosing the Company You Keep

YOU CAN DO it all, not at the same time. And not alone. Community is something you create for yourself and for others. It can bring perspective and balance, encourage you to communicate, and even help to shape your identity. Community is inherently unique in that it requires you to seek to find it, then nurture being part of it as an engaged participant. While a community is made up of individuals, it also has collective strength.

Joan Kuhl, author of *Dig Your Heels In*, founder of the global female leadership program Stay to Lead, workplace strategist and champion for girls leadership and advancing women in the workplace, shares, "Community is about connection, a connection that empowers us together—meeting us with what we need when we need it and in ways we may have not imagined possible for ourselves."

One of the most wonderful things about motherhood is its ability to unify from the very start. During your pregnancy, a community can help you celebrate wins big and small with shared hope and energy that is fueling. It can make you feel less alone during the most vulnerable moments of your pregnancy and deeply connected to other mothers. As one contributor shared when speaking about her mom friends, "It is something that just swallows you up to lift you up." But your community cannot be made up of just pregnant women and working mothers. Pregnancy is temporary and exhausting. You'll continue to need community post-baby, and we all cannot place the burden of support on the community that needs it.

Pregnancy is a necessary part of all our communities, including at work. To perpetuate society (i.e., our big community), pregnancy is normal and quite literally essential. Importantly, a sense of community, including at work, cannot exist if it doesn't feel safe. Often with pregnant women, as a society we skip to the good part of celebrating a woman at work when she has her big belly, but it is not truly an inclusive community if she is not first safe and welcome.

Community is created at your workplace, but also within it through the power of colleagues who become friends, mentors, and advocates that extend far beyond it. In fact, a work community without a collective supportive spirit can ultimately lose teammates, including pregnant women and someday working mothers. One anonymous contributor was working as a midlevel associate at a law firm in New York City when she mentioned she wanted to have a child within the next few years:

> A group of associates were hanging out casually when the conversation inevitably veered toward life goals and plans.... I was struck by the reaction from some of my colleagues, both men and women, who automatically pointed out the most likely damaging impact it would be to be pregnant while an associate. "Think about the hours! You'll be tired with the pregnancy, so how will you be able to meet billables?" One actually said, "I just assumed you'd want to accomplish more before you switched to the part-time track."

*I was shocked by the lack of advocacy, even from my peers.
It made me question whether I should push my timetable out,
to give myself time to "prove my worth" before "taking this hit
to my marketability." But then I also thought that the stakes
would be even higher if I were a partner and tried starting a
family. It struck me again that these were my peers having
these thoughts, and I automatically assumed that I wouldn't
find much support from the partners. And I was angered by
the constant touting of the firm's leave policies, when in practice employees felt that building a family was detrimental to
their career prospects.*

*I ultimately ended up leaving that firm, for multiple rea-
sons, but the tenor of the conversation and the adamant beliefs of my peers helped leave an impression that pregnancy or
being a working mom would automatically have a negative
impact on career progression. . . . I look back and I realize how
a true mentor and ambassador could make such a positive
impact and ensure that a pregnant woman could feel supported and valued. . . . And it saddened me that too often, and
not just in law firms, ambassadors aren't readily visible or
available.*

In my first study of four hundred women who worked full time
while they were pregnant, 50 percent of women had a positive change
in opinion of their employer/place of work during pregnancy and 10
percent of women said they experienced a negative shift. The impact
is significant.[1] When digging into the why, there was a correlation between comfort and community at the intersection of managing expectations. I asked women to say whether factors like "company
policies regarding maternity leave" or "flexibility to work from home"
exceeded or underdelivered on their expectations. Six of ten reasons,
including both of those, were quite neutral—generally met expectations. But four had a significant gap, meaning that they had an impact
on the change in opinion of their employer during pregnancy—and

three of four (bolded below in order of gap) were very personal and community driven:

- **Support from coworkers**
- Flexibility regarding doctors' appointments
- **Support from manager/employer**
- **Firsthand guidance from coworkers**

Even the second, "Flexibility regarding doctors' appointments," could have come down to whom you work with versus policies at a workplace level. While big-picture policies and resources are necessary to support you and all working women during pregnancy, individual relationships matter, and you can help to create them. Creating community is about connecting with colleagues and creating resources. While you can outsource, gather information on your own or from your employer, your community in your unique place of work, with all its quirks, is a powerful one—from specific recommendations to general support with a helpful frame.

What is important for you to think about now is who is part of your community today—both in your life and especially in your work. In addition, think about your place of work and whether it cultivates a sense of belonging for community to exist—that is, it needs to create the cultural safety, security, and support for you to bring your authentic self to work. Ensure that it is a place where you are seen and can see others for their unique perspectives, and you are able to be proud of what you do and who you work with.

Jaime Carrington, head of sales training and communication at a large organization, has five children under five. After years of trying to get pregnant, she had four embryos left. A year after her quadruplets were born she had surprise baby number five—a tremendous feat, and yet her moment of impact was something simple.

I was carrying quadruplets and my company allowed me to park in the handicapped spot at the front-door entrance instead of parking blocks away in a garage and walking to the office. At the time I felt awkwardly different, as only the EVPs and CEO parked in front of the building, but looking back I see the care and concern the company leaders were showing me in that small act.

I felt embarrassed during my pregnancy. I had moved from New York to California for this job and found out I was pregnant on my second day at work. To be carrying a high-risk pregnancy at thirty-nine after just accepting a new job was frazzling, to say the least. Today I feel such deep appreciation for the way coworkers rallied around me—recommending night nurses, bringing me baby swings, sharing clothes their kids had outgrown—it brings tears to my eyes because now I know that's what mamas do, they look after other people whenever there is a need.

In this chapter, you have heard the why of community; now we will go deeper on how to find and build community and, importantly, how to pay it forward. There are several groups that can make up your community at work. There is your inner circle of several key players, including your partner, your work BFF, your "board of directors," and your community including your allies. Each part has a distinctive and complementary role to play. There are also your teams. As you learn about each role, think about how they can work in tandem with one another. Notably, if you are in a very small organization or an entrepreneur, you can treat these terms more broadly, utilizing the guidance to bring in resources from beyond your place of work to support it.

Let's build your community by starting close in.

THE INNER CIRCLE

The inner circle is paramount to your community and includes only people you trust. This can be friends and family, and professional resources like coaches, therapists, trainers, and health experts. You need people who will celebrate you, are willing to challenge your assumptions, give expert counsel when you ask, and be there to catch you if you fall.

Jourdan Dunn, mother, model, actress, and philanthropist, whose story is in the conclusion, shared with me:

> *"I found out I was pregnant in the airport before a family holiday. Carrying this information on the flight, there was a lot going through my head. I was thinking, I can't do this right now, my career is taking off, what will people say? It wasn't until I started to think about what I really wanted, and no one else, that I knew I would make it work.*
>
> *I was, however, dreading telling my mum. I knew it wasn't what she wanted for me at eighteen, a young mum like she had been. After a roller-coaster of emotion, I remember her saying, "I've got you. We're in this together." Today she is an anchor in my support system. I always looked up to her as a single mum who worked, but one day she corrected me and reminded me of my grandmother and others who were part of my every day, like she is for my son, Riley. I have leaned into my family support system. For women who don't have that, it doesn't have to be a bloodline; you can create that community for yourself. Create it with people who get it and love you.*

Your inner circle does not need to be huge and it is based on one-to-one relationships. One of the integral members is your partner. Whether this is your spouse or someone you have chosen to help you raise your child, a partner is someone you love, who loves you and makes you feel safe, and who will consider your child's needs as paramount. If both of you are working, your partner's career will have a relationship to yours, and frankly they will have to understand and develop their own relationship with your baby and their work. Having a conversation about how you'll navigate both of your careers amid pregnancy and child-rearing is important, not just once, but as your relationship to each other, and to your work, evolves.

Contributor Alexandra Cosan shared the challenges of new motherhood with her wife, while concurrently navigating her career and responsibility as a breadwinner:

As a same-sex couple with my wife carrying our child, I felt guilty about taking maternity leave for anything greater than two weeks. I also felt like I was going to be judged for taking more time than a man may have for paternity leave and felt like I constantly had to justify my role as a mom despite our daughter not coming out of my uterus. I feel grateful that I had a very supportive boss who encouraged me to take more time and to focus solely on being a mom. This was incredibly difficult to fathom as nurse leader in an operational role that keeps my phone buzzing twenty-four hours a day, seven days a week, and requires real-time decision making that directly impacts patients' lives. I knew I would have to completely disconnect—partial disconnection would be too difficult.

I am already fearful of going back to work and trying to balance the responsibility while having to defend myself from others' thoughts that "Well, isn't her mom home with her?" Erin, my wife, my person, has always been my number one priority, but I haven't always been the best about translating that feeling into action with respect to work. Now having her and our daughter, the action has to come too, however I also need to continue to do well and excel professionally so that I can support our family financially. I am proud and happy to do this, but it is a heavy burden.

There are financial and physical considerations to discuss with your partner during pregnancy. What is our budget? Are both of us going to continue to work full time? How will we cover medical, childcare, and other necessary expenses? Who will be home when? It is also important you take this big moment to discuss both of your career aspirations and how you want their support (or not). Again, this is an ongoing conversation as you navigate your lives independently and as a family.

Kathleen McDowell, senior partner manager at Pinterest, like many contributors to my research, shared the incredible importance and appreciation of their partner at the intersection of pregnancy and work: "I truly have a parenting partner in everything from babies to bedtime to the mental load. Tim encouraged me through countless interviews the year I was expecting our daughter. After that maternity leave, I officially started my role at Pinterest. We were pre-IPO, and I felt as though I had a lot to prove—and I jumped in with everything. I flew to San Francisco to lead a CMO meeting just a week or two back from leave, was pumping in airports, the works—and Tim didn't miss a beat. He managed our nanny's schedule, did bedtime with two babies under two, all while cheering me on each day. I was very grateful then, and still am today."

Margaret Zakarian, president of Zakarian Hospitality, television producer, and mother of three who works every day with her husband, chef and restaurateur Geoffrey Zakarian, shares the following advice about managing time and giving full attention.

It is imperative to plan times when all the work stuff gets shut down. You must be strategic depending on what your work is, when your peak times are. I learned along the way not to schedule the "off" time when my attention in the office or with customers was most needed. For example, in the height of the busy season at one of our restaurants, making family time Friday night at seven p.m. serves no one well, because we as parents are struggling to force ourselves not to think of everything that is needed on the job. The time away ends up being a huge additional stressor. You are stressed that you are not working, and you are stressed that you are only half paying attention during designated family time. It's a lose-lose.

Plan the "off" time when you can logistically pay atten-
tion, relax, and have fun with the family. The kids feel every
nuance, so set it all up for success, and then you will get the
win-win you are looking for. Same goes for date night and
self-care.

Margaret also shares the even more pronounced importance of setting an example for your family, who see your work and life blended, often with theirs. "When thinking back to when my kids were quite young, I remember the mom guilt being strong.... One day my husband stopped me in my tracks and said, 'This is a gift, your children seeing you work so hard every day. You are setting an example.' That was an aha moment. You always hear children are sponges, sucking up their environment, so perhaps through our day and night entrepreneurship, we have been helping to instill from an early age the art of dedication and perseverance. From then on, the guilt was there, but less. I know we are contributing in a positive way, rather than just being too busy!"

Up next, the work BFF. This is the friend with whom you share a lot more than your to-do list and what you're having for lunch. They are there for you before, during, and after the workday is long over, someone with whom you can truly be yourself, including at work. No one can underestimate the value of the work BFF, both during pregnancy and beyond. Erin Weibel shared, "I have been pregnant at the same time as my work BFF twice. We have bonded over the shared experiences, and she's been key in giving advice as she tackles issues before me. Having that support system to cry to or laugh with directly across the desk can't be matched."

A tremendous number of women I spoke to say that having friends at work was what made or would have made a difference at work for them during their pregnancies. Temi, a director of marketing and contributor to my research, shared with me how her work BFF served as a lifeline during her pregnancy:

I always knew what I wanted.... I married my first boyfriend from college by twenty-three and got my MBA by twenty-six, to start my career in brand management. We were enjoying being married but living young, carefree lives.... After a couple of years at an elite consumer goods company I felt like I had proven myself enough and could "get away with" going on maternity leave. Everything was happening as it was supposed to ... until the lunch break.

It was my first pregnancy, and I snuck away to have my eight-week checkup. There I was informed that there was no longer a heartbeat. I was in shock, alone, perplexed that at twenty-seven years old having a child would not be anything but smooth. I was scheduled to present at a big meeting that afternoon, and so my manager became the first person besides my husband to know I'd had a miscarriage. My manager was incredibly understanding and kept everything confidential, but when I returned to work the next day, I was not the same bubbly office personality and my work BFF called bullshit.... She not so gently asked me WTF was wrong with me. She was concerned, and I let it all out.

My private life had been incredibly separate from my work life, but the two have been intertwined ever since that lunch break. In hindsight, my ability to show up as my full, authentic self began its formation during this time.... If there is any silver lining, it is that some of my colleagues became close friends, and opening up about my own struggles allowed me to be a comfort to others who shared grief about miscarriage, IVF, or surrogacy. Find one person you trust in the workplace to be honest and transparent to.... My work BFF [was] the first person who helped me unpack what was going on and navigate returning to myself in a really nonjudgmental and nurturing way. She was also my comedian and hype woman who lifted my spirits when I was at my lowest point, and for that, I will forever be grateful.

Your work BFF can certainly be an ally, but there can be a distinction, and in your inner circle you need people who can advocate for what you need, protect you, and champion what's right, often with their power. Allies seek information and understanding and then when needed (and wanted) can spring into action. Allyship for working women and pregnancy is essential. The burden must be shared and encouraged throughout all levels and types of organizations. For many women, that allyship can be found in unexpected places.

Callie Reynolds, a vice president at an account management firm, shares her story:

Emotions run high in the TTC/infertility community, and we can't help but feel a lot of things (often raging resentment) when we hear a friend is pregnant. Doubly so when we hear "I wasn't even trying" or "I didn't even know I was pregnant"—it's like taking a bullet.

I'll never forget a friend and colleague coming into my office for our weekly one-on-one when she told me she was expecting. What she couldn't have known in that moment is that just hours before, our doctor informed us that our positive pregnancy test was a "pregnancy of unknown location" (horrible name), aka ectopic and therefore not viable. . . . Unsurprisingly, I was devastated by all of this and completely overwhelmed. I had already gone through several IUIs and was on our first round of IVF. It would take three more rounds to make us parents. In that moment, there was no concealing it. My eyes welled, my throat filled with a massive lump, and my face flushed.

As I spewed my infertile guts at her feet, she sat and listened patiently. Her reaction was calm and supportive. Once my mouth stopped moving and I was left staring at her red face and wet cheeks, she uttered the best possible words she could have said: "I have your back. If you need me to cover for

*you or back you up, I'm here." She didn't give me advice or try
to fix it. She simply offered support. It was one of the most
thoughtful and generous gifts I could have asked for. She was
my ally. She checked in on me. Never pushy or prying, she
wanted to see how I was and if I wanted to talk. She was also
delicate in sharing her updates. I was so lucky to have her and
the handful of other allies in my corporate corner along the
way, whether it was slipping out for bloodwork, sneaking out
of the TSA line, hiding injectable meds, skipping a business
trip for a procedure, or just having a shoulder to lean on.
These allies did have my back and got me through it. Since
then, I vowed to always be the ally for others.*

*So my advice? If you're struggling with this secret, find an
ally. If you're not, remember not everyone's journey to parenthood is easy. If you don't need an ally, be an ally.*

As you review your inner circle in preparation for navigating
pregnancy at work, consider who's in it today and whether there are
any gaps. Do you have people at work who are allies today or could be
if you needed them, especially right now? In addition, think about
whether there is anyone you need to kick out of the circle. Pregnancy
at work can give you an energy boost, but it can also be a super energy
suck. You don't need anyone around you who is going to drain you
further. Some people at work you just work with and that's okay. All
of a sudden they aren't going to become your new work BFF, but be
aware if someone who's close in could affect your pregnant at work
mojo—they can be replaced.

BOARD OF DIRECTORS

You should have a board of directors for work. In fact, you should
have one for life, and especially during your pregnancy. This is a
group of individual contributors that together create a broad spec-

trum of support at work and in life. Their mentorship extends to sponsorship, with support going beyond a sounding board for ultimate advocacy. They may be people who tell you what you *don't* want to hear—but are later glad they did. Your board can evolve over time, but these are generally not short tenures. They may know one another, but they may also only be connected through you, handpicked to guide you in big decisions. Some of your board members may be controversial or offer completely different views from one another—but ultimately that is their role, to give perspective and to push you to choose who, when, and what you need for yourself. They are honest, authentic, and can be kept close in or at arm's length.

Pregnancy is a good time to review this board. Some roles you might fill: A working mother whom you aspire to emulate. A male counterpart or someone without children you may need to have open discussions with about their lens. Someone who has known you for a long time, perhaps a former manager or coworker, and someone who is new to your life but with whom you have a very deep connection.

How many people you need on your board depends on your capacity and what each member's life and work experiences bring. Some people might need five to ten board members, while others might feel like three offers them a broad range of perspectives. Depending on the size, your board of directors may include some members that you speak to with consistent frequency via text and others that you only set up time with in person when you need them. What's important is that there is a genuine connection, understanding of expectation, and follow-through on both your parts to meet that expectation with sincere gratitude and mutual respect.

When Ann Gottlieb, president of Ann Gottlieb Associates and a member of my personal board of directors for more than a decade, reflected on her own pregnancy at work, she remembered a crucial moment and person of support:

> *Fifty-one years ago I was pregnant while working at Estée Lauder. Though there were quite a few women at the firm in*

1969, there were only two who had children, Estée herself and one other. I knew of no other working women my age . . . all housewives or teachers, thus there was no established code of behavior. So I hid it as best I could and had a lot of anxiety once I started to show. I worked very closely with Mrs. Lauder, spending much time in her beautiful office. My greatest memory was a dream I had when I was well into my eighth month, that I my water broke while sitting on Estée's white satin sofa, a nightmare really.

I started at Lauder in an entry-level position and early on developed a relationship with Mrs. Lauder, who recognized in me a talent for the business. By the time I became pregnant, I had already been promoted once and was assured that I had a future with the company. I was truly frightened that having a baby would jeopardize my future at a company I loved, and felt fortunate for having cultivated a relationship of support. Even today many work situations mirror mine.

This book would have been impossible without my cherished board of directors. They know me personally and professionally, with a balance and tension that I trust. They have a unique lens to see the traits that my closest friends and family see at home and know must be true at work, though they haven't seen them in action. Keep in mind that board of directors members often bring to the table that they know our places of work *and* ourselves with a degree of nuance that makes their advice particularly resonant, and with the ability to unlock difficult situations and rare opportunities, including pregnancy.

WORK TEAMS

When creating a community at work to support you throughout your pregnancy, there are two teams to consider. "Team 1" is your peer group, and "Team 2" is made up of the direct reports you manage

respectively. The order is important. Many leadership experts, including Dasha Rettew, president of Reservoir Advisors, a coaching
and team-development firm for founders and C-suite executives, use
these teams to help executives align and strengthen to one another
and within their organizations before and during key milestone moments. To learn why these two teams are important, let's hear directly from Dasha:

> *The most successful leaders understand that their first team
> is not their direct reports, but their peer team, who they then
> prioritize alignment. Especially when a major transition is
> imminent—for example, your maternity leave—alignment
> with your Team 1 requires a steady cadence of communica-
> tion around goals and ways of working in service of the
> goals. Getting aligned as Team 1 is one of the best ways to en-
> sure the success of your Team 2. Your hard-earned invest-
> ment in Team 1 makes your Team 2 the biggest beneficiary of
> the clear mandates and resources you've set up for them and
> their cross-functional partners prior to your time away. Once
> you've done this, you leave a strong Team 2 set up for success
> in your absence. This principle of prioritizing Team 1 applies
> to moments when your mindshare is necessarily focused else-
> where, as well as when you're physically away on leave. The
> mindset shift (that your directs are not your Team 1) is essen-
> tial to your success and to theirs. Also remember, your di-
> rects are equally important to your first team's success while
> you're out.*

To fully complete the example, as you prepare for your maternity
leave, you could partner select members of your Team 1 (your peer
team) with the specific direct reports, or peer team members, you've
chosen as your key deputies to manage your responsibilities in your
absence. Too often the burden to keep it all going and battle cross-
functional stakeholders for time and resources falls on the shoulders

of Team 2. For Team 2 and your direct manager, you need to communicate clearly, as you will read in chapter 4, but you also need to make the success of the business a shared opportunity and responsibility of your two teams, the positive results of which both should take credit.

Your manager is also part of your team, and you are part of theirs. Enlisting your manager into your community can help you have a smoother pregnancy in the workplace. Your manager can help you navigate the highs and lows and support you tactically, emotionally, and physically. They can also help you come back to work after baby if that's what you decide to do. You don't have to force a relationship, but together make some adjustments and acknowledgment for this phase. In the best cases they will lead you by following *your* lead, provide resources you might not even know you have, and strengthen a bond that will last way beyond the months that you share your pregnancy journey. In the worst cases, you may pivot because of how they treat you. Somewhere in the middle, you'll learn together for now, and so that you both can continue to support the community of pregnant and working parents at your places of work.

CREATING AN EXTENDED COMMUNITY

It can take time to build your community, especially in these closer-in levels, and even then you may not find everything you need. Consider this an opportunity for you to go beyond your place of work and find resources and belonging to supplement it and connect you to others. This is what women like the creators of community platforms HeyMama and Scary Mommy and blogs like *Fertilust* and *The Corporate Mama* have done by building online communities to address needs discovered during their pregnancies and to uplift so many others.

Jill Smokler, entrepreneur, influencer, and *New York Times* bestselling author, is a community builder. As the founder of Scary Mommy, Jill grew her one-time mommy blog into one of the most influential digital parenting properties in the world. Relevant and re-latable, Jill led the way for unfiltered conversations about mother-hood. The creation of Scary Mommy also happened at a crucial moment in her life. Jill calls it her "accidental career":

> I started Scary Mommy when my youngest was a month old, and I had a twenty-month-old and a four-year-old. My ex was working in Chicago three days a week, so I was drowning in kids. I had just moved into a new neighborhood that was very conservative, and I stuck out like a sore thumb. Yet I just assumed that everyone was in the same place as I was with their values and outlook. And they were not.
>
> One day, I went over to thank a neighbor for cookies that she had dropped off. I said thank you and jokingly said that I was happy to get away because "my baby was a kind of an asshole." She gave me a look that made me feel like I shouldn't exist.
>
> I had no friends in the exact area where I was, and I could only go a five-mile radius. I was looking for things to do while my kids napped, and I was on my maternity leave from Anthropologie, where I was a graphic designer. In fact, I remember the day at work I found out I was pregnant, because we would get a sample of the shipments to the stores in advance, and I opened a Maine summer seafood cookbook. I could not make it to the bathroom fast enough. I got a pregnancy test and that was that.
>
> I started the blog for friends and family to follow, and it became my sanity quickly. I was lonely. It was just me writing about my kids, then there were people commenting. There was no trolling, it was just people wanting to support others. I became obsessed with it, but I could control it—you can shut down the computer—but I also met people in real life. They needed it and I needed them. It started for me to find like-

minded people—people who thought that it's okay that parent-
hood is not always happy and glossy, sometimes it's messy,
and often funny, not perfect. People felt relief in that.

On reflection, Jill shared that her biggest lesson was "the importance of having people who get where you are especially when you
become a mother. This includes people at work."

Jenn Kapahi, entrepreneur, co-CEO, and founder of Trestique,
also struggled to find the right support during her pregnancy. She
told me, "Growing up on an organic farm gave me a very wholistic
perspective on health and medicine. When I became pregnant I
struggled to find OBs, colleagues, and friends that I could identify
philosophically with.... Not until midway into my second pregnancy
was I able to find a midwife who would support me and allow me to
feel 'normal' when making choices for my own body that were contrary to popular vote. It was a huge relief to have a conversation and
to feel safe and supported." Her advice: "Keep looking for others you
can connect and relate to, it makes all the difference in your self-
confidence and convictions! For me, I made a conscious effort to join
a private moms group and organized a class with home-hosting rotation. This allowed me to meet moms and build real relationships. This
special group was honestly everything to me and we are still friends
today!"

Seek out resources that you need, including digital communities
and in-person groups that allow you to connect with people with
shared experiences but unique workplaces. Most importantly, make
it intentional.

BUILDING INTENTIONAL COMMUNITY

With the intimate nature of pregnancy, you may find that even more
than usual you need your community around you to be genuine and
based in transparency and trust that goes both ways. Katya Libin is

the cofounder and chief growth officer of online community platform HeyMama, which has the ambition to fundamentally shift the way mothers are supported by connecting them to one another. She shares the following tips for building an intentional community:

- Find a few intersections of your life circumstances that you are passionate about. It could be connecting women who are in your industry or in your neighborhood. Whatever it may be, circumstances in life are powerful forces to build community around.
- Whether it's a Zoom, a monthly coffee, a weekly lunch, a quarterly roundtable, or an annual retreat for a company, there are many flavors of connection and community building. The key is consistency. Give people something to rely on and make the format and goals apparent to all. Get buy-in from a few key people and use that momentum to build the group from there.
- Make it personal: community building is all about relationships, and each person in your community wants to feel special. That doesn't mean faking connection or trying too hard; it means being intentional with each person and learning about who they are and what matters to them. Remembering the little things allows you to pick up where you left off, even if you haven't seen someone in a while. Keep in touch in between gatherings, and always express gratitude for those who contribute to your growing community in ways big and small.
- Remember why your community exists. The point is for people to feel connected, to grow, learn, bond, evolve, contribute. Remind those around you that their opinion, contributions, and value is big, and it's why you're all coming together. If it's a new relationship you've cultivated, don't forget to tell that person that they are

valued, and you are always eager and ready for their opinions.

- Reach out to anyone who inspires you. People are way friendlier than you'd expect, even the ones you think are "super important people" who have no time. The only way to build community is to go outside of your comfort zone, be intentional with who you contact and why you are contacting them, and then get out there.

Part of building an intentional community is about finding what's right for you and what you need right now, not anyone else. With that in mind, reflect in this moment about how you, pregnant or not, can bring so much to your community—your views, your energy, your abilities, and more. Community is a reciprocal relationship that helps us all feel less alone.

Sarah Steele is head of brand marketing at Bugaboo North America and founder of the blog *The Corporate Mama*. Three days before she was about to begin a new job she found out she was pregnant with her first child and was terrified to share the news, especially because she knew she wouldn't qualify for FMLA and would potentially go without paid leave when her son was born. Sarah reflected on the power of community:

I shared the news first with HR, and then again with my manager during my next trip (I worked remotely in a different state). We worked through the official discussions/paperwork, but a crucible moment occurred when a teammate, sensing my discomfort, having shared this information as a female in a young, fast-paced/long hours company, pulled me aside and said, "You're not alone in this . . . literally." We took a quick walk through the office, where she introduced me to three (!!!) other women who were also newly pregnant but all of whom had been with the company for a while. She then shared that she too was pregnant! This was unusual and unprecedented at our small organization, but having those women working alongside me made me feel that I had support and comradery. . . . I don't know that I would have made it without that squad of working moms at my (virtual) side!

Because of the reciprocal responsibility of community, including at work, we all have a role to play. Along with advocating for resources and visibility even when we don't need it, we also must do our best to recognize when those around us need help. But figuring out what to do is something that many women felt they could use some further guidance on.

I asked Sarah to for advice on the best way to ask someone if they would like help regarding pregnancy:

Pregnancy is such an incredibly personal topic, and whether someone is a first-time expecting mother or this is their fourth rodeo, every soon-to-be mom will have a different level of comfort expressing their desire for help at work. When considering how to offer your assistance, or gauging whether someone is even interested in your help, I would simply ask. Pop by their desk or send a quick message asking if they'd like to walk to grab a coffee, and during your time together, you may lightly and in a friendly tone express that you'd like to support them in whatever way they are comfortable with during their pregnancy at work. Whether it's connecting them with an associate resource group, lending an idea on preparing for maternity leave, or being a second trimester walking buddy, you're just a few desks away, should they ever need the support. The ball is then in their court to take you up on it, without feeling as if they were put on the spot.

Even if you have amazing people around you at work, for you or for them it may still be jarring to talk about your pregnancy. Andrea Lavinthal was working as the style and beauty director for *People* and People.com when, the day after she found out she was pregnant, she was spotting and rushed to a doctor's appointment. "I didn't get back to my desk until about two hours later and my mind was racing. The last thing I could focus on was work. And even though I'm very close with some of my coworkers, I couldn't share what was going on with me. I felt alone and scared." Yet in hindsight Andrea shared that having the support of her coworkers was the best thing about being pregnant at work. It's okay if it takes time to decide how, when, and why you want to let others in.

COMFORT THROUGH COMMUNITY

Part of building intentional community throughout your pregnancy is getting comfortable asking for what you need, understanding and appreciating what others may need from you, and letting people help you too. You need to build relationships intentionally, but you also need to intentionally let people in. You cannot do this alone, and sometimes, especially at work, our biggest fear is letting anyone see us as weak. Asking for help is not weakness. It's just a need—a sounding board, an escape ladder, or even just a push out the door. Adina Kagan, head of media and insights at Chanel, reflected on her experience while pregnant with her daughter:

> I was working at Tiffany & Company as vice president, global marketing. . . . There was no mistaking it. I was enormous. I looked nothing like the pregnant women who grace our screens. So, at thirty-nine weeks, it had become clear that my cultural frames of reference had failed me. The sheer diameter of my body was a shock, unthinkable really. And so incredibly uncomfortable. Yet I was a professional. One who was going to prove, even in pregnancy, that I could do it all, unfettered. I was down to one last pair of stretchy pants that fit, and I could not, would not, enter a maternity store again. So I was

going to show up, pushing the limits of that elasticized waist-band, every day until my due date.

I was so focused on masking my own discomfort, I hadn't considered the discomfort I was creating for others. Fortunately, I was surrounded by a nurturing and empathetic team of colleagues who looked at me and saw not the consummate, inspiring professional I aimed to project, but rather a friend who was, in fact, pushing the limits of her health. That's when the real role model of this story stepped in—my boss. With her trademark grace, Caroline casually approached me with the kindest, gentlest (yet no doubt carefully considered) nudge. Long before flex work arrangements were at the forefront and without mention of official HR policy, she simply offered her confidence in my ability to do the work I was doing in the office as effectively, yet perhaps more comfortably, from home.

She deliberately made it a small moment—not a plea or an insistence, just a thought. This thought was just the seed that needed to be planted in my willful head. And it was the thought that was front and center when I woke the next morning, looked down toward the view that blocked my toes, and decided it was time to stay home. It would be another two weeks (eleven days past my due date!) before my now twenty-year-old daughter, Erica, was born. Yet all these years later, I am reminded of the importance of Caroline's gentle nudge every time I find myself in the position to support a woman who needs a friendly reminder that it is more than okay to take care of herself.

You are letting people in to support you in your community, but they are not taking over. Remember that even the strongest mentor, the most inspirational advocate, and your work BFF don't make your decisions—they are your advisers, not decision makers. You are the mother of your child, the director of your career—not anyone else, no matter how aspirational or inspirational they are, or frankly how many awesome kids of their own they have while also crushing it at work. The community you surround yourself with is a source of support. It is not your pool for crowdsourced solutions. Recognize what you want from them, but also what you don't.

Libby Wadle, whom we met in the previous chapter, shares, "Everyone wants to offer you advice, and it's great to have some reference points, but sometimes you have to experience things for yourself to know what you need, and you might not know what that means until it happens. When you are working, it's wonderful to have people around you who give support—you can visualize what life might be like five or ten years ahead of you through examples at work, and you can share experiences, but you definitely shouldn't do things just because of the judgment of others."

When Libby was pregnant with her daughter Sylvie, who is now twelve, she was sorting through advice on what type of help she would need when the baby was born, including with breastfeeding. In fact, Libby's own mother led her local chapter of the La Leche League, a "nonprofit organization that organizes advocacy, education, and training related to breastfeeding."[2]

Instead of advice, Libby reflects that as a leader her role is to create a spirt of comfort, community, and normalcy that allows women to integrate as who they are—with all parts of their lives—and not to feel isolated: "Working moms are normal—this is important." One of the things that she does for her team? "I start conversations with what's on my mind," she says. "I share more of myself than just the CEO. I know that my words have weight, but I also know me, just showing up as me, does too. Leadership has become more accessible, barer to people; there is vulnerability in that, but there is also more humanity."

One of Libby's team members, Ellie, who was pregnant for the first time during the interview, shared that "her ease is inspiring."

That ease and flexibility is essential to a spirit of community; it allows you to choose your own adventure—and to learn and communicate what *you* need.

WHEN COMMUNITY CHANGES CULTURE

While you have your inner circle at work, the people you call your "friend friends," not just "work friends," others on your wider team may ask to be included or may insert themselves in your journey, and they *are* part of your work community. You should ask yourself, in what way—if any—are you comfortable inviting them into this moment with you?

One of the best ways to illustrate this is the work baby shower. During both my pregnancies, I gave my inner circle a heads-up about what I wanted to occur regarding the celebration, drawing some boundaries and specifying timing. Basically, I did not want to shout to the whole world, "So my high-risk pregnancy probably means I will run out of here sometime around thirty-six weeks, but I also have a horrible fear of people being in my business and of something going wrong." In addition, instead of my private registry, I shared the fact that I had an empty bookshelf in the nursery and that it would bring me joy if people who wished to contribute would gift a book that they loved reading either when they were little or to their children, and to write their name inside so that I would think of them when I read it. It was very special to pull a book from the shelf—and, yes, you do need multiple copies of *Goodnight Moon*—and think of my colleagues, often in a different light than I would ordinarily. Another excellent and neutral idea women referenced was a diaper fund, available on many websites. While the dollars can be used for anything the mom needs privately and given in any amount, it is a tangible and simple gift appropriate for the workplace.

Whether big or small, these experiences can also have an important added benefit. If it's built properly—individually for the collective, and with an intentional approach, community can change workplace culture for the better. Pregnancy at work is a visible moment of joy, something personal that is memorable and special. Rachel, a corporate educator, said, "I loved sharing my pregnancy journey with my co-workers and even with my unborn baby. It was special to know my children were with me on so many flights, adventures, and presentations."

There is an element of community building in these moments of celebration that reminds us we are all just people with lives outside of work. As contributor Aya Kanai shared, "I remember at my baby shower at work, someone walked around doing little videos of advice from parents of older children. I saw the president of Hearst, colleagues at other publications, cross-functional partners, my teammates, all sharing messages in such a warm and heartfelt way. It was so powerful and visible. It felt like a very human moment, a great unifier.... While it was extremely valuable to me, it was also to everyone there who saw it as a moment to celebrate and share in at work—and lowered a barrier."

Long before that moment, Aya recognized and took mental notes of the women around her at work, inspiring her in the day-to-day. "I remember being an intern at *New York* magazine and seeing women like Sally Singer," she said. "She gave me examples of what was important and what wasn't. It was a formative experience. I saw her as someone who was really focused on her career, passionate about what she was doing, yet weaving the chaos of motherhood into it—and happy about it.... Later in my career I also remember that Joanna Coles's sons would come into our office, and you could tell they were proud of their mom, but they joked with her and made us all see her in another light. We watched them grow up—it let me experience another dimension of someone I admired, and still admire."

These moments make us human. Aya adds, "I love when I am walking down the street and I see someone so put together pull a bag of Cheerios from their purse—it's humbling in the best way possible."

These little moments are a recognition of something much bigger. You are part of the community you create for yourself and the women around you. It is the community we create to pass forward with gratitude, empathy, pride, and energy for movement forward. A surgeon, executive, and mother of two shared, "The best thing about pregnancy and work is normalizing visibility, the fact that you can crush it at work while being pregnant. I think it was nice to bring a little bit of humanity and kindness into the boardroom. Babies do that even when they aren't born yet."

We are part of flipping the script in our varied places of work and unique careers, sharing possibility in our communities of support. Think about your interns (or when you were an intern) as you reflect on Sarah Angelo's experience:

I am only a junior in college now, but growing up the only thing I wanted to be was a mother. Yes, I knew I'd have a job at some point, but with my mom as a stay-at-home parent, I always wanted the same for myself. For a while, I wanted to be a nurse because I could have days off during the week and a flexible schedule for my kids. Everything just revolved around my dream of motherhood. This summer, I worked at a venture capital firm and one of their start-ups in Silicon Valley. My team was made up almost entirely of working mothers. Sometimes, one of our team members would text, "No childcare today, bear with me!" or "My kid is sick, may get delayed today." So even though I am nowhere close to being a mother, I understand that being a working mom is hard. But it is not at all impossible. In the two months of my internship, I felt extremely empowered. For the first time, I saw myself as a real working woman in the male-dominated world of Silicon Valley. I realized that throughout my childhood, I really saw motherhood and work as mutually exclusive. But today, I sit here writing this, excited to succeed in my career and motherhood at the same time.

Community is about connection. Building connection in this time in your pregnancy is powerful and a foundation of trust for the short and long term. This trust not only creates a better work environment, but it builds your confidence and the confidence of those around you at work—for safety to fail, to be vulnerable, to be proud, and to be willing to openly communicate all these feelings, as you will see in the next chapter. Community in all parts of your life also creates a positive reciprocal spirit of hope.

Jennifer Richardson, while working full-time, navigated her auto-immune disorder, severe endometriosis, ten unsuccessful rounds of IVF, and one jubilant pregnancy of her daughter, Caroline, with the love, support, and elation of her Monroe, Louisiana, church and sister church in Ceigo de Avila, Cuba. Jen shares, "I used to think that hope was a passive verb, no action required . . . just hope. But then it struck me—like a lightning bolt—hope is an exchange, you give hope, you get hope. Simple. I began to focus on all that is good, even if seemingly insignificant. . . . I have always been optimistic, but it's now on another level. My community is my strength, and I am a strength in my community."

How many of you have had someone in your life, possibly your own mother, say to you, "Many hands make light work"? This always is in the back of my mind when something feels heavy and when it feels light. When it feels heavy, how can I get my hands around it? Do I make myself stronger? Use a tool? Ask for help? Who can I lean on in those moments? When it is light, is it because of a talent or a skill that I can use to help others? Or is it because of the community I have around me? There is a reason why we "build" community versus just have it. You are not alone.

QUESTIONS FOR REFLECTION

Does your place of work cultivate a sense of belonging for a larger community to exist—that is, cultural safety, security, and support to bring your authentic self to work? Is it a place where you are seen and can see others for their unique perspectives and are proud of what you do and who you work with?

Do you have a board of directors? Notably, do you have anyone you need to kick out? Do they know they are part of your board and what you want from them? Take the opportunity now with gratitude and grace to share. The energy of mentorship, allyship, and friendship goes both ways, and it's important we acknowledge it to keep it going.

Carry Strong Stories

LAUREN HARRIS

I am a single mother by choice (SMC), which is not only a path to motherhood but also an identity. It means being part of a community of women who for whatever reason decided to pursue motherhood and create a family on their own. It also means that the families we create aren't traditional, and we go into this process thinking of answers to impending questions from family, friends, and well-meaning strangers!

I began trying to have a child when I was around thirty-eight and found out I was pregnant the day after Mother's Day a year later. I work in a close-knit middle school, so it was about at that point that I wondered if people would ask questions or suspect as I tried to hide being pregnant, mostly because it was still early in the pregnancy. I tried to decide how I would answer questions that hadn't yet been asked by my colleagues, who knew my dating life mostly consisted of good stories to tell over a drink! The summer came and went, giving me more time to get used to being pregnant as well as to come up with how to answer my colleagues' questions now that I looked pregnant.

On the first day of school in September, I wondered if I'd be able to get through the whole day without having to answer questions, but at the same time thinking of what my colleagues might ask and coming up with possible answers. If I could just get through the staff meeting I could retreat into my office, where the colleagues/friends I worked with already knew all the answers. As I left the meeting, a colleague stopped me and quietly asked, "So how did you do it?" This was where I was supposed to be caught off guard or even shocked. The funny thing was I wasn't either of those things. This colleague, with whom I had worked closely, was in a long-term relationship with another man and therefore was also not in what society often deems as a traditional relationship. Maybe that's why it was so easy to answer. I very easily told him I used a sperm donor, to which he said, "That's great, good for you!" At that moment when my pregnancy world and work world collided, this thing I thought would be such a big deal turned out to be the antithesis. Now, seven years later, I easily talk about my SMC journey and my daughter, whom I lovingly refer to as my donor baby!

TRACY LOCKWOOD BECKERMAN, MS, RD, REGISTERED DIETITIAN, YOUTUBE HOST, AND AUTHOR OF *THE BETTER PERIOD FOOD SOLUTION*

I help women get pregnant for a living. As a registered dietitian who specializes in fertility and women's health, I meet with women struggling to regulate their periods and get pregnant. I even wrote a book, The Better Period Food Solution, *to teach women how to manage and fine-tune their periods through real food and nutrition education.*

Some may think the biggest challenge of my job is detecting the underlying nutritional issue causing a blip in a woman's reproductive health. But for me, that's the easy and exciting part. The biggest challenge, in my opinion, is to remain somewhat anonymous to my clients in a world where life is publicly broadcast through the likes of social media. I feel that it's my responsibility not to let my personal life interfere with my professionalism and individual counseling. But my friend, it gets complicated. I have to stay on top of my social media game for the sake of my business. And constantly being visible on Instagram was inevitably going to make my secret harder and harder to hide. Insert my growing baby bump.

I was fearful that my pregnancy would upset clients who were actively trying to become pregnant themselves. While I was super excited about my own news in January 2020, I was uneasy with the fact that I was sitting across my desk from clients, with a somewhat noticeable and somewhat round secret. If it were up to me, I would have kept my pregnancy a secret until the baby arrived to spare these clients potential pain, jealousy, and hurt. I would have worn extra-baggy clothing and stayed behind my desk during the entire session for nine months to conceal my bump—literally anything! Little did I know that I would not be in an office setting for much longer. As 2020 unfolded to become a sh*tstorm, the coronavirus allowed me to keep my pregnancy news to myself as businesses moved virtual. Thankfully, my phone calls and Zoom sessions never showed my growing belly, and I was able to share my news with clients on my own virtual terms.

Once I jumped over that hurdle, the next challenge I had to overcome was how to deal with the haze of anxiousness swirling around the unknowns of pregnancy and the pandemic. To learn coping strategies and bond with women going through similar motions, I mustered up the courage to join a virtual support group for pregnant women led by a skilled, open, and warm social worker.

I was dragging my feet before joining because the concept of a virtual support group didn't align in my head with my experience. How could you connect with someone through a computer if all you've ever known was in-person support? But after the first session, I felt lighter, and my shoulder tension started to ease up. Because we were all growing little, tiny humans at the same time, I was comfortable opening up to a Zoom full of strangers from all around the United States. I started to look forward to these weekly chats as we all discussed looming thoughts and fears around pregnancy and the coronavirus. Turns out we were all in the same boat after all. I quickly felt supported, heard, and validated all thanks to my strong wi-fi status. I knew all these pregnant women could relate to what I was also going through.

This support group ended up being exactly what my mind, my body, and my baby needed to help normalize a very abnormal time in our lives.

LASHÃDA DICOSMO, CEO AND FOUNDER OF 1 COVE

I was born and raised in a neighborhood on the South Side of Chicago that outsiders would label as difficult. It was only after I moved geographically and professionally that I truly recognized the disparity that separated my childhood world from what I am now able to provide for my children. Throughout my career I discovered the importance of bringing your whole self to work. That is what I identify as true diversity, being authentically you and staying true to your values. It takes courage. While surrounded by people with industry experience, my life experience added value that informed my approach to business. I sought mentorship from familiar faces, those with similar backgrounds, and noticed that no one within my team looked like me. It was then that I realized that I had also become the "safe place" for my colleagues to ask questions about Black culture and motherhood. In addition to my job, I became a diversity advocate within the organization.

I'd had my first child eight years earlier, so I thought I was prepared for my next working motherhood experience. In one year, I got married, was pregnant with my second child, was a bonus mom, and had just purchased a home. It was exciting, but not easy. Following my approved maternity leave, I hired a nanny and had the necessary conversation about balancing the parental load with my husband. When I came back, I was back into the full swing of things—this included my usual flexible work location (home and office). Perfect.

Upon my return, however, things felt different. The strategy had shifted, I wasn't included in key meetings for my business, and I think the team became concerned about the balance of family and work. It wasn't because of performance—the amount of success I was having with my accounts surpassed my other colleagues. My manager told me that I had to come back into the office full time. My husband worked long hours and traveled for work, my older children were in sports and other crucial developmental activities, and my parents lived almost eight hundred miles away. I had no intention of giving up my flexibility and relying on a nanny to raise my children, so I gave up my job and found another one.

For me, my story affirms my decision that family should always come first. In hindsight I wish I would've spoken with my husband more about what we could've done collectively when my job expectations changed. I still felt strong while making that decision, but it was a chink in my armor. I personally felt like maybe I should've toughed it out. In hindsight, no new mother should ever have to feel like that.

The best thing about working while pregnant was the sense of pride that I felt knowing that I could do both. Yet there are so many new mothers and existing mothers who are still in the corners of the office or on the phone whispering about when to share their good news. When you are a Black woman, workplace politics are already complicated. Even with the introduction of paternity leave, men don't have to wait to announce that they are expecting a new addition to their family because the age-old assumption is that their partner will manage the leave. Take the time to process.

In reflection on my experiences, I encourage women to create goals for both family and career, including their significant others in the decision-making process, to give yourself grace, and to be authentically supportive of other moms at work.

CHAPTER 4

Communication

*Creating Confident and Comfortable
Conversations*

COMMUNICATION SKILLS ARE essential—you probably have experienced the impact of good and bad communicators in your day-to-day at work and at home. A good communicator is clear, concise, and compelling; they express what they want you to hear and give space for you to listen and reply. They engage you and make you feel seen and heard. From a presentation to a meeting to a virtual group chat, words have influence and leave an impression. They build trust. As a good communicator you feel in control *and* open. A bad communicator at work doesn't read the room, lacks credibility and authority, and is often a horrible listener. Distracted or just disinterested, they detract from conversation, or they make it their own in a way that means they are only interested in one side. In our personal lives we observe the differences as well, including with our partners and best friends. When communication works well, it creates ease, reduces stress, and builds relationships with lasting effects.

Pregnancy is one of the most significant times in your professional life when your private life is made public. While many personal circumstances that may affect work need to be communicated, including about health, often details can be kept to a circle of those it may impact. But that belly, even one that isn't there yet, can feel like a bull's-eye. On top of that, even though your pregnancy is something to celebrate (remember it IS!) many women felt the need to downplay their joy before they even say it out loud. Jill, a communications strategy expert and a pregnant mother of two, put it best when she said, "Being pregnant at work felt like a series of uncomfortable conversations."

I spoke to women in remote roles who shared a common sentiment of relief that their jobs behind the screen have given them—from protecting fertility treatments to hiding morning sickness and simply removing fear of perception. One woman shared, "I just raised my camera angle and I felt like a genius." Another theme? "The exhale." That is when you are home by yourself and you just let that belly out, or when you finally tell people why you've been having so many appointments. A working mother I spoke to who ultimately adopted her child said, "The long road was exposed at work when I announced I was flying to meet my daughter around the world and would be completely unavailable for more than twenty hours. It was both so abrupt and personal, but also like a valve was released."

Sometimes, releasing the valve means unleashing all the communication on the other side of the equation. The many things that are said *to* you. These comments are often unsolicited and generally unhelpful, although some occasional gems shine through. But some comments can be so triggering that you don't know what to do with them—they percolate and can drag you down or set you off.

The relationship between your personal life and your work is yours, and so is how you want to communicate it. This can include setting boundaries around which information is up for discussion, and owning your narrative. A trailblazing chief marketing officer told me, "Everyone at work knew that [my daughter] was my priority. There was a freedom in setting that expectation." This time requires ongoing conversations, plural, not just one, because every experience is unique, carrying emotion and tangible details. Keep in mind that these are two-sided conversations between individuals like you and your place of work that can be eased when normalized, but that are still crucial to personalize.

In this chapter we will break down the stigma and awkwardness around discussing pregnancy, with a focus on critical self-advocacy and how to control *your* information. We'll discuss three communication styles to encourage your comfort and to guide those around you to follow your lead—and to listen. In addition, we will cover how to manage the input you're getting from others, including discerning benevolent discrimination at work. Even some of the best communicators shared the feelings of isolation during their pregnancies at work and a need for a boost of confidence. The insights and tools in this chapter can help you anticipate what you may need in order to feel comfortable to communicate.

STRATEGIES FOR COMMUNICATION

I remember thinking and overthinking how to keep everything secret when I was trying to get pregnant, then how to reveal my news, then how to prep for my review when I was about to go out on my leave, and then how to transition my team for my leave—and how it all felt like it was in a time warp, the only things that mattered in the moment. These important but common communication events happen in all types of workplaces every day, and we should be able to have them with a hell of a lot less pressure.

In my first study, while half of women who worked full time during their pregnancy were very comfortable announcing their pregnancies at work, half were only somewhat comfortable, with 16 percent feeling uncomfortable to very uncomfortable. If they were comfortable, they were statistically more likely to have an increase in confidence. Pretty obvious, but easier said than done. In addition, women often reflected in the research how they felt "awkward" talking about their pregnancy at work in every phase, not just the initial announcement. Only one out of two women felt comfortable transitioning to their leave.[1]

For being pregnant at work to be normalized, we certainly need to be able to talk about it. And as you will learn, you can share your news with joy—not shame, guilt, or an "I'm sorry."

Sara Daly-Padron, a Human Capital practitioner who was introduced in chapter 1, shares her powerful memory of this very phrase:

> I was twenty weeks pregnant with my third child and doing my best to keep the news under wraps a little longer. As a mom to two-year-old twins, I knew the pressures (and joys) of working motherhood and how a pregnancy announcement triggered a countdown to maternity leave and left the question "Will she return?" hanging in the air.
>
> I was actively recruiting a VP to join my team at a New York City-based financial firm and excited when I found the perfect candidate. I also knew the important role a manager plays in the successful onboarding and integration of new hires and how difficult being a new hire at a large organization could be. I felt tremendously guilty about the fact that I would be leaving for maternity leave shortly after she started. With each passing day, my pants got tighter and my guilt got stronger. The time had come to break the news. So, on a sunny afternoon during her first week on the job, we walked to Le Pain Quotidien for lunch with the dual intent of welcoming her and sharing my news (which was obvious by then).
>
> As excited as I was about welcoming a new baby to my family, I committed to focusing on her and tempered my news. I briefly stated the obvious and focused the conversation on

how I would support her and the team up to the birth and beyond. I pressed on with the conversation, discussed defining her priorities, and kept our talk all business. I felt relieved and successful in sharing my news and keeping the focus on the projects ahead of us.

Fast-forward two months and this new hire shared her own news of expecting her first child. What stood out was how she shared what was one of the most exciting moments in her life. She apologized to me. She assured me that she didn't know when she interviewed. She reassured me that she would work tirelessly until her leave.

It struck me in that moment that my own announcement may have taught her to minimize the joy and maximize the commitment to being "all business." While conveying commitment is surely important, it should not be at the expense of sharing the joy.

My response to her was clear: "Do not apologize to me or anyone. Congratulations! When you tell others at the firm, say 'I'm excited to tell you I'm pregnant' and end it—no further explanation or equivocating needed. There is time to work out the details."

That was a seminal moment for me, one in which I recognized how high the stakes are in these conversations and how our own actions and reactions can shape the culture for working parents.

I write this story nearly six years later and can still hear her apology ringing in my ears. And she's not alone. I coach women every day on how to have "the conversation" with their boss and hear so many variations of "I'm sorry." As a manager I wish I had recognized the impact of the message I was sending to the young women and men on my team when I minimized my own joy. I am grateful that now, as a coach, I have the privilege of helping others affirm their commitment and share their joy.

The first step in communicating around pregnancy and work is to realize that the freedom from discomfort comes at the intersection of control and letting go. The second is to develop your communication as a skill. This is a moment when even the best communicators are put to the test because you're dealing with things that you haven't dealt with before, even if this is not your first child, because of the personal nature of the news and its importance. If you can find comfort and confidence throughout your pregnancy, particularly in what you say, you are benefiting yourself in the moment but also investing in your future. Strong communication skills at work are key to creating gravitas that lasts, getting what you want, and specifically getting what you *need* during this important time. There are a lot of opportunities to practice, as you'll see in part II.

To develop your skills for now and the future, I think it's helpful to think about communication, including regarding pregnancy and work, with six classic questions: **Who**, **What**, **When**, **Where**, **How**, and **Why**.

First the **Who**. Who are you communicating to, and who are you as a communicator today and specifically in this moment?

To give you confidence in communication, there are many different types of self-assessment tools available for you to support your career (and personal) growth. They are both widely available online and best facilitated with a coach and/or communications expert. For the sake of this book, I was inspired by the highly cited *Change Style Indicator* (CSI) by W. Christopher Musselwhite, PhD, and Robyn D. Ingram, PhD. "The CSI is an assessment designed to determine an individual's preferred style when addressing change and how those around them may respond to their style."[2]

Communication is a two-way street, and I appreciate that this tool considers both directions. Kathy Kennedy, DrPH, MA, introduced in chapter 1, explains, "Just as with DiSC or MBTI (other self-assessment tools), if you can find a way to understand the personality and preferences/reflexive tendencies of the other person, the Change Style Indicator can help you to craft a communication that will stick for them and get them to engage with you. It can apply well because family building by an employee will cause *changes* that impact the workplace because we bring our whole selves to work." Keep in mind that we can all behave differently when dealing with change.

There are three types of communicators on a spectrum. Note that some women I have spoken to are generally one style, but during pregnancy they lean more toward another. Where they usually were comfortable communicating in a certain way, they leaned a little more conservative (**conserver,** below), for example to reduce risk, or a little bolder (**originator**, on the next page), because of timely news.

Conserver. This style of communicator prefers the known to the unknown. If you're a conserver, you like structure and knowing the rules of the game. You also prefer things to change gradually—evolution versus revolution. For you to feel comfort and confidence, you may want to do your research before you share news of your pregnancy at work, have your questions outlined based on what you know, and, with your board of directors or a confidante, know what you want expected outcomes to be, with a timeline (but remember to have some flexibility based on your needs).

If you're a conserver, you can imagine it might be tough for you to deal with a missed deadline or to advocate for something outside of the rules. On the other side, if you are communicating with someone who is a conserver, you need to push them to see the bigger picture and to flex the rules for what you need. If this is the person you are communicating with, how can you give concrete and organized points to give them security about the unknown and minimize uncertainty?

Pragmatist. This style of communicator prefers to take an objective approach, meaning that they take themselves out of the situation. They like functional change and can see multiple perspectives but prefer what will work and be practical. Think about someone at work who is a pragmatist—they like to organize ideas into action, they cooperate and build on past experiences. They are also open to multiple sides. If this is you or whom you are communicating to, watch out for a tendency to compromise to a fault—which often is accompanied by the feeling that something is off, that it's not sitting right with you and you don't feel conviction when communicating.

With regard to rules as a pragmatist, I encourage you to find the middle ground. Think whether you want to be a bit more of a conserver—do you you want to bend or shift the rules only slightly—or do you lean toward being an originator and challenge rules or come up with new ones altogether.

Originator. This style of communicator is the closest on the spectrum to big change. Originators prefer a faster and more drastic approach. If this is you, then you like to initiate something new and are unafraid to challenge the status quo.

If you are communicating with someone who is an originator, they can help you to project your experience into the future (likely with enthusiasm) and be willing to take risks. However they also may not carefully think through the realities of what is needed including considering established policies for a particular workplace. One of the possibilities that could be an issue in the window of pregnancy is missing the short-term impacts, both for the individual originator or for the organization.

Being a good communicator is about what you say, but it is also about comprehension. Of course, to have comprehension, you need to have a good listener on the other side. If a message is delivered based on their preferences, it's more likely to "stick," as Kathy shared, and it's more likely that those you are communicating with will follow your lead.

Alexandra Gonzalez Repetto was "petrified" to tell her boss that she was pregnant. She had just started a two-year master's program funded by her company, and had a confidante tell her that she should drop out before it started because she "wouldn't be able to handle it":

I was so nervous I waited until twenty weeks to tell anyone because I felt so ashamed. The week before I told my boss I received horrible feedback that I was not meeting expectations preparing for a specific presentation, and that I was letting my usual stellar work fall flat. The stress of being pregnant (and super sick all the time), plus transitioning to balancing work and studying was getting to me. I was in tears as I headed to class that evening. As soon as I got to class, the female executive who was my professor saw me completely off and clearly upset. I immediately confessed everything—my pregnancy, the feedback, my total anxiety about being pregnant at my level. Most women I knew who had kids were very senior, and I was a midlevel manger still developing my career.

She listened, then immediately gave me a plan, but not without reminding me to take a huge deep breath, and that I wouldn't be the only pregnant brand manager or student ever to pass through this program, and to take the pressure off. She told me, "You've got this for you and your daughter," and that it was positive exciting news, but affirmed that it was a lot, and I just needed a plan and a way to talk to my boss so he would get it.

I wish in that moment, and the many after that when I felt embarrassed or nervous, that I would have reminded myself of how much I was carrying. I wish I would have known that I was not and will not be the only one. While there were smaller moments when I felt scared, anxious, worried, I also felt a strength to advocate for myself and my hard work to make this little girl growing inside me proud. In the end, I completed my master's and returned from maternity leave to a promotion. The action plan and those deep breaths from that senior executive changed my perspective that day and many days since.

I met Alex when I was working full time, teaching after work one night a week, and my second son, James, was tiny. I continued teaching because it was important to me, but it was also borderline nuts. I found it hard to show up with energy after a long day and struggled with missing bedtime; but teaching felt, and still feels, purposeful and important.

That night, I saw Alex walk into my class. She was usually an excellent student—engaged, a good partner to her classmates, fully prepared each class—but on this night she was off. During a break I pulled her aside. Tears formed in her eyes and puddled behind mine because I could feel her stress. I acknowledged that "this is a lot." I knew her communication style from class, and I knew that she was a pragmatist, whether or not she (or I) had the words to define it. She needed me in her circle, someone she could trust—not to tell her what to do, but to help her decide what she needed. She needed to discern her own communication style and that of her boss. Then she had to decide what to do.

Let's move to the **What.** What is the specific objective you're trying to communicate? Are you stating an update or information with nothing for the receiver to act upon? ("I am doing fertility treatments. This will mean early morning appointments that cannot be moved.") Are you asking for support? ("I would like to set you and the team up for success when I am on maternity leave. I have some ideas about what might work best but would like to go over your expectations for the projects and the team when I am away.") Or are you simply asking for a listening ear? ("I need a friend right now.")

When communicating what you need, be organized, be concise, prioritize your messages, and be clear. Ask yourself, what is stated fact, what is up for discussion, and what do you want from the other side of the conversation? By thinking through the questions and having clear answers (I write down bullets), you can keep your emotions under control and really think through what you want to say and what you don't.

By the way, being human and vulnerable in these moments is only natural—don't put extra pressure on yourself to have perfect delivery, but if you think through and practice, ultimately you will be expressing what you want to say the way you want to say it to the best of your ability.

Now let's talk about the **When** and **Where** of good communication. Homing in on the right timing and location is also part of how to best execute a conversation. You want to be in the right mindset and unrushed. If you have a regular meeting either in person or virtually, or even better can take a walk away from your place of work with your boss or coworker, it takes some pressure off. Of course, sometimes with pregnancy and matters of health time is of the essence, so do not let waiting for the perfect moment stop you from making it happen. This also means that while it's helpful to appreciate and anticipate the perspective of the other side, do not let it hold you back from sharing what you want, how you want to, and to ask for what you need.

Finally, the **How** and **Why**. How do you want to share your information and how do you anticipate the message will be best received? Do not diminish yourself for the other person or make limiting assumptions. "I am thrilled about my news that I am pregnant, but I am a private person so would like to share the news only to my team and not make a big deal about it." "I appreciate that you are here for me. What I need right now from you is to focus on work. I will let you know if I need time to discuss my pregnancy further with regard to work."

Alexa Levitt, senior vice president of human resources for the Entertainment Group at NBCUniversal, reflected on the How challenge in her own conversations at work while pregnant: "Here I was, eight months pregnant, working in HR, and I didn't know how to have these conversations. At that moment I shifted my mindset away from asking for permission, and now I use my platform to speak openly and with pride about the pregnancy journey and to create the space for others to do the same." And that, in essence, is the most important part of the How and Why: there may be many reasons why in the specific conversation, but the big ones can be defined by your critical need in this moment for self-advocacy.

ASKING FOR WHAT YOU NEED

Self-advocacy is about sharing what you want to share, on your own terms, and when you need it. You do not owe anybody any explanations. The goal of self-advocacy is to protect yourself—and ultimately your baby.

To learn what effective self-advocacy can look like at work, let's look at four women's stories. Consider each person's communication style and the six questions of effective communication—the who, what, when, where, how, and why—to gain perspective and grow your knowledge about communication, which will lead to greater capability for self-advocacy.

Kelty Heilman was living in South Florida working in sports television. She now works for Warner Media. Kelty shares:

> *I have always felt pressure to be visible in the workplace. Always available, capable, reliable. Even when a season of my life required my priorities to shift. In the meeting where I told my boss that I was pregnant with my first baby, he jumped up from behind his desk and came around to give me a hug. I was greeted with genuine happiness. He and I did not have the best professional relationship, but I could feel his sincere joy in that moment. But it turns out that one person's brief reaction to the announcement of a new baby doesn't translate into greater understanding of pregnant employees' needs in the workplace.*
>
> *Instead of looking back on that year and remembering tentpole events like key presentations, partner events, or company initiatives, I remember how awkward I was made to feel. Like most other mothers I know, I had shown up with morning*

sickness. Led presentations with Braxton-Hicks contractions. Flown across the country at thirty-six weeks pregnant to attend meetings that had me on my feet for three days. My perspective was that sometimes you simply have to go out there and play hurt. I thought if I behaved as I always did, I would be treated the way I always was. But the amount of unsolicited feedback that my pregnancy attracted in the workplace was astounding. Comments on my physical size. Colleagues publicly voicing opinions that I wouldn't be returning to work. Suggestions that, absent a lactation room, I should pump breastmilk in the bathroom stall when I returned to work.

The final blow was learning that my employer, a Fortune 100 company, had announced twelve weeks of paid maternity leave beginning January 1 of the following year. When I gave birth ten days prior to January 1, that benefit did not extend to me. To frame this more completely, even though I was the only pregnant woman in the office, my baby's birth occurring ten days before the start of a new policy meant that I was simply out of luck. I did return to work. And when that same boss who was so pleased that I was having a baby less than twelve months prior walked by my wide-open office door without so much as a "hello" . . . multiple times a day . . . for a week . . . I decided that this wasn't the best place for a working mom.

Flash forward . . . New employer, new boss, new baby on the way. The curveball of my mother's terminal cancer diagnosis coupled with my husband being out of state for a thirty-day job training meant that I was suddenly balancing more than just being a pregnant working mom. When I was at work, I would be completely focused on my work responsibilities. Then I would race out the door to my ninety-minute commute and the anxiety would start. Would I make it to day care pickup? How did my mom's latest palliative care appointment

go? Did we have any groceries? I hoped the dog had managed
to survive another day inside for eleven hours.

One afternoon, my boss stopped by my desk to chat with
me about a new assignment. And in a moment of exhaustion,
I told him that I couldn't do it. That there were too many
things on my plate. Anything new had to wait two weeks until
I had some more bandwidth. It was embarrassing. All those
years of "leaning in," and what I needed right then was to lean
out. You know what he said? "What do you need from me and
how can I help you succeed?" And he didn't just say it in that
moment—he has said it at all the important moments since.
Playing hurt has its merits, but so does speaking up to an em-
ployer who listens.

Kelty's boss asked, "What do *you* need from *me* and how can *I*
help *you* succeed?" highlighting the contrast between her experiences with two different companies, managers, and roles. But also, as
she got pushed to the limit, she advocated for what she needed. She
adds, "Looking back, this story makes me feel very accomplished and
capable. I feel strongly that normalizing pregnancy in the workplace
is important for those who come after me. I wish I would have advocated for myself more in my prior job. It was my dream job and I loved
it. It was hard for me to give it up because I wasn't supported. I wonder if I had spoken up, if I would have been able to stay there and had
success under a different boss."

Kathryn was eight months pregnant with her first baby when her
office changed locations. She would now have to take a subway and
a ride on a company shuttle van. She recounts:

We can all attest to how awkward climbing into the back of a
shuttle van is. Imagine doing so eight months pregnant and
over seventy-five pounds gained!? Day one, I got to the shuttle
early and was first in line for the front seat beside the driver.
Success! Day two, I was a little later and had to sit behind the

driver's row, but I selected the seat by the door in the first row. Not so bad . . . I can do this.

Day three, everyone was all the wiser and arrived to line up early so as not to have to sit in the back row, or worse, wait for the next shuttle and risk being late to work. I was not in on that memo and came at my regular time hoping I'd get a similarly comfortable seat in the van. Not only did everyone look at their phone when they saw me waddling toward them through the revolving door and again while I passed each one of them to arrive at the back of the line, but once we started to board, no one offered me an accessible seat. They ignored me as I tried to squeeze and fold to fit in the back row, to no avail. Not one person offered me their seat when I proclaimed to the driver that I couldn't fit and would have to wait forty-five minutes STANDING in line for the next shuttle. The doors closed and everyone kept their eyes straight ahead and ignored me in my condition as I took my place at the front of the line and steeled myself to wait for the next shuttle. When I described this deplorable behavior to my OB at my next visit, she immediately started typing a doctor's note saying that I would be working from home for the final month of my pregnancy. And just like that, my relationship with that shuttle van and those inconsiderate people was erased.

I wish that I would have known that I could have advocated for the right to work from home before even setting foot on that shuttle. I was fiercely dedicated to doing a good job and riding that shuttle every day, even though I had already accepted a new job, for which I had negotiated a start date after the baby came. Advocate for yourself and your comfort. Pregnancy requires an incredible amount of strength and fortitude. . . . In fact, during pregnancy, I felt so special and powerful. Like I could do anything. Build a human? And a career? No sweat!

In response to the question in my research "Who would you like to thank for support during your pregnancy?" Kathryn answered, "Myself. I didn't lose sight of myself, my drive, or my personal or professional goals while enjoying the life-changing experience of becoming pregnant and being a mother."

An anonymous contributor was pregnant while living in Brooklyn on active-duty orders as a sergeant with the Army National Guard. She recounts the moment she learned how to advocate for herself:

I was pregnant with my first child. I was young and had only been working with my supervisor, who didn't have any kids, for about two years. It was early on in my pregnancy. I had a few appointments. At first my supervisor was okay with me leaving early. Then one day he questioned me about it, whether I "really" had to go. I didn't want to get in trouble, so I didn't. I still regret not attending that appointment. I am currently pregnant and have been in my position for many years. I no longer ask. I schedule them and inform my supervisor.

This seems simple, but this is a big change. This contributor also shared that she is incredibly open about her pregnancy in order to encourage other women to ask for what they need. One of her male colleagues later shared with me that because of her, their company no longer questions their pregnant colleagues' abilities, even in the field, but they do offer to do the physical, "definitely not mental," heavy lifting. Overall, they follow their pregnant colleagues' leads.

In our final story, a senior financial services executive reflected on the pressure that was put on her, and that she put on herself, as a midlevel professional on a private equity investment team, both to manage the expectations of her team and to meet the demands of her work.

I pulled an all-nighter when I was six months pregnant with my first child the day before my thirty-second birthday. I was

*leading a large-scale but short-fuse project across the whole
team, and honestly, we probably got more done because nobody was going to leave before the "pregnant lady" did. The
senior managing director who had dumped the project on me
apologized profusely, but he got fired two months later. I didn't
really get upset at the time—I just was trying to get done what
was necessary—but in hindsight, it was appalling that they
would have put me in that situation. I work at a bank, and I
get that it's intense, but let's be honest, we're not saving lives
here. There is not a chance that I would have come even close
to doing something like that for my subsequent pregnancies.
I would have absolutely pushed back. There is also no chance
that I would let something like that happen to someone on my
team now. In hindsight, I would have told my younger self
that I would have been "successful" without risking my child's
health or my own health.*

The women in these stories had basic asks—for maternity leave,
for a seat on a bus, to attend doctor's appointments, to ensure the
health of their baby—but they had a big impact on comfort and confidence. The first step to self-advocacy is to evaluate the importance
of the risk in your situation. Pregnant or not, the "extreme" situations, like an all-nighter, we are put in at work need to be fact-checked.
Is the urgency merited? As a leader of a team, how can these situations be avoided or reframed for the ongoing mental and physical
health of your team? As a team member, evaluating how to manage
expectations of urgency and your impact is a skill.

What can you do if you are faced with a situation like this, where
there doesn't seem to be a solution that doesn't impact both your career and your health negatively? The health of your baby matters
more, but it isn't always easy to see, or to navigate the guilt associated
with making the right choice. Frame your thought process with the
concept of "Will this matter?" from chapter 2: Will this matter later

today? (Probably.) "Will this matter tomorrow?" (Probably.) in a week?... In two weeks?... In a month... six months... a year from now? Assess your options. You don't necessarily have to decide between the health of your baby and your career, but this exercise might help you think about what you need to decide to do now and when you need to assess again or think of alternative solutions. Also, ask yourself why you're willing to say yes to work, even if it impacts you and your baby's health. Because it matters to you? Because it matters to the group? Consider how you can you achieve the "yes" in a different way.

Remember too that you can change your mind. Before, during, and after a decision that can impact how you mentally and physically feel, it's okay to change your mind about its importance and about what you want to do about it... for you. Just communicate this rationale, be open to the level that you feel comfortable sharing the why, and be empathetic to the impact of your decisions on others.

You're not alone in decision making and even communicating if you don't want to be. While what you do to protect yourself, your child, and your ambitions is your decision alone, you don't have to make it in isolation. Your inner circle, board of directors, allies, and just good people around you can support you as you advocate for yourself.

ADVOCACY FOR SELF-CARE

Rachel Nicks is a Juilliard-trained actor, trainer, doula, lactation counselor, mother of two, and the founder of Birth Queen. Birth Queen "educates, supports, and empowers Black women, parents, and birthing people, enriching the Black birth experience and saving lives." Rachel founded Birth Queen to be a resource that Black women and birthing people can trust. "They can be confident knowing there is someone advocating for them and breathing new life into the birth world with funding, education, and support." Rachel shares, "As a founder, I am a Black woman who has given birth to two beautiful Black sons, but I know that my experience every day is that of a privileged Black woman, and that I must use the power and influence I have to inspire all women and absolutely my people."

Rachel, whose career made her pregnancies "a living example of the intersection of work and pregnancy," is often asked for advice from the physical angle as a trainer, but she says it starts with what's inside.

"I am a huge advocate of self-care personally and professionally, what makes me feel good about myself. It's never about someone else, it has to be about you—your pelvic floor to your fingernails. Feeling good about yourself has to come first. For mothers, this includes processing your birth story *and* loving your body, healing from the inside out, your heart, your mind, your vagina, then you deal with the flat stomach, after you heal your insides. Nothing about fixing the outside is going to fix the inside."

Self-care is also about prioritization and advocacy. The problem is that often on top of feeling guilty, women don't think they deserve it. Many mothers put themselves last on their list of responsibilities and feel that at home and at work they need permission.

Rachel adds, "When I returned to work to do a play when my son was three months old, I was breastfeeding and I remember saying to myself, 'You are an Oakland girl, there is none of this "do you mind?" . . . You do what you need. It is not a question. Do not ask for permission, ask for what you need. Stop making it more than it is. It is a need. My baby needs to eat. Period.' Can you imagine if people in office meetings were raising their hands asking for permission to go to the bathroom?"

Just as this is true for taking care of your baby, it's true for yourself. Advocate for what you need and give yourself grace in asking for it. Like so much of motherhood, you must get out of your comfort zone. "Will it be uncomfortable?" Rachel asks. "Yes, but challenges change us. Having a baby is not comfortable, parenting is not convenient, but it is a journey of growth—and stretching. . . . That's what's so beautiful about motherhood—the growth."

To foster this growth means truly recognizing what you need (and what you don't) at home and at work. Leslie Forde, the founder of Mom's Hierarchy of Needs and a mother of two, offers a framework solution sparked by her own experience returning to work after her second child.

She shares, "I was completely burned out. Even though I had the experience of my first leave and return at work, it was different. I had taken on a big promotion when I was pregnant—a crucial role in a dynamic, fast-paced business, which was exciting, but it also meant that when I returned, in the span of twelve weeks everything had changed, including my team, with added pressure."

In the moment I thought the answer was to work harder, to throw the hours at it—because I was capable and that's part of how my career grew pre-kids. But I quickly found myself trying to shield my co-sleeping baby and toddler from the glow of the computer at one, two . . . three a.m. I became hollowed out. I was a depleted, tired, angry zombie person. So I left the job I loved, I took a huge pay cut for a four-day workweek, and had only one direct report. It took over two years to rebuild from burning out emotionally and physically. Around that time, I met with the founder of a wearable device to manage stress, for some advisory work. We discussed moms as a possible audience, and when I said, "There's Maslow's Hierarchy of Needs and then there's Mom's Hierarchy of Needs," a light bulb went off. That night I drew the Mom's Hierarchy of Needs and realized I had reached that low because I was trying to do the impossible. All the things that we prioritize with vital importance are never done.

The Mom's Hierarchy of Needs helps mothers visualize why it's so challenging to make time for self-care, interests,

and healthy relationships with other adults while raising
kids. It's a way to think about how and why we spend our time
as we do. At the bottom, the most fundamental priorities—you
are responsible as a mother for your children's well-being—
then you have layers of their activities, your household. Next,
your professional role, healthy relationships with other adults,
and self-care. And at the top of the pyramid, your interests—
fun, hobbies, new skills. Each of those top categories plays its
part in helping to keep you grounded. There is no "extra space"
for our mental, physical, and emotional health unless we give
ourselves permission to take it. When you become a mother,
your discretionary time disappears. And when you do get it,
it's often unpredictable and interruptible. But that doesn't
mean that you don't need it.

When I'm "toast" and not even close to the top of the pyramid, I
also call it my "wilted flower" or "a dying star" state—inspiring, I
know. But just like a lot of the advice in this book, the biggest thing
for me is recognizing that feeling. When I get to that point, or even
better if I can predict that I will potentially get to that point, I know
it. I need time, a reset, to be plugged back in. I look at weeks ahead and
instead of saying, "I'll push through and then collapse (like a dying
star)," I see what can come off the plan, where a "block" needs to be—
a night with nothing or conversely doing something totally new; a
movie night with my kids; a midday walk with no guilt, no multitask-
ing, and in protected time. Having this allows me to do more (because
I want to), versus depleting myself until I'm running on empty. I
also know that when I can get to the top of the pyramid, all the parts
of my life benefit. I become fueled, overflowing with energy and
growth.

You are not "getting away with something" when you take care of
yourself in those carved and protected moments—you're allowing
yourself to have the capacity to be the best for you and those who

need you. In those moments you are also connecting with your sense of self, as you will read in chapter 5, protecting where you feel most "you" and evolving it by choice, not by force. It's imperative that we recognize the need, and that those we share our childcare responsibilities with do too. We are setting an example for those around us, including those in our places of work and our children, that having time and space to be yourself matters.

So far we have been defining the communication styles and process for both you and who you are communicating to, but what if you're in a situation where the ball's not in your court? It's important for you to think about what you may experience and how to handle communication when things are said to you.

COMMUNICATING YOUR BOUNDARIES

The reality is that sharing the news of your pregnancy and advocating for your needs is not about what you *should* say. It is about how you want and *need* to communicate—creating boundaries that serve your communication goals and dictate the narrative of your pregnancy in the workplace. Sometimes the initial plan goes out the window and you don't feel that you're in charge of the narrative—maybe your boss inadvertently shares your news and you end up having to fend off intrusive questions—but remember that you are in control, whether that means immediate action, letting it go, or blocking out the noise.

There are also parts of your pregnancy that do not require any communication with anyone at work, and you deserve that respect and privacy. Stephanie Sandler, president of a global consumer insight agency, and Libby Kountzman, architect and interior designer, are mothers of two, and here they share their story about how slightly opening the door about trying to conceive and being pregnant felt like "an open house Zillow posting in the spring, everyone checking us out with myriad of questions beyond the floor plan."

In a nonheteronormative relationship such as ours, when we shared news of each pregnancy, we encountered a fascination with the mechanics of how it works. Along with that came a barrage of intrusive, insensitive, and oftentimes overstepping questioning that felt suspiciously akin to a desire to attend an AP-level gay conception class starring us rather than seeking to understand or to provide support, kindness, or love. At times, we marveled at how often we felt as if we were being cross-examined on the witness stand, or two new animals delivered to the Bronx Zoo on a Saturday in the summer.

What was unsettling to us was the level of intimate details of our pregnancy journey strangers and colleagues felt emboldened to ask: Whose egg is it? Did you use an anonymous or known donor? How many rounds of IUI and IVF did you go through? How many healthy embryos do you have left? Did you choose the gender? What are the terms of the relationship with the donor? We could go on and on.... These were questions that people would never ask a straight couple who announced their pregnancy!

As a couple, one of the steepest learning curves was navigating how not to answer unwanted questions and let people know they were simply crossing a line, both of which were initially difficult as we were typically caught off guard and not wanting to make the other person feel uncomfortable for asking. Quite frankly, we continue to deal with this line of questioning in subtle ways, like when people ask us who our daughter looks like or where does she get her curls from . . . What they are really asking is, whose egg did you use? All these questions put us in the uncomfortable position of finding the right language to shut down the line of inquiry—it's insensitive, sometimes ignorant, and invasive.

By far the most disappointing situation we encountered was when a trusted boss and mentor used TTC against us.

Due to the numerous fertility appointments and need to step out of the office, one of us decided to share that we were TTC. Not long after, this boss awkwardly asked about the timing of a pending embryo transfer, which was used to inform departmental layoffs. In essence, our IVF schedule became a part of the company's schedule for a reorganization. I mean . . .

When we think about our journey to parenthood, it has been an unexpected learning curve. Our greatest confidantes and supporters have been other women who have shared their experiences about boundaries and communication with us, oftentimes in the context of the workplace. But the biggest lesson we've learned is that we are protective of our family's origin story.

The Reverend Caroline Jinkins experienced both an outpouring of joy and unwanted commentary from her congregation at news of her pregnancy:

I am a pastor, and when I announced my first pregnancy, my congregation rejoiced with me. After my twenty-week ultrasound I learned that my baby was small for its gestational age, which resulted in more ultrasounds and nonstress tests as my pregnancy progressed into the third trimester. I felt great and gained a normal amount of weight, but I was very concerned that something was wrong with the baby's growth. Every time someone commented how little I was, I didn't hear a compliment, I heard a critique that I might not be nourishing the fetus inside my womb. I gave birth to a healthy daughter by C-section, and when I returned to work the church comments resumed as people wondered, how did I lose all the baby weight so quickly? I couldn't say endless breastfeeding, stress, and compulsive walks with the stroller, because I was too exhausted to respond.

When I was pregnant with my second child, the church again felt involved with great expectation. Women would

*touch my belly under my clergy robe and reminisce about
their own babies. This time, the baby was growing at a normal rate, however I physically struggled with health issues
and discomfort as my body had aged a few years since my last
pregnancy. One morning after worship a grandmother (whose
daughter had birthed premature twins) asked me if I was sure
I wasn't having twins. I smiled on the outside, but on the inside I thought to myself, if she only knew how much I had worried about my weight, not out of vanity but fear that I wasn't
eating enough! If she only understood how happy I was that
this baby wasn't dangerously small!*

*After my son was born healthily, I let all those mixed feel-
ings go. I wish I could go back and tell my pregnant self to
drown out the voices of complex comments and unsolicited
advice. People will be excited and jealous for you, people will
project and critique you, but none of it will affect your ability
to mother and raise a precious child. Surround yourself with
people who know when to keep their mouths shut, and listen
and nod and smile at the rest!*

Unfortunately, the intrusion can start before the Push and even
before the TTC. Elisabeth Bromberg, a senior vice president of strategy and planning, shares her powerful personal story that encourages us to truly think about the workplace as providing a safe place
no matter our stage (or desire) of the journey to working motherhood.

*I'm thirty-five, and I've never tried to conceive, been pregnant,
or had a child. And I have no idea if I'll ever be able to. I struggled with an eating disorder for twenty years. When you put
your body through trauma like that for as long as I did, there
are lifelong physical consequences. . . . And as a female of
child-bearing age, I'm usually naturally included in the workplace conversations about babies and pregnancies, the planning of the office baby showers, and all of the general excite-*

ment that typically comes when a coworker is expecting. I don't remember my answer to the question, "So do you want kids?" when asked during such events, probably something breezy and dismissive like "We'll see!" But I do remember how I couldn't shake the question. It wasn't the inquiry itself (no harm intended and certainly not the first time I'd been asked), but the setting. My career had always been a safe space, where I could define myself by my professional accomplishments versus my relationship status or other esoteric success standards for women. So I started to wonder: Is my fertility a KPI here too?

Unfortunately, things will be said to you that may trigger you—from rubbing you the wrong way to inciting complete outrage. If you do anticipate any tough questions, talk with your partner or a member of your inner circle; even if no one ever says them to you, it is helpful to lift of the burden of the expectation. Think about a "party line," something that is the deliberate way you want to—to be frank—put someone in their place. Hopefully these things are said with the best intention, and those can be learning moments, but you must recognize when it is more than that. An anonymous contributor shared:

One Friday during my second trimester, I was scheduled to go in for a doctor's visit in the afternoon to check on my baby's size and weight. My doctor was concerned that the baby was underweight and possibly had IUGR (intrauterine growth restriction). My boss at the time moved our morning meeting to the afternoon, and I then emailed her that I had a conflict. She stormed into my office and snapped at me, saying, "Can you please schedule your doctor appointments during lunch, not during office hours?" I had already been experiencing tremendous stress from having to go to the doctor every week to check on my baby's weight, and I was shocked that she lacked

any empathy, and even went further to make me feel guilty
for going to the doctor. I have since left my job and am grateful
that I can take care of my children. I decided to leave my posi-
tion primarily because I felt it was important to be with them
when they are young, but sometimes I do think back at this
interaction and how it solidified my decision to leave.

Even things that are said with no malintent can have a negative
impact. In fact, some comments and actions can go so far as to constitute pregnancy discrimination, and it is important for you to know
your rights and understand how you are protected.

DEALING WITH DISCRIMINATION

The U.S. Equal Employment Opportunity Commission (EEOC) defines pregnancy discrimination as involving "treating a woman (an
applicant or an employee) unfavorably because of pregnancy, childbirth, or any medical condition related to pregnancy or childbirth."[3]

For the purposes of this book, it is important to recognize both
that discrimination exists, and that if it happens to you or to members of your team, you should have the confidence to assert your
rights. Turn to your human resources team when applicable, seek
guidance from support organizations, and if necessary, solicit special-
ized legal counsel. I encourage you to visit the EEOC website (www
.eeoc.gov) to ensure you have up-to-date federal information, and to
check your state guidelines and leave requirements, which vary con-
cerning your rights while pregnant.

Here is an abbreviated reference on pregnancy discrimination.
The EEOC states: "The Pregnancy Discrimination Act (PDA) is an
amendment to Title VII of the Civil Rights Act of 1964. Discrimination on the basis of pregnancy, childbirth, or related medical conditions constitutes unlawful sex discrimination under Title VII. Women
affected by pregnancy or related conditions must be treated in the

same manner as other applicants or employees who are similar in their ability or inability to work."[4]

The PDA is enforced by the EEOC, and "forbids discrimination based on pregnancy when it comes to any aspect of employment, including hiring, firing, pay, job assignments, promotions, layoff, training, fringe benefits, such as leave and health insurance, and any other term or condition of employment."[5] In addition, "impairments resulting from pregnancy (for example, gestational diabetes or preeclampsia, a condition characterized by pregnancy-induced hypertension and protein in the urine) may be disabilities under the Americans with Disabilities Act (ADA). An employer may have to provide a reasonable accommodation (such as leave or modifications that enable an employee to perform her job) for a disability related to pregnancy, absent undue hardship (significant difficulty or expense)."

Although smaller employers (fewer than fifteen people) are not required to offer pregnancy or other disability leave under Title VII or FMLA, they may be required to do so by state law.

Lastly, "It is unlawful to harass a woman because of pregnancy, childbirth, or a medical condition related to pregnancy or childbirth. Harassment is illegal when it is so frequent or severe that it creates a hostile or offensive work environment or when it results in an adverse employment decision (such as the victim being fired or demoted). The harasser can be the victim's supervisor, a supervisor in another area, a coworker, or someone who is not an employee of the employer, such as a client or customer."

Employers cannot ask you if you are pregnant or plan to be. You do not need to tell anybody that you are pregnant, and you cannot be fired because you are pregnant. Remember that discrimination or harassment with regard to your pregnancy could take place at work events, with customers or vendors, at conferences, on work travel, or in other ways outside your primary workplace (or virtually). If you feel that you have been subjected to discrimination or harassment, make clear notes of incidences and conversations and give a report to your HR team or a senior team member. If you aren't happy with their response because there's either no response or a poor one, take your concerns to another senior resource. This is only a brief summary and does not constitute legal advice. Familiarize yourself with your rights and do not be afraid to exercise them.

Another unique behavior to consider is "benevolent discrimination." This is when pregnant people are penalized or devalued or have decisions made for them through microaggressions and undiscussed assumptions. Often, these represent misunderstandings or a lack of communication. Through my research and interviews, I found that the women who were subjected to benevolent discrimination knew that there was no malign intent; in fact, the perpetrator was likely "trying to help." But ultimately there is a big disconnect between the intent and the impact.

When Julia Sanabria was pregnant, she was a senior associate at a law firm hoping to make counsel, the first step toward her goal of making partner. But a colleague's well-meaning comment almost impeded her progress. She recounts her story of "The Well-Intentioned Saboteur":

> I was sitting in a conference room, about seven and a half months pregnant, with the partners in my department. A very high-profile project we had been expecting for a while had just come in and we were staffing it up. I had attended the pitch and my skill set made me the perfect person to work on it. The plan had been for me to do it, but we had also expected it to come in much earlier in my pregnancy. As we discussed it, one very well-meaning partner said, "It is too much stress on Julia to do this deal this late into her pregnancy." I sat there stunned. On the one hand, I appreciated what he was trying to do, but on the other hand, I wanted to do the deal. I didn't speak up in the moment. I was completely caught off guard. I didn't know how to deal with the situation because I know the

partner who made the comment thought he was speaking with my best interests at heart, and I know it came from a good place, but I also know that it was exactly the kind of deal I needed to work on to achieve my goals. There is a longer story that explains how I did end up doing the deal, but I walked out of that initial meeting without being assigned to it.

Julia reflected on this story with a poignant point for you to keep in mind: "In retrospect, I'm glad this happened because I had been worried about bad intentions harming me in pursuit of my goals, not good intentions. I think about how many times conversations like that probably happen when the woman in question isn't in the room, unaware of what they will miss. In that moment, I wish I had been able to think of a way to speak up for myself without feeling like I was alienating someone who was an advocate for me, even if it wasn't working in my favor. My advice would be to speak up, but to do so in a way that acknowledges the intentions of the other person while also explaining how the protection they are offering is becoming a hindrance."

If you find yourself in this situation during your pregnancy, think about how you can both acknowledge the effort of the other person and that you would like the decision to be your own. Share that your decisions at each point are not blanket statements—one time that you lean in to an additional assignment might not mean that you can take on everything, pregnant or not. In addition, when you are deciding to do things in your job that can have either a real or perceived impact on your career now or in the future, there is nothing wrong with acknowledging that. Take a moment with your leader, or those who may have an impact on your career or day-to-day assignments, and remind them that you are committed, and in this moment you are feeling great and are not limited at all by your pregnancy—or that while you need in this moment not to go beyond your day-to-day commitment, you are still very much part of the team and will let everyone know if anything

changes that would not allow you to hold up your side of your responsibilities at work.

This leads us to the last, but very critical, part of communication.
You need to listen—and so do the people you are communicating with.

LISTEN TO LISTEN

There's an important lesson I teach my students as a communications professor: listen to listen, do not listen to reply. To truly listen,
you need to meet, hear, and then respond. I also give the same advice
to employers; for example, if your employee is pregnant, meet her
where she is and follow her lead. Hear her voice her needs. Respond
accordingly. For you, you can encourage your manager—or whoever
you are speaking with at work—to follow this pattern. The goal is to
encourage the act of true listening—not solving a problem on the spot
or asking questions to the point of exhaustion. By prompting true listening, you're shaping the conversation so that it is about you; otherwise, it becomes about them—their frame, what they hear, and what
they want to say *to* you.

Try this yourself next time someone on your team shares news of
their pregnancy, personally or professionally. If you're unsure what
kind of reply they are looking for, try asking. It might be saying nothing at all. Someday with your own experience now behind you, you
may find as an employer or manager that you have gone through a
similar pregnancy experience to theirs, but remember true listening
means focusing on the other person instead of making the conversation about your own experience. It's easy to do so and with the best
intentions; you may be trying to be empathetic, but it can make the
other person feel dismissed.

"I remember sitting on my bed, head in my hands, weeping and
anticipating the weight of the conversation I didn't want to have,"
shared Rachel, a contributor to my research. She had gone in for a
twelve-week ultrasound and discovered that she'd miscarried:

To say I was upset is an understatement. I had two healthy pregnancies prior and had zero physical signs of loss. Nothing. This was the day I discovered what the term "missed/ silent abortion" meant. I knew many people who had miscarried, but now it was mine and my soul was devastated. I had to tell my boss and I was not prepared for her reaction....

The week prior to my miscarriage, we worked a trade show together. She knew I was pregnant and ensured that I didn't lift anything heavy or overexert myself physically. During this trip, she shared with me that she had several miscarriages prior to her two children. I shared that I had not, and naturally, my heart broke for her. We discussed being working mothers and how that (hopefully) positively impacts our children. I really felt we connected.... It felt good, at least for a few days. But now I had to have a conversation I had never had before. Since my body had not let the fetus go, essentially I could pass it at any time before my dilation and curettage (D&C) procedure. So the plan was to take a few days off and have the procedure the following Monday. I could not stop crying long enough to call her, and knowing how busy she always was, I sent a text. "I lost the baby. I have to have a D&C. I am beside myself." She called and I mustered a "hello." Then, she spoke. "I am so glad I shared my experiences with you so you know that I understand what you're going through."

That was the first thing she thought to say? ... She then proceeded to tell me how sorry she was and to take the time I needed. I could barely muster a "thanks?" and we hung up. I threw my phone in my nightstand, curled up, and wept. She made it seem that my loss was insignificant to hers, a mediocre miscarriage. And it cut deep. In hindsight, I truly don't believe she had ill intentions, but it doesn't take away the impact. When I hear of someone's loss or suffering I simply say

"I am sorry. I am here for you if you want to talk or just want someone to listen." The impact of our words is profound. Speak wisely and be kind.

Throughout the highs and lows of pregnancy, a supportive listening ear at work can make all the difference between staying at a job and moving on. Julia Descoteaux, an e-commerce leader formerly at Kiehl's, recounts a surprising moment when her boss affirmed her value:

I was just about to go on maternity leave when our president, Chris Salgardo, called me into his office. I had been with Kiehl's for about a year and was working a lot—eight a.m. to ten p.m. sort of days doing the job of three people, as we were understaffed and trying to hire. I didn't think he even noticed me on a day-to-day basis. I wasn't quite sure what to expect, but he asked me where my head was and whether I was considering coming back to Kiehl's at the end of my maternity leave. He didn't say it to pry, but from a very compassionate place, as if he understood (as a male) the struggle that we females have when trying to juggle hormones, family obligations, and professional ambitions. I remember telling him rather honestly that I didn't quite know what I was going to do, and he said he was fine with that. He gave me a promotion and a bonus in that same meeting, and I was shocked. I had never felt so valued by a person or company.

I remember putting a pin in that moment. . . . The feeling of appreciation that I had for compassionate management really dovetailed into how I wanted to be as a leader in the future. I felt more confident later in my pregnancy than I ever had in my career before.

Communication is a tool, and being a good communicator is a skill, which means that the more we practice, the more we improve. In this important moment, both professionally and personally, use communication to your advantage. Find confidence and comfort by using the who (including recognizing style), what, when, where, how, and why questions. Set boundaries and ensure that if something doesn't feel right, to advocate for what you need or protect yourself in instances of harassment and discrimination, including benevolent discrimination. Finally, listen and encourage listening.

QUESTIONS FOR REFLECTION

How are you going to navigate your timeline for communication in a way that doesn't make you feel uncomfortable or put unnecessary stress on you?

What communication style do you relate to most?

If you could—without any risk—say anything you wanted to your colleagues, what would you share in this phase of your journey? What's stopping you?

Carry Strong Stories

DR. SARAH ORECK

I'm a reproductive psychiatrist, which means that I work mostly with women around hormonal transitions in their life, and particularly around pregnant people and the transition to motherhood. I live in Los Angeles and have a private practice.

The first trimester of both my pregnancies were extremely challenging. I worked with pregnant coworkers during training and assumed the only challenging part of pregnancy would be those very last weeks marked by extreme fatigue, significant weight gain, and when birth was just a few weeks or days away. What I didn't realize until I was pregnant was that I assumed pregnancy wouldn't be hard to navigate at work except when it was so visible that I couldn't hide it.

I never considered that I might be one of the few with hyperemesis gravidarum, and I certainly minimized the challenges of sharing the news with patients, especially in my field. During the first trimester of both of my pregnancies I experienced debilitating nausea and dizziness. It affected my concentration, and over several weeks, my mood. Despite the all-day sickness (I think one of the biggest issues in cultivating empathy is the misnomer "morning sickness," as it isn't reserved for one part of the day for most), I assumed I would be able to maintain the same pace and workload. I was thankful that I wasn't a surgeon performing hours on my feet and thought, "I'm a therapist, I sit in a chair all day—I won't have any issues getting through this."

For the very first time in my professional career, I had a very difficult time being fully present for my patients. As the weeks progressed and my case of all-day sickness lasted eight to twelve weeks in both of my pregnancies, it started to erode my profes-

sional self-esteem and left me feeling at times that I was a less effective therapist or physician.

It was also uncomfortable in my field to tell patients and potentially burden them with a pregnancy that might end in loss. I should mention that many of my patients are either attempting to conceive, have experienced loss, or are themselves pregnant. Throughout many of my sessions with patients, I felt like I was hiding a very important part of myself and my experience, yet there was no room for disclosure in my mind given the risks to viability.

Although I resisted, I realized that the only thing to do was to slow down and take care of myself. This was extremely challenging as a business owner with plans about growth and scaling my practice. This was certainly what was needed, and it relieved a great deal of pressure. It was also the break from work that I needed to fully face the impending changes to my identity—that perhaps physician or doctor would no longer be the first word I used to describe myself (and maybe should never have been) and, instead, I would soon first become a mother.

MARGARET BROWN, LEADERSHIP ADVISER AND COACH

With my first daughter, I thought I had "mastered motherhood," because I was still able to hold on to so many of the things I did before her—brunches in Brooklyn, Kusama exhibits, travel adventures with my stroller in tow. My career also continued to thrive. The more praise I received on my ability to "do it all," the more I felt I was "doing it right." As I navigated the complexity of life, I continued on autopilot, applying the mantra I had always relied on: Just get through this next [insert big thing]. Whatever it takes, power through.

When I became pregnant with my second daughter a year later, I doubled down with the same approach, seeking safety and comfort in what I had always known. But as time went on, I slept less, took on more, and for the first time was pushed well beyond my ability to "power through." Moreover, I felt different. I was different.

This internal struggle was compounded by radio silence leading up to the end of my maternity leave on what role I would be coming back to—a humbling contrast to the support I had become accustomed to throughout my career. Feeling invisible and alone, I reached out to a former manager, mentor, and friend, who graciously helped me return to the job I previously had temporarily. Shortly thereafter, I moved to another role without much clarity on my future. It was clear to me I was on a different track . . . and then the pandemic hit. My life spiraled into what felt like a never-ending roller-coaster in the dark, and after many tears and sleepless nights, I left a career that had become a security blanket of external validation.

Once this veil was lifted, it became clear that my hardest and most important work would be to authentically embrace who I am through every stage of life. Around that same time, I was introduced to a saying often attributed to Paulo Coelho: "Maybe the journey isn't so much about becoming anything. Maybe it's about un-becoming everything that isn't really you, so you can be who you were meant to be in the first place." These powerful words helped me to reconcile that this was my "undoing"—enabling me to let go of this narrow construct of identity so I could let in the depth of who I was (and all of us are) truly meant to be . . . complex, ever-changing, and powerfully aligned with our truest self.

JESSICA MATLIN, DIRECTOR OF BEAUTY AT MODA OPERANDI, COFOUNDER AND COHOST OF THE *FAT MASCARA* PODCAST

Since I was a little kid, one of my favorite films has been the 1987 comedy Overboard. *In short, Goldie Hawn plays two roles. We first meet her as Joanna, a rich female heiress. She swans about on a massive yacht, where she wears fabulous outfits like a red deep-plunge swimsuit with glitter sunglasses. She paints her nails red. She smokes. She has heaps of free time.*

Then there is Annie. This is who Joanna becomes after falling off her yacht, getting amnesia, and being "rescued" by a poor, widowed handyman seeking revenge—Joanna berated and stiffed him on a job on her yacht. Now as his "wife," she would be unwittingly repaying him by cooking, cleaning, and taking care of his four unruly boys.

As a kid watching this on VHS, there was always something about Annie that made me queasy. It felt like I was seeing an honest depiction of what motherhood could be. It looked exhausting. It seemed thankless. It turned Goldie Hawn—gorgeous, effervescent Goldie Hawn—into a frump, wondering how she ended up in this place.

When I was pregnant, my biggest anxiety was around having a healthy baby—I want to get that out of the way. But aside from that, one of my most looming fears was what would happen to me once I had a child. I knew I wanted to have a family, but I didn't want to feel like I was hit by a truck at the end of each day. As an introvert, I worried about my "me" time. I was worried I would be a shell of myself, and there would be a distance between me, my husband, my daughter, and the people I loved each day, because I would not have anything more to give. The well would be dry.

Since I had my daughter, Lake, I think about my own mother all the time. She was not an Annie, but she certainly didn't have much time for herself. My mom was a working mother, and I remember her coming home, immediately putting groceries away, starting to fix dinner, then cleaning the kitchen, then doing the laundry and ironing whatever we needed for the next day, and taking care of herself dead last. The one moment she would be giving herself a quickie clear manicure or opening a People *magazine is precisely when I probably scratched at her door to remind her about a school project that "might be due tomorrow" or uncorked my anxieties about the new school year. She was always giving. If it wasn't physical labor, it was emotional, and while she never said this to me, I'm sure it was exhausting.*

Now retired, my mom has a lot more free time on her hands. One of her favorite things to do is send me little bits of wisdom and spirituality, often mined from social media. Some of it's good. She recently sent me a poem about how the days are long, but the years fly by, but once those "busy" years are over, there's a quiet that sets in that may surprise me. I won't wake up to the sound of my daughter needing me every morning. I won't stress out about leaving work early to pick her up from day care, her smiling face always awaiting me. In eighteen years, who knows how busy I will be, how many emails will be in my inbox, how many friends will still want to get together "with the kids." I can only pray my own mother will still be here, texting as she does, multiple times a day, asking about Lake—these days I quickly ping her back while I am also firing off emails to my boss and trying to remember what it was the day care teacher asked me to bring this week. My apartment won't look like a cheerful obstacle course. This is the busiest, possibly most stressful time, but in the fog of exhaustion, I am realizing it may also be the very best.

CHAPTER 5

Identity

Losing and Finding Yourself
Through Working Motherhood

SOMETIMES AS A working mother you are really going to crush it and other times you are going to want to pull a blanket over your head and cry. It used to make me nuts when people at work would say "Enjoy this phase" as I clung on to a fine thread when James was a year old, and his sleep regression continued for five more months. I remember having a meltdown staring into my closet trying to get dressed for work. Even trying to pick out a shirt would trigger my confidence and make me ask myself, "Who am I?" But yes, just like your child will only say "I love you" and hold your face with their tiny little hands for so long, they will also eventually sleep through the night, and your sense of self will reconcile with your pre- and post-baby self, who is also a work in progress. Acknowledge that the little things can be the big ones, and that ephemeral joy and sorrow can be quickly forgotten or have lasting impact on who we are.

Lauren Tetenbaum, LMSW, JD, PMH-C, is an advocate and therapist certified in perinatal mental health who specializes in life transitions affecting millennial and young women. Lauren explains, "From my practice and my own experience, I've recognized there is a shift that happens when you become a mother, or even as early as preconception or pregnancy. This shift can feel dramatic for some women, while for others it can feel like a constant series of adjustments, throwing us off while shaping our evolving identity. We take so much time crafting who we are at work—through education, thoughtful career moves, how we show up to others—in order to ultimately set ourselves up for success. The identity shift can feel disorienting. However, these moments are just that: moments. They provide opportunities not only for self-reflection—to redefine our purpose and reset our ambitions—but also for self-compassion."

This is the final chapter of the principles. Much like the first chapter, it challenges assumptions. It also is a place to save space. In chapter 1 you were encouraged to think about what you are capable of and embrace what you can look forward to as you both change and stay very much who you are throughout your pregnancy. As we conclude part I with this final Carry Strong principle, you will hear stories of women with a wide range of experiences, including many who felt lost, and truly found themselves, in the journey to working motherhood.

FROM WORKING WOMAN TO WORKING MOTHER

Identity is an evolution. Even with clear values or established missions, many of the women that I have spoken to have said that introducing motherhood into their carefully crafted definition of success can take some getting used to, whether the change after this major life event is subtle or dramatic.

Contributor Lynn Fischer says, "My view of self-worth completely shifted with motherhood. Yes, I wanted to excel at work; I still had dreams and ambitions and goals. And yes, my boss's opinion of me still mattered, but it was no longer 100 percent defining (or even accurate, at times). As cliché as it is, I became part of something bigger and more important than me, and my self-worth pivoted to 'How am I defined by how I raise this vulnerable, tiny person?' *That's* what matters."

She continued, "The flip side of the coin above, which is, 'Who the f*ck am I if I no longer completely self-define through work, which I've done for the last thirteen years?' To be real and transparent: while there was a relief to a new way of self-defining, I struggled (and still struggle) when I compare myself to women in the workplace who have made different choices."

Maryam Nazemzadeh, MD, shares, "My work is my identity. It allowed me to continue being myself until I felt comfortable with my new identity as a mother. It helped me feel like myself. I always say that I have two children; my first is my career and my second is my daughter. I had to give both equal attention and both had to learn to love one another. There was no shame or guilt in that."

Lastly, I was moved by thinking about the flip side too. An anonymous retired senior executive for a major bank told me, "I never meant to have a career, but I never doubted I would be a mother."

Seoan was living in Seattle, a clinical research scientist at the Seattle Children's Hospital working on several pediatric neurological diseases such as epilepsy, hydrocephalus, and traumatic brain injury. Shortly before this story, she interviewed for graduate school to pursue a PhD in neuroscience. Seoan told me:

I grew up in a very traditional culture (South Korea in the eighties and nineties) where little girls were encouraged or even expected to eventually *become SAHMs (stay-at-home moms) no matter what profession or career you may dream of. There is even a phrase called "hyun-mo-yang-cheo," which literally translates into "wise-mother-kind-wife," the golden* standard we are all supposed to strive for. Coupled with the fact that I was the eldest girl in my family (with one younger sister and lots of baby cousins), I had always thought that when motherhood eventually comes, I would be fully and emotionally prepared for an automatic switch to that identity.

While on maternity leave, I have found all the operational tasks familiar and easily doable (perhaps minus the breastfeeding, sigh!) but what caught me by surprise was how unnatural or nonautomatic it was for me to shift my identity from a career-driven, aspiring neuroscientist to the said "wise-mother." The moment that caught me so off guard that I can still vividly recall it was during my firstborn Sofia's first week of Montessori school. At pickup, I was gathering all the dirty bottles and soiled cloth diapers when one of the teachers called for "Sofia's mom" several times before I realized she was referring to ME! I recall turning around and acknowledging, "Oh, Sofia's mom! That's me! I forgot. No one's called me that before!" followed by a nervous laugh. Having had my own identity of an independent, career-driven woman for such a long time, I realized that it took conscious effort to integrate this second identity into my existing one, and that this process is not seamless.

I think when we talk about "nesting" or preparing for the baby, we tend to focus on the day-to-day operational tasks. What I wasn't prepared for was the switch of identity—how it took an enormous amount of conscious effort to add this new identity to my existing one and effortlessly switch back and forth as if they were mutually exclusive. It's okay if this doesn't feel natural to you at first, or ever! It doesn't make you a bad mother or someone with less maternal instinct. We are all different and what is right for you and your family doesn't mean it is right for another.

FEAR AND TRANSFORMATION

There are two big themes (and big emotions) that mark the transition to motherhood—fear and transformation. Naming them is the first step to navigating them. Arianna Taboada, a perinatal health researcher and the author of *The Expecting Entrepreneur*, has run a consultancy since 2015 that helps entrepreneurs make their transition to motherhood while keeping their businesses thriving.[1] She says, "Even though physically you are pregnant and then not, it is not a light switch with identity."

I was working with new mothers in some of the most vulnerable situations women can find themselves in all while they experienced pregnancy, postpartum, and tried to make sense of the resources available to them. When I went into private practice, my clients were self-employed with a different level of resources, yet their challenges and need for structure were still so clear.

Around that same time, I had my own child and discovered that I could make myself my own client. Because of my professional experience I thought of myself of having way more access to create the support I needed around me as a business owner, but nothing could have prepared me fully until I experienced it—and transformed.

My training has all been in the United States including two traineeships funded by the federal Maternal and Child Health Bureau (MCHB), but my birth experience was in Mexico, where there is a centuries-long tradition of birth workers and the space they hold beyond the birth experience, especially with regard to identity. In fact, in the region where I gave birth (Quintana Roo), they call this immense transition la pequeña muerte, *or "the little death." It's not something morbid, it's the normalization of life and death and in this new*

life coming forward, you need to make space for that opportu-
nity.

Arianna describes the biological, psychological, and social changes
you may experience, including with regard to work.

Identity transformation is within all those layers. Your brain
is transforming, your body is transforming, and so are your
thoughts and beliefs. What I tend to see with entrepreneurs,
although everyone goes through this, is that their primary
identity is through their work; they feel the big sense of pur-
pose with their work. Adding motherhood is something that
requires meaning-making to bring into part of her identity,
an exploration with affirmation, and it takes a while to get
used to, and even to identify when it's happening.

Amy Henderson is a mother of three and the CEO of TendLab,
where she works parents' groups at companies like Salesforce, Accen-
ture, Airbnb, Lululemon, and many others, to make work "work" for
parents. Amy also started the FamTech Founders Collaborative, a
network of over 160 founders who are solving for the needs of caregivers. Armed with the revelation that parenting develops career-
critical skills, Amy wrote *Tending: Parenthood and the Future of*
Work in 2021 to claim the value of parents in the workplace. Here is
her story of transformation and discovery:

I never really thought all that much about having kids. In
fact, one of the reasons I married my husband was because he
wanted to be a stay-at-home dad. Then, when I was six
months pregnant with my first child, and the pregnancy was
riddled with complications, my doctors said to me, "You can
have your career or your kid, but at the rate you're going you
can't have both." I didn't feel like I had a choice. I never wanted
to be, or thought I would be, a stay-at-home mom. But there I
was, and it changed me.

I went back to work when my daughter was two and my son was three months old. I needed to. We couldn't afford for me to stay home any longer, and I felt that if I remained at home I might completely lose myself in the ongoing invisible work. I might disappear. Back at work, I felt deeply invigorated. I don't know if I came back to life because my work was visible to others or because I reconnected with the person I had been before I was a mom. I was shocked at how much more effective I was. I was exponentially better than before.

Then, when I was pregnant with my third, and I would soon have three children under four, my whole family got sick. I was in the kitchen mopping vomit off the floor with one kid on my leg and the other beside me crying. My father-in-law, whom I also was caring for, walked in the back door, saw my pregnant belly hanging low to the ground, the vomit, the crying, and said to me: "You know, the frontier women during the Dust Bowl, the ones who never saw any reprieve, a lot of them went crazy and killed their families and themselves." And in that moment, I felt I understood those women. And I had this sense of righteous rage: why is this still so fucking hard? In that moment, I knew I needed help and I couldn't do it alone. But for some time, my shame prevented me from getting the help I needed. It wasn't adding up: I was better at work but struggling fiercely to stay afloat with the responsibilities I was carrying. And I wondered if it was just me, or if other parents were also grappling with what often felt like insurmountable challenges.

This crisis, in combination with all that I'd learned in my recovery from PTSD after my time in the Peace Corps, led me to create TendLab. Our mission is to transform our culture's perception of parenthood's impact on career performance. In founding TendLab, I interviewed hundreds of parents and discovered that parenthood was forging us, creating the *opportunity for us to become more potent versions of our former selves. While it's harder to be a working parent in the United States than in any other developed country in the world, and there is an epidemic of shame among working parents, parenthood, possibly more than anything else, neurologically primes us to develop skills that are critical for success in the modern workplace. When a parent has the support they need, they are likely to develop skills that are not only valuable but essential.*

Amy's advice as you go through this experience: "Don't second-guess yourself—there is transformation possible when we face the things we are afraid of."

There is both freedom and risk to transformation, and as the name of this chapter implies, there is what is lost, as Arianna shared, but in that space, there is what is found when experiencing a life event as big as pregnancy. In identifying what we need and discovering who we are, both immediately and over time, we often cultivate a stronger, more resilient version of ourselves. It is important to recognize this power and not to default to comparing yourself to society's expectations, or even your own preconceived ones. As you read the next powerful story from actress Ana Villafañe, think about your own test-drive, and make sure you're in the driver's seat.

The thought of becoming a mother was always terrifying to me until I played one onstage. In playing Gloria Estefan on Broadway, I had to embody the story of a woman who miraculously managed never to sacrifice her personal life for her professional life. I then developed a very maternal relationship with the actor playing my son onstage and a shift occurred. Almost as though I got to "test-drive" the feeling of motherhood at a lower level, and it sparked something inside me that I had never considered a priority. I still fear the severity of it all. Nothing can ever compare to or prepare a person for the real thing. I can only conceptualize, and it is over-whelming to think about. It is part of my growth and acceptance journey. This unspoken pressure is something women go through both collectively and privately on some level, and all of humanity literally depends on it.

It was September 30, 2014, and I had just booked my dream role, starring in an original new musical on Broadway, which meant I had to uproot from LA to New York City. I had two weeks to move. I was chosen out of thousands of girls all over the world to play Gloria Estefan, and I felt the weight of responsibility on my shoulders. Ironically, in dedicating my life to my job, I unlocked several hidden compartments within myself. In adolescence, like many I struggled with my identity and had a lot of fear. As a young actress in LA, I had been severely mistreated and abused by men in the industry. I had been led to believe that I alone would never be enough. It took the many challenges of surviving the physical, emotional, and mental demands of becoming a Broadway star overnight for me to discover who I was. Especially as a woman. I learned my value and my worth. By the time I walked out of the Marquis Theatre for the last time in August 2017, I had completely transformed.

Reflecting on this story, Ana shared:

I feel proud. I feel more comfortable with the fact that I am allowed to have multiple dimensions. I feel that somewhere along my journey I subconsciously had tied womanhood and motherhood to weakness. (Yes, I am ashamed to admit this.) As a little girl I was a tomboy, and as I grew up I felt this unnecessary need to always be "hard" or "strong" or like "one of the guys" to be successful and to feel strong. I then jumped into an incredibly male-dominated industry and felt my value only came from the outside. But playing a mother onstage

opened different strength. Ferocity I had never imagined.
Something untouchable and un-fuck-with-able. Something
the people who hurt me and hardened me can never feel. It is
like being part of this greater, extremely exclusive universal
club. A sisterhood of strength that I now am ready to join
whenever my life takes me there. I am in no rush to start a
real-life family, but I am no longer afraid of my womanhood.
That is a major shift.

Gloria Estefan herself told Ana that she had wanted to be a
mother since she was a little girl: "Of all the aspects of my life, being
a mother always came first, and I found a way to walk that tightrope
despite the fact that it was the hardest on me. Balance has always
been my key word."

A CLEAR MISSION

As women, our various identities can run off a list: "I am a friend, a
sister, a daughter, a wife, a teacher, a leader, a mother," with motherhood compounding the list of labels society gives us, and we give ourselves. I know I'm not alone when I say that, for me, it often feels like
a never-ending list where I am failing at everything on a bad day and
stretched to my limits on a good day. I shared this with Virginie
Nothard, international career, leadership, and business development
coach, trainer, stress therapist, and speaker. She explained, "Sometimes without a mission we are living our life through our titles. We
have so many of them that we can lose ourselves through them. If a
business folds, I feel like I lose part of me, or if I have a baby, I gain
one, but does that take away from my others? Instead, within these
titles you have a different opportunity every day to focus on your
mission. It's fuel to do more. It becomes a vessel where you live your
purpose, and you make an impact."

This idea of our identity being a "vessel" made a huge impression on me. I used to think of myself as having all these titles, things that I do, including responsibilities to allocate time to. If you picture a cup full of water, I had one big cup and then had a bunch of little cups that I could pour myself into. People would question how I could do it all, and frankly most of the time it felt like I was pouring out everything and had an empty cup I would shake to get the final drops or peer wistfully into to get whatever was left. I was longing for something for *me* that was separate from all those cups. I realized that what I needed to do was change my perspective.

Instead of having one big cup that represents my finite time and energy, what if instead each part of our identity had its own little cup, and each cup had varying amounts of fuel in them every day, or even at different times of the day? With that starting point in mind, they all pour *into* the vessel of myself that *because* of all my many facets is often overflowing, and they often fuel one another. Instead of giving myself away and pouring from an empty cup, I literally am self-fueled and embrace all my titles at the same time, as both a responsibility and an opportunity. If this seems overly optimistic, consider it a way to prioritize your day. If something isn't in service of that mission, the big vessel, why are you doing it? You do have finite time but you also have unlimited potential.

You may have heard the Pinterest-friendly adage, "Your purpose guides you, mission drives you." As your identity shifts and transforms with pregnancy and motherhood, having a personal mission statement can serve as a grounding motivation for you to connect all the ways you define yourself, and to reconcile something that one multihyphenate contributor defined as "the overwhelming list of who I am." Together with vision (where you want to go) and goals (what you want to achieve), a mission connects identity (who you are) to impact (the living legacy you want to have).

My personal mission is to help people and organizations reach their full potential for positive impact. I use my curiosity and leadership skills along with the joy of connecting people to do so in a very personal way, so reaching that potential is self-directed yet supported. I feel the most frustrated when I see potential being constrained. I would never have been able to fully craft this mission without my experience in my career as an executive, but also without my experiences as a mother. It suits me as a professor and now as an author. For someone who is very goal oriented (and a runner who likes a clear start and finish), I love that this mission has no end date either for myself or for others.

To craft your own personal mission statement, be specific from the start, to force yourself to make choices. Your mission statement should have three parts: your skills; your purpose, or the reason why you're doing what you're doing; and your compass, your direction or plan to make it happen.

For example: My personal mission is to use my _____ and _____ skills for the purpose of _____ and I am going to do it by _____.

Of course, you don't need to fill in the blanks right now as it can be overwhelming. How can you distill the big question of "who am I?" to Mad Libs®?

Margaret Brown is a leadership adviser and coach who is dedicated to helping mothers elevate their approach to work, life, and everything in between. Her own story inspired her to support women as they navigate their own career-life journeys and help them to define their missions.

Her advice: Take the time to think about it now, when you are tapped in. She shares, "For every hour you spend obsessing over the colors of your nursery or next promotion, take the same amount of time to really get to know yourself today. Motherhood can be your greatest 'mirror' and the most powerful inspiration for authentic reflection, growth, and transformation. Go deeper than checking the box of society's expectations and ask yourself the hard questions: What are your strengths? What do you value most? What experiences do you want to have in your life? How do you want to learn and

grow? How do you want to give back to the world? And most important, what do you want to be remembered for?"

Having a personal mission statement can also transform your
work from a day-to-day job to a purposeful, more connected endeavor. Alicia Yoon, founder and CEO of Peach & Lily, told me, "I felt
an additional sense of purpose in my work. I started my business out
of passion for our mission—to empower people to transform their
skin. We also believe in giving back and making a positive impact,
whether that's planting a tree for every Peach & Lily Collection order
or helping to stop sex trafficking by partnering with Restore NYC.
With a baby on the way, making a positive impact to help create a better world felt even more personal."

One of the fears women have when thinking about the impact of
motherhood on their careers is that it'll be a limiting factor, a cap on
their capability. Your personal mission statement is not one more
thing that you're putting on your list, another ball you're afraid of
dropping. Instead, it's a way to create an achievable future for you,
your career, and your family—concurrently, and even better, comple-
mentarily.

FIDERE

Confidence comes from the Latin *fidere*, which means "to trust." A
"self-trust" is what many women in hindsight shared they felt or *wish*
they would have felt before or throughout their pregnancies. They
spoke to "self-rejecting," but also to their pride in overcoming self-
doubt. There is a tremendous sense of pressure for women when they
are pregnant at work, but if we flip the sentiment, pregnancy also deserves its own sense of accomplishment, both by others and yourself.
How can you find this confidence and stable ground?

Callan Blount Fleming, CEO of Spark Collective, is an ICF-certified
coach, speaker, facilitator, and consultant with more than a decade of
experience in development of leaders and executives, organizational

design, equity and inclusion, and women-centric initiatives. She built her company while becoming a mother. Callan reflected on identity and its intersection of confidence, and how to find it:

> One of the best pieces of advice I've ever received is to "act as if..." If you have a goal to be a CEO of a start-up, act like you already are—hone the idea, build connections, get scrappy, inspire a vision. If you want to run a marathon, act like a person who already does—regularly train, have healthy eating habits, drink water, sleep eight hours a day, etc.
>
> For a lot of the moms I work with, they really liked who they were pre-mom, and many of them were hoping to hold on to their pre-mom identity and add "mom" onto it. Typically, I end up talking to them around six months to one year postpartum when they realize they're changing as people and professionals. They often come to me saying: I'm not sure who I am anymore. This is the moment they get to "act as if." They get to decide what they value now, what they really care about, how they want to parent, and what their family mission is. And perhaps they even get the important chance to mourn the parts of themselves they valued but that are no longer central to who they are. It is an awesome moment for self-actualization; in taking this step back, you get to work, parent, love, play, simply exist on your own terms. "Acting as if" can be liberating. As James Clear says: "Every action you take is a vote for the type of person you wish to become."

This "acting as if" links back to your mission—what would you be doing if you were living your mission to the fullest? Inherently this also can mean embracing risk.

Christie Hunter Arscott is a leading international authority on women's leadership who has worked with thousands of early career and executive women around the world. She is a mother and the author of *Begin Boldly: How Women Can Reimagine Risk, Embrace*

Uncertainty, and Launch a Brilliant Career. Christie shares my ambition of looking at points of attrition in the pipeline as she powerfully articulated "fissures" as opportunities for retention. Christie
shares:

> *I didn't enjoy pregnancy, had a horrible birth and difficult
> physical recovery, moved away from my husband with our
> six-week-old baby and did long distance for fourteen months,
> struggled to breastfeed, didn't sleep train, didn't have set nap/
> bedtimes, didn't decorate a nursery, and didn't stop working,
> including traveling for work. I didn't know what I was doing
> with my newborn, but I did know what I was doing at work,
> and that gave me the energy to keep going and to be okay with
> the unknown of motherhood. It was a refuge.*
>
> *There is no one way to mother, and yet there is an over-
> abundance of information, opinions, and literature on what
> is right and what is wrong. Without a doubt, some resources
> can be amazing, but I've seen so many beautiful souls get lost
> along the way ... while not trusting themselves and their in-
> stincts.*

Her research has highlighted that risk-taking is "enlightening, empowering, and the antidote for self-doubt. "Mitigating risk holds us
back, but reframing it, especially as women, gives us agency to act."
This includes reframing self-promotion as "courageous advocacy,"
networking as "connecting," and thinking about failure as "essential."
In *Begin Boldly*, Christie defines three mindsets to cultivate an
appetite for risk that ultimately leads to growth: curious, courageous,
and agile.[2] She says:

> *Women often think they need to have all the answers, but they
> need to instead have all the right questions and approach
> them with the right mindset. Just as the three mindsets can
> help you build a brilliant career, they can also help you find*

joy and meaning in motherhood. Curiosity allows us to admit that we don't have all the answers and instead just need the right questions as we navigate the path of pregnancy and motherhood. Courage allows us to understand that even when we feel the least self-assured we can have courage in the presence of fear. We can take courageous action and make bold choices in the face of doubts that will inevitably exist in our journeys. Confidence is the output of courage and doesn't exist in isolation, it is cultivated through action. Agility enables us to understand that our identities and our lives aren't fixed, they are fluid, and just as our children are changing, we are changing too, and the more agile and adaptable we are the more we will enjoy the adventure of motherhood.

For me, courage has meant embracing not knowing what's next, trying something new, and being always willing to ask for help. I never could have imagined the capacity for love that I have felt as a mother, nor the conviction of my strength and resolute ambition to be the best I can be for my sons and myself. This carries over to everything I do, including my work. It doesn't mean that I don't get "stuck" (often) in times of change, but it does mean that I can reframe this feeling with being curious about why—and getting "un stuck" for now and the future.

Dr. Sarah Oreck, who we met in the previous chapter, tells us, "No matter what our field of expertise, transitions are very hard. I think it's important to check in with what you're feeling and try not to avoid the challenges that come with transition. The transition to motherhood has been called matrescence, which is likened to the amount of change and transformation that occurs during the adolescent transition. Although it may seem like you're alone, all new parents experience some level of transition and transformation, and there is help available. If your regular support systems aren't providing the space that you need, consider starting therapy or join a support group."

Sarah shared that her mother and her own therapist were her support. "My mother was physically and emotionally present to help with the transition that she herself had undergone thirty-four years earlier, and my therapist gave me the space to navigate the less acceptable feelings that come with the transition to motherhood, including sadness or anger at the loss of certain features of my identity and independence, but also to enjoy the blissful moments of expanding love and connection."

You can be a warrior, but you do not need to be a superhero. Unfair expectations of triumph in pregnancy can hold us back just as much as unfair expectations of failure. Work can be a bolster and a constant of your identity, just as motherhood can help you grow as a teammate and as a leader. It is not just about what you may lose, it's what you might gain—energy, empathy, efficiency, and maybe even yourself.

Meghan Duggan is the president of the Women's Sports Foundation, a three-time Olympian, a seven-time World Champion ice hockey forward, and director of player development for the New Jersey Devils. In 2018 she was the captain of the Olympic gold medal American women's hockey team and married her wife, Gillian Apps, three-time Olympic Gold medalist who was a member of the Canadian women's hockey team. In 2020 and 2021 they welcomed their two young children.

Meghan reflected on the powerful transformation of pregnancy concurrent to her incredible career:

> I often think about that time in my life as "BC," before children, who I was before, what my priorities were, and the power I had in my life versus after. The experience of pregnancy and the birth of my child was life changing. It was about being empowered in my body, my mind, and inherently who I was. The transformation was about the depths of who I am and what I was capable of, but I also remember this epiphany of thinking about every mom in that moment. That they have gone

through this too, you feel so connected, and that they are all
badasses—I wanted to call every mom I knew and say they are
awesome . . . and I did reach out to a few and thought, "What
a group to join." Becoming pregnant and being a mom—it made
me feel more powerful than ever.

I asked Meghan to reflect on all that she has accomplished with regard to how she now feels as a mother: "You just can't compare. I've
been blessed to have some wonderful experiences, ones that I worked
hard for, and prior to being a mom, winning a gold medal was the
greatest day of my life, but then then marrying my wife, the birth of
our son, then our daughter, make winning an Olympic gold medal
look like an average Wednesday."

One of the greatest bosses I have ever had, Leslie, always told me
she disliked the word "empowered." In fact, we often used the term
"powered" with each other, fondly. This is because empowered often
means someone else needs to give you the authority or power to do
something. Asking for help, support, resources, space, time, anything
is all valid, but who you are, your identity, is up to you. So, as I close
part I, I encourage you to Carry Strong, self-empowered by who you
are today and who you will become.

QUESTIONS FOR REFLECTION

What is your personal mission statement? Revisit the start
of this chapter and identify your skills for the purpose of your
mission and how you are going to do it.

Considering motherhood with regard to your identity, what
do you know you will gain, and what do you wish to gain?

Carry Strong Stories

MICAELA BIRMINGHAM, WRITER, DIRECTOR

I live in Brooklyn in a neighborhood along the route of the New York City Marathon. While pregnant with my first child in 2007, I watched the race, as I do every year, with tears of joy and admiration for the elite athletes and the pack of forty thousand others running 26.2 miles. That year, the race was won by British four-time Olympian Paula Radcliffe. Paula had had a baby ten months before the race, which is an epic feat if you consider the grueling training it takes to run a 2:23:09 marathon. For context, most mere mortals take over four hours to finish the same distance. When I saw Paula win, I thought to myself, "If she can win, I can finish that race." So three months after my baby was born, I started training for my first marathon. It wasn't pretty, with a nonexistent pelvic floor and the need to wear double sports bras to hold in a pair of nursing breasts. I didn't follow a training program, I just ran when I could, most of the time with a jogging stroller. The most mileage I put in on a given run was nine miles. Any marathon runner will tell you that is less than half of the recommended training distance to prepare, but with a newborn at home, it was going to have to be enough.

By the time of the race, my baby was eight months old, two months younger than Paula's at the time of her win. I hauled my nursing pump to the starting line and pumped in the first-aid tent, much to the shock of the Red Cross workers. It was freezing and awkward, but there was no way I was going to run for four hours with engorged breasts weighing me down. My running partner, Laura, was a dear friend and seasoned marathoner. She tried her best to shield my pumping from the view of the curious yet mortified onlookers.

In keeping with tradition, the race starts with a cannon blast and Sinatra's "New York, New York" playing on the loudspeaker as tens of thousands of runners emerge from the Verrazzano-Narrows Bridge. We were off to the perfect start. Then at mile seven, I got a surprise. My period came back for the first time and with a vengeance. Mile seven! I had nearly twenty more miles to go. Should I stop? Laura definitely thought we should stop and find a drugstore. But there was no way I was going to let period blood stop my race. We kept going. The occasional well-meaning runner would tap me on the shoulder and say, "Miss, you are bleeding." I would say, "Thanks." And keep running. We eventually hit a water station, which allowed me to do a little "dump and spritz" into my crotch, which by this point had seen better days.

Eventually, Laura and I stopped thinking about the period altogether and focused on running. My socks and shoes were red, but it didn't matter. We were going to make it. And we did. We crossed the line right on schedule in 4 hours and 7 minutes. The last two miles I paid dearly for not training enough, but I somehow willed my legs to keep running. I have Laura to thank for sticking by my bloodied side when she could have finished much faster on her own. That is a friend you keep for life. As they say in racing: "While doing it you feel like you might die, but as soon as you cross the finish line you feel reborn." After a brief finish line hug, Laura promptly escorted me to the nearest first-aid tent to request a tampon.

Since then, I have run the New York City marathon four times, and with proper training and a second baby have achieved a personal best of 3 hours and 56 minutes. I like to think I have made my mark on the streets of New York City and on my own stamina. There will be many more "mile sevens" in life, but as mothers, as women, and as friends, we learn how to just keep going, even when it's not pretty.

ALI STAGNITTA, ON-CAMERA REPORTER FOR HOLLYWOODLIFE

My coworker had been with our company for nine years and got pregnant. My boss and manager were both incredibly supportive of her, and we were all so excited. When her three months of maternity leave and the extended paid time off was up after having her daughter, she returned to the office with a brave face. But in the middle of the day she looked at me and said, "I can't do this." Crying in the bathroom, she said her husband told her it would get easier, and I remember her voice cracking as she told me that he started crying to her too, saying, "Do you think it's easy for me? I miss her so much, I only got two weeks of paternity leave, but I have to do this." I remember encouraging her to have it all, that she inspired me and that this was something she would conquer. I told her to ask to work from home a few days a week and try to split time, that our employers would be understanding. I don't know if she ever asked to do that.

The next day, she quit to be a full-time mom. I remember feeling very disappointed that she felt she had to and that perhaps there was fear for asking to do both—to be a mom and to work. She started freelancing, which allowed her to enjoy her own schedule while spending time with her child, but it made me question a lot of things for the first time. I had never experienced those decisions she had to make. I was scared. I wondered how I would handle that kind of emotion and guilt down the road, and would I be strong enough to ask for what I want and need? And would my employer allow it?

MANDI TUHRO, FNP-C, ICU RN

I was thirty-seven weeks pregnant when we took our first suspected COVID-19 patient into the hospital. I spent the month before I delivered skimming the news and watching this virus that started very far away slowly get closer to home as my delivery neared. I delivered at thirty-eight weeks and worked until that day. As I was sitting in my postpartum room nursing my baby, I watched the hospital maintenance staff drilling holes in the windows of the hospital rooms, creating negative pressure apparatuses to house patients, and from that moment on, the tiny knot that had been in my stomach slowly grew a little larger and a little heavier each day.

Once we brought the baby home, it was my husband and me against the world—or at least against this newborn. We had planned for my mom to come and stay with us to help, but we decided it wasn't safe because of the pandemic. . . . I'll never forget that I ran out of vaginal pads one week after delivery and needed my mom to bring me some, and the store limited her to two boxes of the ones they had left. That same day, our grocery delivery person sent me a picture of the bare shelves at the store and that knot grew a little heavier, a little larger.

I watched my coworkers in the ICU battling COVID-19 as I was battling my own issues at home as a first-time mom with little hands-on help. We struggled with breastfeeding, and in-person lactation consultations weren't an option and the phone advice just didn't work. I got very little sleep for months. Honestly, my baby is just over a year old, and I can count on one hand the times he has slept through the night. As the end of my maternity leave drew closer, that knot became larger and heavier as I absorbed blows from people asking how I could go back to work and wasn't I scared? Of course I was, but I was and am the breadwinner of my family and couldn't afford not to go back. I returned to work as the pandemic surged. I was taking care of the sickest patients I have ever seen, working in conditions I never imagined, under stress I couldn't handle while trying to take breaks to go and pump milk for my baby. No one besides my coworkers who had also recently had babies understood. When I was at work, I was desperate to be home with my baby and husband; when I was at home, I couldn't shake the stress, sadness, and anxiety that my job was burdening me with. Before the pandemic, working in an ICU was sad sometimes, but I could leave work at work, but then everything changed.

I knew journaling and words would never capture the desperation I felt, so I decided to take a picture: me in clean PPE. Scrubs, face shield, respirator, sitting on the exercise ball I had spent so much time on trying to soothe the baby while breastfeeding him. The rawest depiction of my experience of being an essential worker and first-time mom during a pandemic. Some people see that picture and take it as a political statement. They get upset. I have had people comment that I don't deserve to be a mother, or they feel bad for my baby. Those people will never understand what I went through.

ANONYMOUS

My boyfriend and I traveled back to his home July 2021 to take a "Baby Tour de Chicago Suburbs." We hadn't seen his friends in three years and a lot had happened. Many had purchased homes and made the migration from the city to the burbs. They got pregnant and had children, while some were figuring out their future baby plans. After a full day of activities playing Restaurant, Teatime, and Baby Olympics, we decided to take a "Rest Day" with friends who didn't have children. The first stop led to a dynamic lunch conversation about reproductive health care. After years of trying and being diagnosed as a thirtysomething with the egg count of someone ten years her senior, my friend had only wished that her ob/gyn and society made it more common to get tested for egg follicle count earlier. Perhaps, had she known, she would have been able to think ahead.

The next day, my boyfriend and I went to go see another friend who recently frozen her eggs under her partner's insurance because her company didn't have coverage. She said that she hadn't told many people because she felt strange not knowing their views on it. By the end of the weekend, while catching up with another friend about the trip, we realized that when it comes to planning for kids, despite society finding it more acceptable to have them later in life and it being possible because of modern medicine, at the end of the day, we still kind of hold our breath and hope for the best.

Many people's first step is to try naturally until twelve to eighteen months passes and then consider more intense measures. In an age of social media, apps, and fast medicine development, I couldn't help but wonder: "Why does women health care seem behind? Perhaps it's the project manager in me, but why isn't it more common to test for reproductive health—is it simply a cost or concern around mental health? And why do we never talk about it?" The next day, I called my ob/gyn to ask her to run a couple of tests to see if my egg count was normal for someone my age. She was surprised to hear this question, because normally patients don't ask to run these tests until after six months of trying, but she agreed. I also planned to see if freezing my eggs was covered somewhere in my work's health insurance. However, I had trepidation about talking to HR on the chance that it could affect any future promotions. . . . Perhaps I am just a project manager who can't stop project managing. Yet when it comes to something I care about, I would like to have a plan—any millennial here with me? Don't be afraid to be proactive. Put your mind at ease, don't be afraid. Data can be very powerful.

PART II

The Five Carry Strong Phases

CHAPTER 6

Phase I

BTTC: Before Trying to Conceive

THE CHAPTERS IN part II each represent a phase of your journey to working motherhood from Before Trying to Conceive (BTTC), Trying to Conceive (TTC), and The Hush, through The Push, to Anticipating the Great Return (or Not). These five common but previously undefined phases provide a time-flexible road map for navigating your pregnancy, as well as a new way of thinking about pregnancy as part of your career that extends beyond forty weeks.

Although linear, the phases are not presented in trimesters. This is because throughout my quantitative and qualitative research, I found that, specifically for work, women were expressing common themes with notable start and end points, but they had different timelines that did not necessarily line up neatly with the first, second, and third trimesters, which are based on the development of your baby, or beyond them. In fact, today there isn't a single resource that considers the many years *before* any of those trimesters at work, including when you're trying to conceive, and the impact of that time is huge. Instead, the five Carry Strong phases represent self-realized checkpoints where you are likely to be navigating decisions about the impact of pregnancy on your career.

If we broaden the intersection of pregnancy and work, the runway gets longer, not just for your ease and control, but so you can think about the two coming together in a way that doesn't seem weird before it's right in front of you. By breaking down this intersection, it is more tangible and less scary. In fact, identification of these phases is the first thing that can help you wrap your head around navigating each step. Labeling takes some stress out of all this ambiguity by giving you something defined and the authority to act within a phase. The thresholds of each phase also create powerful moments for reflection.

PHASE I: BEFORE TRYING TO CONCEIVE (BTTC)

Phase I begins when you decide you want to have a baby someday but aren't quite ready to start trying to conceive. This phase is pre-preconception in the medical sense—you might be years away from pregnancy mentally, physically, or both, but the desire to have a baby is there, and that's a good thing to know. Here you have an opportunity to evaluate your personal and work situation and what you want to do about it—even if the decision at this point is to do nothing at all. This phase helps guide work conversations to normalize discussions about policies for future families. It's better to investigate your workplace maternity policy now instead of when you're six (or sixteen) weeks pregnant.

PHASE II: TRYING TO CONCEIVE (TTC)

Many women describe this phase as a "mind f#$k." Most women go from trying hard to not be pregnant to trying hard to be pregnant.

Others are instantly zapped to an abrupt "Whoa!" with a faint plus sign or double line. With that perspective, trying to conceive is either remarkably simple or complex with regard to work. I still give pause to the fact that someone could be trying to be pregnant for years at work without anyone knowing what they are going through. This time is a big deal. There is the headspace alone of this big (private) priority in your life that could affect your work, or, depending on your circumstances, a significant number of appointments for monitoring or fertility treatments, which also may affect you physically. In addition, there are restrictions you may need to consider because of timing or risk factors, including work travel or your work environment. The end of this phase is the BFP—the Big Fat Positive. Getting a BFP is so huge for every woman, but at work, it can be a trigger—instead this is a moment that can use a guide, so it can have the option to be more positive, like the test itself.

PHASE III: THE HUSH

If TTC is a "mind f#$k," The Hush is often a bigger one. The Hush represents the period of time between finding out you are pregnant and deciding to share the news—The Big Tell. This phase is different for everyone, but every single woman I interviewed had a point of view on it—especially as it manifests at work. During this time, pregnancy feels "very real," but often only to the pregnant woman, which is a tough load to carry. As in TTC, The Hush encompasses a combination of the mental and physical considerations of your day-to-day, which of course includes your work. Decisions on when to share at work can be both a necessity and a choice, exciting and scary. While it does focus on the physical pregnancy implications at work in this phase, this is a period where even if you are not the "carrying" partner, navigating your family's pregnancy can be complex and inevitably leave you feeling soon to be exposed.

PHASE IV: THE PUSH

The Push is the phase after The Big Tell to when you have your baby. The Big Tell is one of the most publicly discussed pregnancy and work topics. To illustrate ubiquity, "How to tell my boss I'm pregnant," or variations of this question, are searched tens of thousands of times a month and are met with short lists of helpful tips, but unlocking it, even in the way you think about it, is so much bigger. This moment, a crucible for many, leads into The Push.

The Push is the period of modern nesting from when you announce your pregnancy to when you have the baby or go on maternity leave. The Push before the push. You are likely to have to-do lists to accomplish with the knowledge now public that time is limited. As the time approaches, offboarding, with clear delegating, is paramount. With most women sharing an energy boost before the final weeks, often there is a moment of true concurrent pregnancy and work "can-do"-empowered effort, but it is different for everyone. During this time, there may also be new health concerns or risk considerations at the end of pregnancy, which may mean that work takes a back seat much earlier then leave. Like the phases in their entirety, identifying The Push as a prolonged period rather than a moment is not only relatable but also the reality, no matter the pregnancy week your Push starts or stops for you. For so many women, the end date, your due date, or when you give birth can be a moving target.

PHASE V: ANTICIPATING THE GREAT RETURN (OR NOT)

This final phase of the working mother's pregnancy journey spans from The Push through to your return to work (or not), although it can truly be concurrent with the whole process. The key word is "anticipating." Mothers will evolve. What you anticipate you will need or how you will act and feel after baby is born will likely change when your baby arrives. However, understanding the possibilities and preparing for this time is helpful now, so when you do get there you'll see options with some clarity. Career-wise, this phase is essential to downregulate the feeling of a distant, looming return to work. It normalizes your return to work (or not) as simply the next step on the horizon—a very normal thing to happen after you have a baby, and this is true even when you chose a pivot that lines up with the birth of your child.

These Carry Strong phases and their defining moments can be summarized in the visual timeline below:

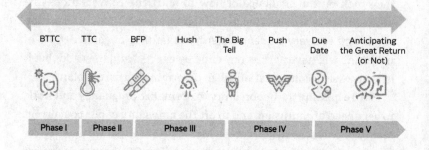

| BTTC | TTC | BFP | Hush | The Big Tell | Push | Due Date | Anticipating the Great Return (or Not) |

| Phase I | Phase II | Phase III | Phase IV | Phase V |

Let's begin with the first phase of the journey to working motherhood: BTTC.

PHASE I: BEFORE TRYING TO CONCEIVE (BTTC)

It is likely if you are reading this book with the word "pregnancy" on the cover that you are or have been in the BTTC phase recently. Notably, if you are beyond it, chances are that your experience in the BTTC phase has implications for your current perspective.

If we take a step back together to when individuals in my research started talking about formative career choices, as you read in part I, 92 percent of college-age women and 86 percent of college-age men believe that parenthood will have an impact on their career choice. Going a bit deeper, what is interesting is that 50 percent of women, one out of two (!), said their desire to have children someday has an impact on their major choice, while 60 percent of men said that wanting to have children someday (some or significant) has an impact on theirs. Yet only 20 percent of college women (15 percent of men) talk about future motherhood often, 28 percent rarely, and 13 percent never.

The bottom line: there is a clear mismatch. I connected with students at the University of Michigan Ross School of Business and as part of their Social Media and Digital Communication in Business class with Dr. Mary Hinesly, chair of Business Communications, and they took on the challenge of how to start the conversation. One powerful statistic they used to highlight the need: "This information is relevant to every student's identity regardless of gender—66% of US adults will have at least one child by age 35," and they add that it is "a necessary consideration when determining a career plan."[1,2]

We're missing the opportunity to normalize pregnancy and work, to get ahead of confusion, and to lift the ambiguity of our concurrent reality of parenthood and career. More specifically, if we make fertility conversations, including testing, part of an OB check-in, it doesn't seem terrifying when you are thirty-six and questioning your ability to get pregnant after a year of trying. The college women I spoke to in my research said, "We are more likely to have had a conversation about a shot for HPV" or "put a condom on a banana" than to have talked about pregnancy, let alone egg count.

The period between deciding you want a baby and actively trying to have a baby presents an opportunity to anticipate the reality of the intersection of pregnancy and work, and you should take advantage of it. From assessing your goals and current work environment to creating financial awareness, there are important considerations that happen in the BTTC phase whether it is in front of you, you're in it, or it's behind you. Thinking about them now will allow you to ease into the next phase and assess whether you're ready to have a baby.

PRE-ASSESSMENT

Before you cross this threshold, you can review where you are in your career and how you might want that to evolve as you embark on your journey to working motherhood. In this chapter, we'll navigate key considerations—your environment and resources; boundaries; financial, physical, and fertility-based implications; and how you want to navigate your goals. To start, you might be asking yourself, "What do I want to achieve *before* I have children?" or "What are the goals I need to accomplish *before* having a baby?" That's a lot of pressure. But if we flip the concept, you might ask, "What do I *want* the impact of having a child to be on my career?" or "How will having a baby (or another baby) impact my goals?"

While it is good to think about the logical steps that set you up for the path that you imagine in the future, remember that life does not stop when you have children. Some things may be temporarily harder to do with your new responsibilities, and it might be true that achieving your goal of completing a certain level of training or hitting a certain salary will help you provide for your future family, but they aren't immovable constraints. There is also nothing wrong with having these goals to drive you. Just keep top of mind that those goals are *yours, you* set them, *you* say when they are met, and *you* can change them.

Revisit the traffic light exercise from part I. When thinking about the impact pregnancy might have on your career and future ambitions, it's good to take stock of where you are now. Are you at a green, yellow, or red light—and where do you want to go? What is blocking you and your ambition? Use your answers to these questions to navigate your personal evolving plan and reevaluate as needed. This is important with regard to goals, but also to the environment that you are in.

ENVIRONMENT AND RESOURCES

A key consideration you might make during the BTTC phase is whether your current work environment is suitable for pregnancy. First, is it safe? But also, who do you spend your day with? Can you imagine what it would be like telling them you're pregnant? To be pregnant? To have a tiny baby? Does it feel good? Do you see examples of what you can project to want and need? Thinking about what you want in your place of work as you take the next step toward starting a family can help you decide if a change is necessary. Culture is key.

Jodi Katz, the CEO and founder of Base Beauty Creative Agency and host of the *Where Brains Meet Beauty* podcast, shares, "I was years from even being pregnant and I looked around at the company's management, the expectations on the staff, other new moms in the organization, and I realized that I couldn't be a mom the way I want to and still have a job at this company. So the path I set from that moment forward was to walk away and craft something for myself that would suit my future family goals. That company 'lost' me years before my first pregnancy test! Because of that experience I *built* a company that leads with humanness: kindness and respect are our first two agency values. And we are always focused on life-work balance—it's literally the reason I started the business, and so it's baked into every move we make as a company.... We ask our parent staff what kind of support they need now. We ask our nonparent staff what kind of support they *think* they might need if they become parents. Having these ongoing conversations allows us to keep nimble and to evolve the way we support our team."

Dr. Jennifer Kangas's story provides another perspective on anticipating the environment in which she wanted to have her second child. Jennifer had her first when she was a third-year medical student at Columbia University College of Physicians and Surgeons.

Columbia is an intense place, and the third and fourth years of medical school were grueling, with or without a young child. When I was applying for pediatric residency programs at the end of medical school, I knew I wanted to have another baby within a year or two and I had a tough decision to make. I interviewed at all the top hospitals in New York City. Although Columbia's program was the most prestigious, it was also known to be the most intense and demanding. More important to me, none of the residents there had children at the time. I ultimately decided to rank several other programs above Columbia because there were multiple residents in each of those programs who had children. I knew residency was going to be incredibly hard, and I would spend countless hours away from my son each week. I needed to have fellow residents who would understand that struggle and who would be supportive if I had another child during residency. I matched at my first choice, Mount Sinai Kravis Children's Hospital, and I have never regretted that decision for a second. I got top-notch training while feeling supported and encouraged by colleagues who could empathize with the challenges of balancing eighty-plus-hour weeks with having a family.

Jennifer's advice captures this phase perfectly. She tells us, "It's really important to consider your family when making big career decisions and it's okay if those decisions are different than they would have been before you had kids or before you were pregnant."

Now is the time to identify the resources available at your place of work to parents and future parents regarding fertility, surrogacy, adoption, and more, even if you may not need them right now. And also what's not offered. It is better to know the range of options that exist today, and we are fortunately living in a changing time for many of these considerations, including what is provided by our government and organizations, and what is integrated with our health care providers. You can have a supportive culture with supportive resources (the best), but also one without the other, and that can be okay for you too! Know where you stand and what is most important to you.

Along with the information itself, do you feel that you are in an environment where you can comfortably ask these questions? If it's not obvious, ask. Even if you have been at your place of work for some time, setting up time with your HR representative, a benefits liaison, or manager and sharing something like, "I feel like I haven't been taking full advantage of what is offered by our organization. Where can I find out more about the benefits offered?" can be helpful. Or you might say something like, "I know that we are a small team. As we look to grow, what kind of benefits are important to you to offer your employees?" Applying for a new job? "I'm thrilled at the prospect of this role, and as I consider what I'm looking for in terms of total compensation and lifestyle to make an impact here for the long term, where, how, and from whom can I find out more beyond salary?"

If someone doesn't answer these questions or doesn't even know where to look, that's something you may want to have in mind as you move into this phase of your life. Of course, you may be more comfortable asking colleagues about their experiences—both for content to fact-check and for whether they respond positively, negatively, or neutrally. Keep in mind all your colleagues. Working for a company with a respectable parental-leave policy matters more to women than men, but I found the percentages are both still quite high—80 percent of women and 69 percent of men share that it is important.[3] It's also not just about parental leave, but all benefits, from health care to flexible work policies, vacation days, and more. Notably, we must acknowledge that different types of places of work are going to have variability within what they can provide, but at the minimum we shouldn't have to be afraid to ask.

Pilar McDonald and Lola McAllister, the cofounders of Project Matriarchs, are doing just that with their "Pledge to Care," which encourages their fellow college students—part of our future work force pipeline—to put it out there and ask for commitments to basic needs for caregivers before there is an immediate need. As college sophomores in 2020 during the COVID-19 pandemic, they created a virtual platform for academic support and childcare for low-income working caregivers. It was a necessary solution in a difficult situation, and one that exposed a greater need for a commitment to change. Today, they are engaging their generation around issues of caregiving to "help [Gen Z] express the way we want employers to support their caregiving employees."

Pilar shares, "When the pandemic hit, I saw working parents, and in particular working moms, suffer. I was fueled to fight for a better, more supportive future for caregivers. Now I am fighting to create a system that allows caregiving and career responsibilities to coexist."

Lola adds, "I remember early on realizing that women leaving the workforce was going to be a huge side effect of the pandemic. We were only starting to grasp the enormity—of both the problem and the opportunity. . . . In thinking about my own experience, I feel a tremendous amount of responsibility. Intentionality. For my moms, motherhood was central to their identities. They were deeply dedicated to both their roles in the workplace and their roles as mothers. I grew up understanding that both roles were important and valuable. My moms had an opportunity to create a dynamic motherhood that wasn't imposed on them as lesbian couples. That's what I want for me and the women of my generation. Motherhood is not a hindrance to what I can provide to the world. It can enrich my life and make me a better human doing whatever work I need to do. It's part of my larger purpose."

Pilar and Lola concluded, "Our ambition with 'Pledge to Care' is to challenge assumptions in order to create a culture in the workplace where employees can talk about their caregiving relationships with work in a way that is destigmatized. We want employers to speak openly about their own caregiving responsibilities, setting the precedent for employees at all levels so that they can do the same. This is an accessible, impactful way that anyone can contribute to the gradual erosion of stigma around the topic of care and the bias applied to caregivers in the workplace. This goes for pregnant employees, non-carrying partners, and everyone within their ecosystem to make an impact for the future."

ASSESSING BOUNDARIES

Creating and communicating boundaries prior to pregnancy can also have a tremendous impact during the pregnancy. Revisiting chapters 2 and 3, think about what boundaries you have today in your work and personal private life. What are the things you are comfortable sharing and what is important to you to keep private—and is this firm, or does it depend on the environment you're in, your relationships, or the length of time you have been at your place of work? Setting boundaries in the BTTC phase with the power of no is a whole lot easier if you set them long before they are relevant.

This also includes the impact of boundaries on work-life balance. Identify how you achieve work-life fluidity today and think about how that could change, and how what you do now might help to set boundaries to protect it. Remember that this includes both resources of energy and time. Boundaries are incredibly personal on all accounts, so don't feel pressure to have the same ones as someone else. Because they can also change over time, consider where you are now and how they may evolve.

FINANCIAL CONSIDERATIONS

As with anything to do with your finances, the sooner you think through them and plan, the better. Specifically with regard to pregnancy and work, you need to think about a budget of both dollars and time. While there are significant costs you may incur while trying to conceive and while pregnant, the longer term, ongoing financial impacts often start in year one. If this is not your first baby, consider the costs that will double (or triple, etc.), the ones that you have already accounted for, and those that may decrease versus those you had with your first child.

Jennifer Barrett, the financial expert we met in chapter 1, explains some of the costs you might consider when planning your pregnancy. She says, "Having and raising a baby can cost a lot more than we think. One of the first things I recommend is to check your health insurance coverage to see what the delivery and potential overnight hospital stay will cost you and how much you can expect to pay for any medical visits ahead of and after the birth. I switched insurance plans between kids and was charged twice as much for my second delivery as I had been for my first—something I hadn't anticipated. It's also a good idea to start setting aside extra savings well before the baby comes to cover unexpected expenses, because they will come up!"

Jennifer adds, "It's also important to talk ahead of time about how much time you and your partner each want to take off after the birth and how you'll cover that financially. When you have a child, your expenses will grow significantly. But your income will likely be lower that first year if you and your partner take time off, since most employers still don't offer full paid leave for new parents."

Keep in mind that this planning extends beyond expenses. For example, the need for a partner to take a leave may seem like a cost at the onset, but it's worth it. Jennifer shared, "That time with a new baby is so important, and it sets patterns that can endure for years. That early hands-on experience and bonding time can make new fathers much more comfortable taking on more caregiving responsibilities. It's important, too, to talk before the birth about your expectations for how childcare and household responsibilities will be divided. A lot of times we have expectations about those responsibilities but don't convey them to our partners, which can lead to misunderstandings and frustration. Talking about it ahead of time can prevent a lot of resentment down the road."

Thinking about childcare in the BTTC phase might feel early, but it will have an important and significant financial impact. This might mean considering the type of childcare that you and your partner have available to you and want for your child based on your support system, work environment, community, and the financial impacts of pregnancy and birth. Consider whether family members will be part of your care plan or whether you or your partner can have a schedule change that may limit total care hours.

Like anything in this time of your life, costs and what you may need financially will change. Your job may change. What your child needs may dictate what you need. Your partner may contribute financially more or less than you do. Other things you have going on in your life together as a family or as individuals . . . so many things are likely to change. But big picture, it's true that taking a moment to reflect now regarding how a job will provide you a budget of time and money for your concurrent family goals may have implications about what type of job you want in the first place.

I can't say this enough: Don't feel limited by this. Just consider that you're processing it now as part of the reality of working parenthood. Planning allows you to do research, save, and reprioritize other expenses to make your family ambitions a reality.

EGG FREEZING

Speaking of planning, research, and prioritization (and financial cost), although this isn't a medically focused resource, I do want to revisit the questions many women in my research had surrounding egg freezing, as there were many, and this topic certainly comes up within the BTTC phase. The following pages are an abbreviated reference with perspectives regarding pregnancy and work as a starting point for an empowered conversation. If this topic is particularly relevant for you, ensure that you take the next step, with specific research and a discussion with your health care provider, including the starting point of fertility testing for women and men.

Let's turn back to Dr. Caitlin Bump, whose advice you found in chapter 1, to tell us more.

What is egg freezing, and should I do it?

"As someone who has been through the process of egg freezing, and as a licensed ob/gyn, my initial response to this question is 'if you're thinking about it, do it,' even in your early to midtwenties, which previously was considered too early. However, the reality is a bit more nuanced, and it is not for everyone. Fertility preservation is the process of preserving oocytes (eggs) and/or embryos (fertilized eggs, if you have a sperm donor or partner but want to delay conception) by storing them at very cold temperatures, essentially 'freezing' them. When elective (not for medical reasons), it is done before the age-related reduction of fertility and before the increased risk of chromosomal abnormalities of the embryo. It is important to note, however, that fertility preservation is not a guarantee or promise of a future pregnancy."

What are the factors to consider with regard to age and lifestyle?

"For women under thirty years old, cryopreservation has generally not been recommended for nonmedical reasons because the likelihood that the eggs will be used is quite low. These women tend either to choose not to have children at all, or do not require the oocytes or embryos to conceive. This, however, is changing. It's being considered more as a 'personal insurance' policy against the potential what-ifs than for medical reasons. Women are choosing to freeze their eggs for personal and lifestyle reasons, most commonly for their career or education, or because they have not yet found a suitable partner." Their partner choice may also necessitate IVF or other fertility methods.

What about cost?

"Those with medical reasons for fertility preservation, such as prior to starting chemotherapy for cancer treatment, are more likely to have it covered by their insurance. More and more companies are covering the cost of fertility preservation, making it more accessible to women, and at younger ages, though this is still not most companies or most women. And few insurances cover 'elective' oocyte cryopreservation.

"Cost is often the defining factor for most people considering fertility preservation, and this cannot be ignored. When researching the cost of fertility preservation, a wide range of numbers come up: anywhere from $2,500 to $20,000. It is important to look closely at what services are offered in that quote, such as consultation fees, medications, lab work, ultrasounds, clinic fees, procedures, number of cycles, and storage fees, to name a few. There are three categories of costs: initial preservation procedure (the cost of everything for the initial process; it generally includes initial fertility testing and lab work, medications, ultrasounds, clinic fees, and the egg-retrieval procedure), storage fees (how much it costs to store your eggs or embryos depends on how long you plan to wait before using them), and then later, IVF fees."

How does the process work?

"Fertility preservation is also uncomfortable (and at times painful), and inconvenient. It requires a flexible job schedule. The first ten to twelve days require injecting medications to stimulate the ovaries to produce eggs. Repeat blood tests and ultrasounds are done, most commonly every other day. The egg retrieval is a procedure that requires sedation and can be uncomfortable to painful afterward, as it involves your physician using an ultrasound, needle, and suction device to extract the eggs. And sometimes it's necessary to do more than one round." But you can and will make it work if it's important to you—and determine whether you need anything from your place of work to do so.

Aya Kanai, whose stories and advice we read in chapter 3, gives perspective from her own experience: "When I first started doing my fertility treatments, my company at the time didn't cover egg freezing. It was a huge expense, but 10,000 percent worth it. So now if anyone asks me about it and their company pays for it, I frame it as a gift—money on the table. Is that month the most fun? No, it's really uncomfortable, but what you get out of it is a major gift. One that can be game changing if and when you want to have kids. It gives peace of mind for a myriad of challenges that can come your way that you can't see now."

Another contributor to my research, Erica First, shares her story with a unique point of view, along with the insights of her boss of nearly ten years, Debra Messing:

I've had a long career as a celebrity assistant, and I have always taken great pride in what I do. I have been working with Debra Messing for almost ten years, managing her day-to-day operations, and she has empowered me to take on more through the years. As a result, I am fulfilled and have reached a new level of professional growth. I've also seen her raise her son as a single working mother, which has inspired me to take stock of my place in the world as a working woman and future mother. Starting a family has always been a top priority for me, but as I got deeper into my career, the years started to fly by, and I felt like I was losing control of my future, with no husband or children in sight. I decided to see a fertility doctor when I turned thirty-five. I was hard on myself and couldn't believe it had come to this. Although I was not ready yet, I got the information.

At thirty-eight, I decided I wanted to be proactive and protect my chances of obtaining the future I always dreamed of. I went to Debra and spoke with her about my plans. The process is intense, with blood tests every other morning, multiple injections per day, and ultimately the egg-retrieval procedure. Her response was, "You can do this, and your squad will be there for you." I went for early "morning monitoring," then worked all day and at night did my injections at home.

Finding the balance isn't always easy, but if you have support from your job and family, you can have it all. So I made it work. That's what women do: we figure it out. As I approach my fortieth birthday, I feel hopeful. I have a great job, amazing friends and family, and twenty-one eggs! I never imagined having a baby alone, and while it is not the ideal situation for me, having the option is everything. It was not easy on me physically or emotionally. But I got through it and the process changed me for the better. . . . There are no words to convey the level of accomplishment and empowerment that I felt.

Debra Messing, actress and Erica's boss, shares the following reflection on Erica's story:

As a single working mother, I often felt, deeply, that I couldn't do it. That it was too hard, too overwhelming, too exhausting. As a new mother, I always felt like I was failing. I believed it was impossible to be both an involved, present mother and a disciplined professional. But then, as they say on Project Runway, *you "make it work." As long as you can admit you need, and can ask for, help—you can. With dear friends, babysitters, family stepping up, a balance can be struck for a time. Inevitably you will be forced to make choices: taking a job or missing a school play. That was an easy one. Walking this high-wire act forces you to really look at what's important to you. Only you can answer that. Erica is a magician. She makes my life run smoothly. And she knows what's important to her. My*

*hope for Erica is that she has confidence in her unique path
and faith that she is never alone. She's got a coven of women
at the ready, for whatever she needs. She's going to make a
magnificent mother.*

CROSSING THE THRESHOLD

Thresholds are tipping points of something new. Anticipating them
and asking yourself what it will take to get there can help push you to
clear decision making. The one we are talking in particular is the decision that you are ready to have a baby. This threshold can be
crossed before you know it. But after this big one, you will cross many
others, making decisions about your comfort in sharing news, even
how much you want to push or be pushed.

Dasha Rettew, who shared her expertise as a leadership adviser
in chapter 3, remembers the moment she decided she was ready to
start trying for a baby:

*It was a September day. I was sitting at a desk in a vision
writing workshop offered by my employer, the world's largest
social media company. I was asked to write where I wanted to
be one year from today. I knew the right answer, but I couldn't
say it out loud. I wrote: on maternity leave with my first child.
I joined the company as a coach and leadership guide to the
executive team as the company doubled in size. My work was
100 percent aligned with my life mission to help executives
build the leadership skills to drive the change they want to see
in the world, and yet in this company, for a variety of reasons,
I wasn't the person I wanted to be. I didn't realize one of my
good friends had a miscarriage. I wasn't healthy. And I knew
I had more to do professionally. I had to break away to get on
a healthier path to pregnancy and to be more purposeful with
my career—ultimately, to return to the company I founded*

several years prior, which was calling me back. The following
September, my vision came full circle.

I remember many conversations with Dasha before this point.
The certainty to try to become pregnant inched along until she
crossed her threshold together with her husband. I asked her advice
in hindsight. She told me, "I wish I would not have judged my gut instinct and probably not fought so hard against it. Know who you are
as a leader and person. Make the best choice for you and your family
based on that, not based on external perceptions or perceived risk. If
you surround yourself with advisers you trust, they'll help you navigate through what are naturally a series of tough questions—the ones
that you need help technically getting through, but that you know the
right answer in your gut is a starting point."

I often ask women who openly want to talk about it, and often in
the context of work, where they find themselves on a 0 to 100 scale
of readiness to have a baby. The funny thing is, even how they define
what the tipping point is varies. For you that might be 51 percent, for
others it might need to be 99 percent or 100 percent ("I need to feel
safe and totally ready"), or 2 percent, just over the hump ("Why not
try if I/we know we want this someday?"). What's most important is
that you have in your mind that threshold, recognize it, and then
manage—along with everything else you have going on—the reality
of the risk *and* the reward of working motherhood. Everything won't
be perfectly lined up, but if you can get yourself to *your* tipping point,
then go for it. I've talked to so many women who share this sentiment
from a contributor: "In the moment it feels like it really matters and
so quickly it just doesn't."

MAKING A PLAN

As we wrap up the BTTC phase, how's your metaphorical house? Is
it in order the way you want it to be in, or close to it? If you're already

flying through the TTC or even The Push phases, is there anything you want to revisit to increase your comfort and confidence?

The CDC has a list of steps to preparing for a healthy pregnancy. The rightful focus is on your physical and mental health—including caring for preexisting conditions, learning your medical history, evaluating your lifestyle, knowing your folic acid intake, not drinking, not smoking, not taking drugs, avoiding contaminants, and making a visit to your doctor. There is one key item on the list that intersects directly with your work: "Making a plan and taking action to achieve your goal of getting pregnant and having a healthy baby."[4]

Planning for your financial, mental, and physical health, plus how work touches each one of those things, sets you up for awareness, prioritization, and actualization during your pregnancy. Having a plan matters. It matters in the scope of your day-to-day but also in your long-term approach for the relationships of who you work with. Those who support you at work are implicated in your success, just as you are implicated in theirs.

For entrepreneurs and business owners, Arianna Taboada, author of *The Expecting Entrepreneur*, introduced in chapter 5, shares the following advice about BTTC for entrepreneurs, and an important summary of considerations for this phase that you can apply even if you aren't one.

"What's interesting is that I see pregnancy as a forcing function; there is a hard deadline, so if you are thinking about what needs to happen before you get pregnant, as a business owner you know what is outstanding, what needs to be tightened up—you know your core business functions, what can use some updates to improve—but it's not urgent until you're on a timeline."

She highlights three considerations to get ready:

1. Consider your financial reality carefully. Look at what your business needs are, as well as your personal financial scenario. Consider whether you have profit reserves that can

be used during leave, what your household financial needs are, whether you are in a state that has a paid leave program you are eligible for, how business (or personal) expenses can be adjusted to be leaner during leave, what creative ways to have cash flow staggered to come in during leave. For business owners, I often see three scenarios play out: a. using profit reserves to cover all expenses and salaries during leave; b. covering expenses but adjusting salary/owners draw; and c. covering expenses and taking unpaid leave.

2. Think of it as a project, blocking out time for system design or system maintenance. Who and what do you need: Are you playing a lot of roles in your business? What support do you need, either temporarily, taking this as a moment to create standard operating procedures, a manual, or are you at a business stage where you need part-time or full-time support, a function to hire for? This could even be support for developing and maintaining those systems that will boost you after you have your baby.

3. Closely look at what your role is. If you had a job description and were revising it, what would need to be on your plate? It's about prioritization—are you doing the job that you want to be doing?

Phase I of the journey to working motherhood is unique in its capacity to engage women like you on this topic before it's right in front of you. It's how we flip the script to make working motherhood normalized and celebrated, a way to open the window so the timeline feels more natural and captures the truly concurrent nature of career and motherhood. Assessing your goals, environment, and other key considerations in the BTTC phase is ideal while you keep in mind your threshold to the next phase, TTC. Remember to reframe the impact of your pregnancy not as what it could "do to your career," but the other way around—what *you* want the impact to be.

The ultimate takeaway is this: options exist. Options give us the ability to see choices and to narrow the scope at the same time, to feel empowered, and to face our fears and uncertainties at this crucial stage. While it requires research combined with organization and introspection, use your options to your advantage. Use the principle of perspective and truly listen to advice, but most importantly, listen to yourself. Your gut will guide you in this time, especially as you edge toward the first major threshold of a Carry Strong pregnancy—the moment to decide you're ready to start trying for a baby.

QUESTIONS FOR REFLECTION

Do the traffic light exercise: Where are you and where do you want to go? Are you at a green, yellow, or red light?

Revisit your board of directors. Do you have someone who can help demonstrate the possibilities for working motherhood? Someone to ask questions about how to think through the first steps, even if just out of curiosity?

How's your "house"? What are the goals you want to achieve prior to and for pregnancy, including for health and career, and why?

Where is your tipping point? Create your way of measuring the threshold to take you from BTTC to TTC and use it to facilitate important conversations with those closest to you.

Carry Strong Stories

ARIELLE SPIEGEL, FOUNDER OF COFERTILITY

I was working a high-pressure job in digital marketing that involved some travel, but usually to fun and exciting places. Once I started trying to get pregnant, however, I had to reevaluate my trips for one reason or another, usually because they interfered with my ovulation—and later, because they interfered with my fertility treatment. However, before I started really taking my TTC journey seriously, I was asked to cover an event in Mexico where I'd be responsible for strategizing all live content across social media. And I knew it would be an awesome trip. But this was at the height of Zika fear, and my husband and I were taking that very seriously. No vacations to affected countries, and certainly no work trips there either. I stressed about how I'd tell my boss that I wouldn't go and that they'd have to send someone else. Not only would it look like I was turning down an opportunity, it also would be letting my managers in on the fact that I was trying to get pregnant—when, typically, one's boss wouldn't be aware of this until after someone was already twelve weeks along.

I decided to rip the Band-Aid off, and a few days later pulled my boss into a private conference room. I told her that I didn't feel comfortable visiting Mexico since I may be trying to get pregnant soon and Zika made me nervous. She was supportive and told me it was okay; they'd figure something out. Of course, I still felt guilty, but I knew I did the right thing. They probably wondered why I still didn't get pregnant over the course of the next two years there. Maybe I'd put the cart before the horse, but that's another story.

KATIE BECKER

About three years ago, I was out at an expensive, intimate, delicious dinner with a dear friend and mentor who is about five years older than me. I was in my early thirties, single after two long, very wrong relationships that I put up with because, you know, you gotta pick someone before thirty-five, right? My friend, my strongest shoulder to lean on, was telling me about her recent embryo freezing—a decision she made because she and her partner weren't ready to make the decision and pull the trigger. They had built an extremely successful, flourishing business with interesting clients and philanthropic opportunities, while allowing them to travel, party, and enjoy the DINK lifestyle to the absolute max.

"Will I use the eggs?" my friend said. "I don't know, but at least it's off my mind. And if that day does come, I am 100 percent outsourcing it." I nodded but realized I wasn't quite sure what she meant. "You mean, a surrogate?" I asked. "Yeah, I don't want to actually be pregnant—I'm too busy," she replied, turning to the approaching waiter to put in our cocktail order. This struck me as a shockingly frank and completely new sentiment in my brain space. Was it distant? Was it delusional? To be perfectly honest, I found it . . . an amazing relief. Motherhood is fraught with pearl-clutching preciousness. You must get a doula or midwife. You must breastfeed. You must hide all screens and sugar for the first two years at the very least. And yet somehow you also must not fall prey to stereotypical maternal guilt. I don't have to be a mom to know the feeling of narrow expectations. That's the kind of suffocation that can turn anything you love, including your work life, into your own personal hell. It's like playing a game of Snake on a phone from 2003—mounting expectations of a singular goal to check off all the boxes.

Why are we always looking for how we're doing it wrong, when modern medicine is giving us exponentially more ways to do it right—right for each of us? My friend knew exactly under what circumstance she would be happy as a mother—a circumstance that would allow her work life to thrive—and, I would argue from personal experience, a parent who knows how to be happy demonstrates one of life's most difficult skills.

It would be three years until I would work at a company with the fertility benefits that would allow me to freeze my own eggs. What I am going to do with them, I don't know yet. But that hummingbird heartbeat of urgency has slowed. Way. Down. Whatever I do, it will work for me. We are inundated with advice for exactly how to live the "best" way, and so often the advice is against our own natural instincts. If there's one thing we can do to honor the women who fought for us to have choices, it is to exercise all those choices to the absolute maximum.

MELISSA DISHART, EDUCATOR

"I want to be a mommy, a ballerina, and a doctor." I had that response ready to go in kindergarten when adults started testing out the age-old question "What do you want to be when you grow up?" Now at thirty-one, I'm none of those things, but I am a proud and passionate educator, coach, wife, and dog mom. Who knew the ballerina thing wouldn't last past first grade?

Just recently, I experienced the abrupt transition from BTTC to TTC when we stopped using birth control. The cross over to TTC gets a little nerve-racking. Every month during those peak fertility dates, tracked by an app and confirmed by an ovulation test, it feels like you apply for your dream job (multiple times) and just wait by the phone for HR to call to say you got it. Except that when you get rejected from this job, you don't get a phone call, you just bleed in your pants. If you manage to land the dream job, nothing in those first few weeks of work is certain. I'll leave the metaphor there, but TTC so far is tough. My partner is the love of my life, and I know he'd do anything for me, but this is an empowered, but lonely, one-body journey. He has no choice but to witness and support me while I pee on sticks and attempt to mentally prepare for childbirth.

In the TTC phase, family planning gets real. It's not just conversations about baby names like before. It's obsessively checking conception versus due dates. It's crying in a parking lot over vague genetic testing results. It's rushing to get house projects done and going on trips with friends. As I google random thoughts that pop into my head at midnight, I'm comforted by the auto-populated questions asked by so many other hopeful souls.

What I do know for certain is that we want this. So badly. While we wait, we'll continue to build our life in preparation of what's to come. Until there's really something to worry about, I'll keep holding on tight to the dream of growing up to become a mommy.

CAITLIN BUMP, MD, MS

"Gravida" means pregnant, from the Latin gravis, *meaning "heavy." A word that carries so much weight. Significance and significant. Important. Meaningful. Teeming with life. And yet, in the middle of my first year of medical school, I chose to have an abortion.*

I was in the process of getting out of an emotionally abusive relationship. Long before I knew I would go into obstetrics and gynecology, I got pregnant. Staring at that positive test, I felt deeply that I could not have any kind of relationship with the father for the rest of my life. The heaviness of a connection like that was unbearable to me. I also intuitively knew that I would not finish medical school if I had a child. And so, I made my choice, took misoprostol and mifepristone, and ended it. I prioritized my safety and sanity, as well as my career. It wasn't an easy decision, but it was the right one for me.

I did not know at that time that having gone through that experience would make me a better doctor. It has deepened my compassion and connection with my patients and has given me an understanding of women in abusive relationships, who come in with their own struggles. I am reminded of the mother of three children, whose birth control failed her and, in tears, told me she could just not afford to have another child. It reinforces over and over again the importance of listening to and caring for each woman who comes to see me, judgment-free.

This is why the language we use is so important and significant. So gravid. It can help patients feel either heard or dismissed, empowered or inhibited, understood or misunderstood. Standardization of language and terminology is essential in medicine. It allows everyone taking care of the patient to be on the same page and understand exactly what is (medically) going on with her. It optimizes patient care and good outcomes. It is clinical and often sterile, and at the same time it can be dehumanizing and hurtful. It is removed from the woman's experience.

It is time we listen to our patients' experiences of how the language we use makes them feel. Does it empower them or blame them? Does it teach them or does it belittle them? Does it encompass their desires and experiences or does it mass generalize?

I don't yet have any children. This is because of a combination of personal choice, prioritizing my career, and not yet finding the right man for me. I joke and say, "I know too much," and yet I would love to have children. I've always imagined I'd have three, two boys and then a girl. I will be a better ob/gyn having the experience of pregnancy (and likely early pregnancy loss given my age), postpartum, breastfeeding, and parenting. And now I must decide at what point to have a baby on my own.

Pregnancy and childbirth are miraculous. Every time I assist a woman who is birthing her baby I am amazed by the strength it takes, the way it happens, and the humanity of the whole process. I know that with my language I can help empower and enable every woman I care for. With my voice. With my support. With my care. I can meet her where she is at. Not only is a new life born, but so too is a mother. With gravidas.

CHAPTER 7

Phase II

TTC: Trying to Conceive

NOW THAT YOU'VE crossed over the threshold and are actively trying to get pregnant, you're officially in the TTC phase. This phase focuses on the realities of trying to conceive while working. (Well, not literally while you're working—although I did hear from women who would realize during their workday that they were ovulating and call their partners to tell them that their plans after work had changed.) While that might be you right now or at least made you laugh, the important part of that anecdote is that during this time there is an active brain switch. You might have flown through this phase, a surprise of BTTC to that Big Fat Positive, but chances are even if not this time around, this information can be helpful to you at some point, or give you some insights into what might be going on for other women around you.

It's no secret that pregnancy is physically and mentally demanding. It is also a natural part of many people's lives. And yet there is a broad range of experiences among women, and even between the pregnancies of the same woman. One of the most significant and dramatic variations in the experience of pregnancy expressed by women and physicians is fertility. The amount of time and effort that it takes to get pregnant is variable, so the time part is something you will personally weigh—and that will weigh on you.

As you learned in the introduction, half of women in my first study said that conception, not just pregnancy post the positive test, had an impact on work, and of the other half, nearly 20 percent were unplanned pregnancies.[1] You are juggling the reality of pregnancy and work now. The goal of this chapter is to explore this important time, because as many women shared, "It's getting real."

There are two parts to this chapter. The first is about framing this phase and the levity that you may feel about your new priority to get pregnant. The second part zooms in a bit closer on the longer road to pregnancy, which can have a prolonged effect on work and require additional considerations for you and for your job. You have heard powerful stories throughout this book from women who've experienced the stress of fertility expectations including the realities of IUI and IVF. Here you'll find more of these accounts, and just a few of the ways you may rethink your expectations of time.

FINDING HEADSPACE FOR FREEDOM

As you're trying to conceive, you may find that this becomes the paramount goal and all-consuming focus despite what is happening in other facets of your life, including at work. The little stick wields tremendous power. In fact, many women in my research spoke about this time as a major "rude awakening" moment where they realized that they did not have control over something they wanted. They couldn't work harder, and they had to be okay with ambiguity—a critical factor in successful leadership. They couldn't network or pull an all-nighter to study something that would immediately mean they were more competent than before.

Personally, in addition to mood changes and how I felt physically, I felt at the mercy of tracking apps, digital ovulation tests, and "pee sticks" as I was trying to get pregnant. For better and for worse these tools gave me a new awareness of my body in a way I hadn't thought about before—but sometimes I also felt a little too aware of each cycle's opportunity window. One of the women I spoke to in my research shared that when trying to conceive her second child, "Each month feels like I have to reassess my work for ten months from now."

In fact, many women spoke about how they would assess their current and future work commitments each cycle. While it's good to project the impact of pregnancy and a new baby on your career based on the length of gestation, that's a lot of pressure—much like the credit we give "work" in "work-life balance." Conception might happen sooner or later then you anticipate. You have to be okay if it happens on the first try, and okay too to reassess, like the contributor above shared, but maybe consider revisiting every three or six months, to think about what that means for your goals and your resulting "impending" due date, versus constantly.

At work, there are a lot of other things that get thrown in the mix. A project might change, you might get a new team, a class might not be offered that semester, or a big opportunity might come up that you've always dreamed of. Things happen, and it's okay if you want to be flexible and okay if you don't. You don't want to think about work and pregnancy in terms of FOMO (fear of missing out). In fact, I recently heard the term COMO instead of FOMO—"certainty of missing out," which I think is more helpful, acknowledging "missing out" and moving on (and who knows, you might not end up missing anything at all). In addition, you can make your "I can't" "I can't yet."

If I've learned anything from motherhood thus far it is that while the best-laid plans sometimes execute flawlessly, they often don't—a lopsided, teetering, overly ambitious block tower that if you take a second to think about it should make you laugh rather than crumble. You can do your best, but sometimes your child will be sick during what was supposed to be your time to shine at work. One hour or one day might feel like it is everything to you at work, a crux of your career, but in reality that one hour or day might be everything to you and nothing to your client, practice, employer, team, or project. Or that moment might be able to be moved, end up getting canceled, or come back to you again later down the road. It. Is. Okay. There will always be more opportunities, and you also will be having your own incredible things happen that you won't want to miss.

What about saying yes to those opportunities when you know there's a chance you might have to say no further down the road because you're pregnant? The same rule of thumb applies—until you have to say no, if you want to say yes, say yes. Think about it this way: Would you answer an opportunity to go to a conference by saying, "Well, I think there's a chance that I will break my leg and not be able to go?" Never.

What about when you're interviewing? Although there's an unfortunate chance that all of us at childbearing age might experience pregnancy bias when we are interviewing, there is no need to let that stop you. The only reason you would be interviewing is to set yourself up in a better position in the first place for when you do get pregnant or when you have your child. Otherwise, it would be part of your assessment in your BTTC that maybe the best move is to stay put and give you stability as you TTC. (Of course, if you are physically pregnant while interviewing, there are reasons to share and not to share, but more on this in chapter 8.)

NAVIGATING INFERTILITY AT WORK

There can come a point when making decisions to perfectly dovetail your career and future motherhood just seem arbitrary. According to UCLA Health, "An estimated 15% of couples will have trouble conceiving—both female and male 'infertility' having an impact."[2] While technically infertility is "the inability to get pregnant even after having frequent and unprotected sex for one year," whenever it is longer than you anticipated based on your medical history, personal desire, and other factors, you may shift your mindset from work having a significant implication for the timing of pregnancy or otherwise as a consideration for TTC to moving work to the last thing that's on your mind when pregnancy is your priority.

There were many women in my research who experienced infertility on their journey to working motherhood, and several of whom had to turn to work for help and support. While this book certainly can't give you all the answers, it can give you stories to inspire hope, balanced with the tangible realities of daily life. For example, TTC challenges might mean that the private/public threshold is debated long before a physical baby bump and can carry tremendous weight. It also can mean that work needs to play a supporting role in lifting you up.

Ginny Bowen Olson, the author of the blog MothersRest.com, a "love letter to moms, both new and seasoned, journeying from sleep deprived to joy-arrived," shares her story:

I'd just landed a promotion from contractor to full-time employment as the senior web project manager at a global nonprofit. I was at work when I got the call. It was our last attempt at intrauterine insemination, otherwise known as IUI. The nurse practitioner and I got into a fight. She'd told me earlier in the day to "go ahead and use the trigger shot" to release my eggs. And now she was calling to tell me to wait until two p.m. to do it. It was too late. We'd just wasted another fifteen hundred dollars. We'd just wasted more eggs. We'd just wasted more pain.

Trying to keep my voice low, trying to keep the tears in check, I half whispered, half shouted into the phone in the hallway because my open cubicle wasn't exactly private. I'd only been working there five months. I was still that new girl, donning the cloak of confidence and badassery to assure everyone I belonged there. Heartbreak, tears, and bitter anger were not the things I wanted to risk my reputation on. Our doctor told us the news we'd been avoiding with our repeated attempts at IUI. He could do nothing more for us. It was beyond time to try IVF.

We'd been trying to conceive for six years. Six years of watching everyone else's bellies swell. Six years of attending everyone else's baby showers. Six years of smiling politely at everyone else's newborns. I'd resisted IVF. Because I was terrified it wouldn't work and that would reinforce an idea I'd picked up along the way that God deemed me unfit for motherhood. And it was crazy expensive.... But it was time to risk it, to put the truck up as collateral for a loan at the bank. To fund this last-ditch effort at motherhood.

I knew I would have to reveal more of myself at work than I'd originally planned. I figured the fifth IUI would work, no one would ever know about my struggle, ta-da, baby on board! I told my new boss about this heavy burden I'd been carrying for six years and what kind of schedule I would need. He was kind and empathetic. He talked about his own baby girl. And how motherhood had impacted his own wife so much that she quit her full-time job to pursue an entrepreneurial dream of photography centered on pregnancy and new life. He asked questions, including the name of the clinic I'd be working with. Which struck me as odd and too personal, but I responded. He then shared that his sister worked at one of the best fertility specialists nearby and encouraged me to check them out.

While we'd already selected our doctor, every time I spoke with the staff I left the conversation with a vague feeling of being cattle-herded through their various steps, like I was inventory being processed. So I called the recommendation. He believed in individual attention for each patient. He believed in personalized care. He believed IVF would work. He was right. We welcomed our son during the Christmas season, and then our second miracle eleven months later. All because I took a risk and shared the most vulnerable part of myself at work.

My advice to women struggling with infertility or walking through the transition of pregnancy to motherhood is to view advocating for your needs as an opportunity to practice the leadership skills you need to succeed in your career. Taking risks, advocating for your health, asking for what your family needs are transferrable skills for your career. Embrace your pregnancy experience as a crucial part of your leadership journey.

A more balanced workload, time for appointments, a break in the middle of the day because there is a lot more going on than your team's to-do list, including emotionally—these are all justified and often necessary when navigating infertility. During this time, your boss could become your advocate, not just for a moment, but for years. Nathalie Carpenter, founder and chief marketing strategist of Well + Luxe and *Fertilust*, shares how her boss unexpectedly became one of her biggest allies as she sought to conceive:

Just after my first two years at Audi, I had launched into fertility treatments. I had abandoned IUIs and had moved to IVF after being branded by my fourth doctor with unexplained infertility. After my second failed IVF cycle, I realized that it was going to be a much longer road than I had anticipated. I was also a little bit caught off guard to realize that IVF doesn't guarantee a pregnancy or a live birth either.

I had been dancing around boardroom meetings and doctor's appointments, hoping that the time spent at the latter was invisible to everyone else. I had overcompensated by sleeping less and working harder to cover the fact that I had a second job: trying to become pregnant. After two years and four treatments, two of which had been IVF, I decided to leave my fourth doctor to work with another at his clinic in Colorado. Traveling to Colorado in addition to general travel for my first job at Audi would make it nearly impossible to hide my early or lunchtime medical appointments. I found myself at a crossroad, and because I was already exhausted, decided to reveal to my employer that I was undergoing fertility treatment. Not only did that feel very personal, but I was also concerned that my employer would see me the way that I saw myself, as a failure. I had been branded a rising star and enjoyed autonomy, leadership opportunities, and upward mobility, and I didn't want to fall.

For two months, the wheels spun in my head long after my head hit the pillow as I wondered how I would break the news and if it would affect my professional reputation and growth. Time was running out, and I would soon have to travel to begin my third IVF cycle. I rehearsed what I would say to my boss for a week—in my head, in front of the mirror, to my husband, and finally on repeat out loud as I drove to work. I must have looked incredibly nervous by the time I found myself in my boss's office, because his first words were, "Don't tell me that you are leaving." My awkward response was, "No, but we are trying to get pregnant and need your help." Clearly that was not what I had rehearsed. After we both had a good laugh, I shared that I would continue to be committed to my career and the company, but that I needed support in working remotely and at times a bit more flexibly. I expressed my concerns about being overlooked for opportunities because I might be seen differently as a mother before I biologically became one. And then the unexpected happened.

I was not only told that my requests would be honored, but I also quickly understood that my fears of an early mommy

tax were unfounded. It is not to say that a variation of the
mommy tax never arrived, it just didn't happen while I was
trying to become a mother. Even then, my executive manager,
an exceptional leader and ally to women, stood by me to lobby
in those instances.

If you're not ready to ask your boss for support in your fertility journey, consider asking someone else who can support you either covertly or as a vocal advocate when you can't. One contributor shared that it was her team leader's assistant who was a close friend and was able to help maneuver the calendar so she could do the early appointments. Even just one person can make all the difference and be a valve to the pressure you may feel. Think about the community around you and who you need in that circle of trust from near and far.

Kristyn Hodgdon and Abby Mercado cofounded Rescripted after their own difficult journeys through IVF and pregnancy loss. The number one global media platform for fertility, infertility, and pregnancy loss, Rescripted is on a mission to reinvent the fertility journey for the millions of people who are trying to conceive, going through IVF, or grieving a miscarriage. Their platform is completely free to join and once there, you'll find thousands of others who get it, with no explanations necessary. "They're Rescripting fertility *together*—because no one can get through this time alone, and no one should have to."

Kristyn captures the power of community especially during the TTC: "They say it takes a village to raise a child. But sometimes it takes a village to become a mother. Despite the images of positive pregnancy tests we see in the media, the truth is, the road to parenthood isn't always straightforward. Those stories need to be told, and those experiences need to be normalized so that we all feel a little bit less alone. That's why finding a community is so important when you're trying to get pregnant or navigating fertility challenges."

Other work-specific advice I heard from women when trying to conceive takes more time than you anticipated is to use work to chalk up some wins. Work wins are things you *can* control; having a moment of success or celebration individually or with your team is a positive distraction that can give you a boost. This was very much true for me. In the TTC and in the Hush phases while dealing with my pregnancy losses, I needed those work wins.

However, sometimes I felt like I needed them too much, and that's where it is important to realize that work can bolster your other stresses and priorities in your brain, but it can't make them go away. For me it was those moments when I had control and could make things happen with people around me toward a common goal, moments that had nothing to do with the fact that my long cycle seemed to be counterintuitive to my very driven brain. I just needed to make sure that those around me didn't see the overcompensating force I needed as a negative to them. I also realized how much I needed just one person to be there for me so that when there was a question about why I was so invested in my work above and beyond my usual high ambition, they could check on me.

TAKING A PAUSE

Lastly, consider when you know you need a break—both in trying to conceive and at work. You don't have to fully stop either to slow it down, regroup, give your brain and your body a rest, and then start again. When trying to conceive, you may need a few days or months to clear your mind of "doing everything right"—thoughtfully planning, monitoring, and restricting. At work, there might be moments when you need to actively deprioritize. If you look back at your résumé, no one ever counts the months you were in one role before another, generally never even the years. No one questions why you may have had to push that degree an extra semester, or why you haven't checked certain boxes by your birthday. You might, and it's okay to care, but remember that time will pass, and you will continue in the direction you desire—just maybe on a different path.

You also may get to a point where you do need to stop trying to conceive or achieving at work temporarily. None of this is failure, it's recognition of what is needed in this phase. The same approach goes for dealing with pregnancy loss, which we will discuss in the next chapter.

Nanda Jayaseelan, vice president of communications at a national service organization, shares how her decision to pause her career made all the difference in her conception journey:

After years in the corporate and city hustle and bustle, my husband and I opted to move to a more suburban lifestyle since we were trying to start a family, even after multiple miscarriages. We began fertility treatments and were both very open about our process with our employers. While my career was not stressful and allowed for a flexible schedule around my treatments, the working environment was toxic. I felt like I was giving 110 percent in my position, but dealing with unpredictable management decisions and outbursts were detrimental to my mental health.

After many rounds of IUI/IVF, my doctor expressed that we could try one more round, but we would probably need to discuss other options if this was unsuccessful. Together, my husband and I decided that I should quit my job if we were truly considering all options to make our last attempt work. That small change seemed to make a huge difference! I was used to giving 110 percent professionally, but making the decision to give myself 110 percent in this extremely personal endeavor was difficult. While an employer can provide benefits and flexibility, a toxic work environment has lasting effects on both employees and the employer. If I could give any advice based on my experience, I'd recommend being open with your employer about the environment they are creating for their employees. If they're receptive, you may be able to ignite real change. If they are not receptive, you should reconsider working for that employer.

There is one more huge thing that I want to ensure you take away from this chapter. That is the idea of celebration—including the fact that you are trying to conceive. When you Carry Strong, you recognize that you are both contributing to your work and taking a step toward creating or growing your family. This is awesome! It's not always easy, but it deserves a celebration. The process, and of course the BFP, the Big Fat Positive and the end of this phase, whether it was a surprise, took two weeks or more than two years, deserves a celebration. You've got this, so take a moment for all you have achieved, and all of what's to come—one step at a time.

QUESTIONS FOR REFLECTION

> What are the things you want to assess with regard to work as you actively try to get pregnant ? Do you have a timeline in your head? How flexible is that timeline and when is it realistic to reassess?
>
> What are you most and least excited about being pregnant?
>
> Do you have the ally you need?

Carry Strong Stories

ALICIA YOON, FOUNDER AND CEO OF PEACH & LILY

I was twelve weeks pregnant and struggling with intense morning sickness, which really is a misnomer as the nausea can happen all day. I wasn't ready to share yet that I was pregnant given that it was still early days. During the midst of a particularly intense "morning sickness" episode, I had an important Zoom I had to attend. I distinctly recall debating whether I should reschedule the Zoom or just take the meeting and somehow try to choke back my nausea. I couldn't really think of a good reason to reschedule, short of sharing that I was pregnant, and decided to take it. I had my video off and was on mute because every few minutes I was bent over my trash can. Meanwhile, I was out of breath from being so nauseous and had to find a way to compose myself whenever I had to speak. This was a small moment among many varied and larger struggles during my time trying to get pregnant, being pregnant, and being postpartum. But this simple moment really captures so much.

There's this incredible and momentous life event that comes with real bodily changes and needs that really cannot be controlled. And yet so much of the struggle and challenge that comes with bringing life into this world is hidden. I remember the contortions I went through to hide what I was going through. For me, the reason for not sharing about my pregnancy was an empowering choice. I wanted the early days to be something that was nurtured and celebrated intimately with just family. Once I was ready, I was able to share openly about my pregnancy and the challenges that came with being pregnant.

However, it's not lost on me that one of the reasons I felt com-

fortable doing so was because I run my own business and I have an outsize influence on the culture we build. Supporting working mothers is part of our culture. I have many friends for whom this was not the case. There was a need to pretend everything was fine through the whole pregnancy for fear that having things like persistent morning sickness, for example, would negatively impact how they were perceived in the workplace. Being hunched over the trash can in secrecy for four months was challenging. But pairing that with six more months of choking back all the fatigue, joint pain, and more, mixed in with the stress of being perceived poorly for not being "tough enough" while pregnant, is a reality for so many pregnant women. This needs to change. Work can still get done—and, in fact, once pregnant women can feel more supported in the workplace, work can get done more effectively and efficiently, as there can be open conversations about how to work around specific hurdles without impacting work.

KAY MCKEAN, THE GOOD LISTENING PROJECT

The first time my husband and I saw Maia was at the office of our reproductive endocrinologist. The doctor pointed out on the ultrasound screen this thin, tiny open circle with an even tinier closed circle attached to it. We were looking at the beginning cells of our daughter, and the tiny, closed circle that the doctor described as glistening like the diamond on a ring was her heartbeat.

It's as though in the doctor's office that day the rhythm of her heart awakened my own inner beat. For years this inner beat, my most authentic rhythm, had been knocking; and while I was always aware of the knocking, I didn't always open the door. On this day in the doctor's office, it was as though this inner beat gave me an ultimatum to open the door or it would be knocked down. I remember thinking to myself in the days that followed: "I hope that *my daughter knows, trusts, and lives by who she is inside. The part of her that feels and is most authentic. And one of the greatest gifts I can give her is my own example."*

With the embodiment of new life came the deeper embodiment of a familiar call to live through what's inside you. I felt this, I knew this, and still, it was (and is) hard to put into practice. I hired a coach with the intention of recalibrating things. I said to myself and to her, "I have six months to get myself and my business in order before baby arrives!" I thought if I could get everything set before she was born, I could come back to myself and my work easily and more authentically. There would be a foundation there for me to pick right back up.

I hear this perspective in hindsight, and I laugh, for two main reasons. First, I see now that how you relate to yourself, your work, and the world can fundamentally shift with having a baby—as it can with any major seismic moment—if you're paying attention. And so the idea that in the six months predelivery I'd have a certain kind of foundation set for a life post the seismic moment feels kind of hilarious now, and fully human.

The second reason I smile and laugh at this story is because my initial reaction to recalibrating my business in response to the call that embodied me after my visit to the endocrinologist now feels miles away from what I understand it looks like to live life through what's inside. I've come to see that feeling driven by the inner beat takes nothing more than sitting still enough to feel what is authentic and having the courage to let it lead you.

LYNN FISCHER, GLOBAL BRAND LEAD

It was early in my pregnancy—post-positive pregnancy test and pre-twelve-week announcement. The day was hot and humid, with the sticky, suffocating heat that typifies a New York City

August. Like my first pregnancy, I was muddling my way through the weeks while suffering from hyperemesis gravidarum (HG), a not-too-common condition that causes severe nausea, vomiting, and weight loss during pregnancy. And when I say "severe vomiting," I mean severe—ten, twelve, fifteen times per day was the norm. (For months!)

I trudged out of the subway and started slogging up Third Avenue, nausea rising in my throat. I got to the corner of Third and Forty-Fourth Street, crossed the street, and thought, "Oh, thank God, there's my first puke planter." And I promptly leaned down and vomited in the concrete container used to hold a small bush. Third and Forty-Fifth? Another puke planter. Forty-Seventh? My favorite. The plant wasn't too healthy, so I had plenty of room in the container. I didn't use each of these puke planters every day, thank God. But there were many days in which I'd use more than one, and it was always a welcome relief to be near one in case I needed to throw up. Oh—and this was all before nine a.m.

I have mixed emotions in retrospect. On one hand, my God, I was so much stronger than I knew! My HG lasted the full nine months of my second pregnancy, and when I look back it's clear I had a sheer determination to Just. Keep. Going. And not only that, but to take on a new position and responsibilities at work, which turned into one of my favorite and most challenging roles to date. And on the other hand, I feel a mixture of sadness and anger too. I wish our society offered more support to women. It's not healthy—both literally and for our culture—to expect someone to perform at full steam while extraordinarily ill. It's one of the driving factors in who I vote for, how I spend my money, where I donate: we need to have better support systems for pregnant women, mothers, and women in general.

WINDSOR HANGER WESTERN, COFOUNDER AND PRESIDENT OF HER CAMPUS MEDIA

I started my company in college with two of my classmates, and the three of us began running the company full time at the age of twenty-one. My husband and I met in college as well and got married at twenty-four. I was told by my doctors that I may have trouble getting pregnant and so to start trying as soon as we felt ready, as it could easily be a two-plus-year process. Fortunately, we got pregnant within a week of going off birth control. I was twenty-five.

At the time, our company had around fifteen employees, most of whom were my age or younger and none of whom had children. I remember especially during the first trimester being terrified that I would miscarry and thus wanted to keep the pregnancy a secret from my business partners and coworkers. I pretended that I had given up drinking for Lent (not sure they bought it) and was trying to kick my coffee habit (they didn't buy that either). I remember one occasion out to dinner entertaining clients when I ordered a mojito at the table and then snuck up to the bar, pretending I had to go to the bathroom, to whisper to the bartender that I was pregnant, and I needed the mojito to be virgin.

I also remember the overwhelming fatigue. In the middle of the day, I would feel a crushing urge to lie down to nap. At one point, I even lay on the floor under my desk with my laptop perched on my belly, trying to work in that position. Reflecting on all of this, it's so interesting to me how I went through such great lengths to hide that I was pregnant. The fear of miscarriage was a very real part of it, but I also think I was worried about what everyone else would think and if they would assume it would negatively affect the company. I wish I had known that my business partners would have supported me no matter what. We all now have children and tell one another everything. . . . Know that these fears and stresses are more common than you think.

CHAPTER 8

Phase III

The Hush

WHETHER YOU'VE BEEN trying to conceive for a while or got that BFP, the Big Fat Positive (or insert your other *F* word), immediately, it's all exciting! You're now entering The Hush. You are pregnant but not yet sharing your news at work, or possibly at all. In this phase, depending on how you feel, you might have a few doctor's appointments to navigate logistically, but you might also have to navigate so much more than that, including at work. While that sushi lunch or team champagne toast might seem like a light topic, it's more complex than it seems. There is also a chance (70 percent, to be exact) that you will have morning or all-day sickness and a high possibility of exhaustion. From that first day you walk into work after the BFP, there is just something different for so many women—the reality of the real nine-plus-month timeline—it's happening!

Since The Hush hinges on disclosure, how long this phase lasts is totally up to you. You may be working virtually as a solo-entrepreneur and inform those you work with only when you are going into labor,

or choose to have this phase be brief and share the news of your pregnancy with your colleagues early on. If you decide to hold off on sharing the news personally and/or professionally, the first thing to keep
in mind is that you may want to get your allies or just one solid member of your board of directors in the loop to support you for the
months (!) you may need them. For context, 50 percent of women in
my study waited until the early second trimester to share, and another 21 percent waited until more than sixteen weeks. With that in
mind, 63 percent of women made some effort to conceal their pregnancy, and a third of those say that they made "a lot of effort."[1]

For so many women, the time after the BFP and before The Big
Tell can feel very tenuous. The Hush itself is a "hush" primarily because of fear: fear of pregnancy loss, which is addressed in this chapter, but also fear of loss of self and a change in perception, plus a risk
of being exposed. The Hush is super personal—something tremen-
dously joyful but also very unknown even if you are becoming a second, third, or beyond-time mother. It's something that everyone
experiences in some respect, but quite literally no one talks about—
that's the point.

Even with IVF, where women were very much aware of the timing
of their pregnancies and have often had a long journey with tremendous excitement at the positive test, the "what now?" when you are
pregnant and heading into work the next day can feel like a lot. One
woman in my research said, "It feels so big, and yet my belly was still
so small!"

Dr. Sarah Oreck shares an expert perspective on when the reality
of pregnancy sets in and why it feels so big at work:

> It points to the tug of war between the desire to become a parent
> and a competing desire to achieve at work and school. This
> dread is a result of the fears of what this added complexity will
> do to the normal order of business, but it's also a reflection of
> our society's difficulties with accepting that a woman doesn't

*have to be childless to be successful, and that being a successful
mother does not require staying at home until your children
are off to college. We have a great deal of work to do as a society
to expand our understanding of motherhood and identity as
women in the workplace and as mothers.*

It's okay for your brand-new pregnancy to feel big, so let's break it
down. Instead of asking yourself, "What should I do?" ask, "What do
I want to do right now?" Rather than plotting out what you think you
should do based on what others have done in your work environment
when sharing the news of their pregnancies, consider what feels right
for you and what is best for you and the baby. Overall, while you have
no obligation to share your news at work, you may feel responsibility
sooner rather than later.

For example, if you could be exposed to something potentially
harmful to you or your baby in your work environment or through
work travel; have extreme job conditions, like night shifts; or need a
physical accommodation, you might need to inform your employer
sooner rather than later so they can help you find solutions.[2] Alterna-
tively, maybe for you there's something you would like to accomplish
and share at work before announcing your pregnancy. While we are
working to shift perception, frankly I found that I wanted to keep my
professional and personal lives separate just a bit longer, and had a
work deadline that was just after my twenty-week mark that I knew
was going to feel like "my moment."

Next let's talk about the physical realities of pregnancy—the well-
known, like morning or all-day sickness and exhaustion, and even the
lesser-known bloating—that often affect The Hush. There are other
conditions, for example preeclampsia and varicose veins, that are
more likely to affect you physically later in pregnancy, in The Push.
Personally, while I had challenges at the end of my pregnancy, during
The Hush I was fortunate not to have a "puke planter" or feel like a
"dumpster fire," as more than one contributor described it. I did,

however, basically eat plain pasta and crackers for three months while pregnant with my first son, and considered sleeping in a bathroom stall because I couldn't keep my eyes open with the second. I knew that there was a bathroom on another floor in my office building and a very quiet bookstore around the block if I needed to make very personal calls.

Instead of thinking of these things as only stressors, because to be fair, they are, think of some of them as tools for your privacy. To lighten your stress, maybe even smile as you are in the corner of that weird private spot "eating only jelly beans," as one contributor shared was how she sustained her baby (and now very healthy toddler) when she could not fathom anything else. I also recognize that there is nothing funny about weeks of ongoing exhaustion and vomiting when you're worried about weight gain or loss for you and your baby. But it is temporary, and essential to communicate with your health care provider when prolonged, which is what makes it both manageable and hard to see the end of the tunnel. You're figuring out what you need right now, because everything keeps changing and work might be the only constant. One contributor recalled that work was a break from her very busy household of two young children at home when she was pregnant: "It was where it was quiet, people were taking care of themselves, and I could go to the bathroom whenever I wanted."

There is a lot going on in your brain and your body during The Hush, with a wide range of impact. This means that how you're feeling either can be managed by yourself or with an ally with little struggle at work, or may literally mean that you cannot do your job.

One day I got a call from a dear mentee. She had trusted me in her own Hush at a large company, had decided to run a small agency with her partner, and was now supporting one of her employees in her Hush. She described how she was torn. A new mother who had experienced her own set of challenges, she now had a pregnant employee who felt so horrible she couldn't even sit up, let alone use her laptop.

The company was fledgling but thriving and she needed her employee. We talked through the options and the checkpoints for conversations for the two of them to have, using a version of the "Will this matter?" exercise from chapter 2. Her employee started to feel better, and after a week of half days, an extension on a project, and some temp support, they got through it. It set them up ultimately for her maternity leave (and development of the policy and plan in the first place). Great story, still lots of tough conversations.

Speaking of conversations, while writing this book a question I heard a lot regarding keeping your pregnancy a secret was "What about the lying?" My answer to that is you're not lying, you're protecting your privacy in a very small window where it matters a lot to you and much less so to those around you. You are choosing what you share and need to remove the burden of guilt.

Personally, I found a tremendous amount of joy in drinking water martinis at company events—it's slightly amusing to have people go from watching whether you will drink to having them be impressed by your bold move of sipping a cocktail. I did also do this with friends, arriving at a bar or restaurant early to tip the bartender to make me a cold glass of water in an awkward glass with an olive. This is the light version of the lying/nondisclosing/choosing what you share. Silly that we do this to protect ourselves and especially as women. Is it really more likely that we are pregnant than that we just don't want to have a drink? But we do and it's okay. While I wish we could normalize not drinking at work social events while we are normalizing pregnancy and work, you just can't overthink it. There are way more complicated "lying" scenarios than water martinis.

INTERVIEWING WHILE PREGNANT

Even if you never interview for a job while you're pregnant, this a pretty good example of the guilt that you may feel when you are not disclosing something that could affect your work and those around you. The main reason you interview for jobs is that you want something different at work—either internally or externally—and you are going to convince someone else (and they are going to convince you) that it's a good idea. The interviewer is judging who you are right now—your skills, what you have done recently, where you want to go, and maybe what your lifestyle is like if it could impact work and your fit in the role they are trying to fill—just like you are interviewing the interviewer. What does pregnancy have to do with that? At first, nothing. Remember, pregnancy or having children at home isn't something that is stopping you from any of your future ambitions. It is concurrent with your career. In fact, pregnancy might drive that ambition even more.

However, there are a few exceptions. Realistically, if your pregnancy is common knowledge or super visible, you might want to acknowledge it for you and for the interviewer (or if you are the interviewer, by the way!). In addition, if you know the benefits you may need during or post-pregnancy at this checkpoint, then it might benefit you to disclose your pregnancy. Lastly, if the role could include risks to pregnancy, that's a clear consideration regarding disclosure.

Also, put yourself in the shoes of the employer. (Strange, I know.) They should want you no matter what—you're awesome, you're a great fit, you're clearly looking for a job while you're pregnant, so there's an extra level of effort going into this interview. But sometimes, a job might turn out not to be right, right now.

A contributor to my research shared a story about being a pregnant applicant. As the months of courting passed, the company got more invested in the search with her, and the applicant got, well, more pregnant. The employer was willing to go out on a limb and say yes to all the applicant's requests that weren't ideal for the company at the time, but ultimately fairly negotiated, because she was the right candidate—yes to remote work, yes to more salary, more vacation, more team support. The employer was also now in a tight spot.

They had a deadline, and this was a lead position that needed to deliver a project in a matter of months, which was also when the person being hired would deliver her baby. Because interviewing was done virtually, there was no real reason to bring it up.

It was time for her to put her cards on the table. It sounded something like, "I'm pregnant, I want this job, I want to do this with you, but I also am not going to sacrifice my maternity leave I need for my health or that of my baby. I can get you in a good place, but not what I know you want from me. I can set up a structure, hire someone to execute, and come back after three months to take it to the next level, but if you have another candidate that can come close to me, then I'm going to stay where I am. Hire them, and then hire me in six months to be their boss."

This particular situation is rare. Remember: You are interviewing that employer and they are interviewing you. You are building trust together. You do not have to share anything, but you might want to, and in fact, it could be an advantage.

Ellen Newhouse, a partner at global executive search firm Caldwell Partners, who went through a rigorous promotion process while pregnant with her second son and was later promoted while on maternity leave, advises, "If you are interviewing when pregnant, just like anytime you are interviewing, remember to highlight your capabilities, achievements, and commitment to a long-term career in the industry. For example, the rapidly evolving financial services sector where I often work mandates a more diverse workforce with inclusive policies and cultures, including hiring and retaining women. Have an open conversation about family benefits or other areas of importance such as workplace culture or potential childcare benefits. Do not be afraid to ask about topics such as the organization's track record of promoting female employees, how it supports working parents, or its relevant employee resource groups. This offers a natural way to highlight how you might add value to this agenda now and in the future."

To conclude, Dr. Nicole Foster and Kathleen McDowell, who was introduced in chapter 3, offer two additional empowering perspectives regarding interviewing and the big picture, both in The Hush and beyond it.

Dr. Nicole Foster:

I had just moved from Oregon to Washington State when I was seven months pregnant. After the first trimester, we wanted to be closer to some family when the baby came. I had interviewed for my job as an outpatient physical therapist at a hospital when I was four months pregnant, in the most belly-hiding outfit I had. As anxious as I was about breaking my pregnancy news to brand new supervisors, they were warm and supportive. However, because I was new to the state it meant I would not have any FMLA to cover my maternity leave. I would be taking eight unpaid weeks away from work.

My last couple of months of pregnancy were full of all the stresses that come with moving to a new state and doing everything I could to feel like a valuable team member at work. We were more than ready for baby, but I must have explained a hundred times why a perfectly decorated nursery for a newborn just wasn't the priority.

I am overall so proud of everything I was able to do while I was carrying my girl. I felt so powerful to be able to work the way I did and make such a big life transition while growing a human. I do wish that I had given myself more grace during that time. The measure of myself as a pregnant woman and new mama had (and has) nothing to do with how many things I can accomplish at once.

Kathleen McDowell:

Timing plays a critical role in how our lives are shaped. You're in the right place at the right time, you meet the love of your life. A friend of a friend has a contact, you land an interview. As for children, what many mothers will tell you about timing is that there is no good time to have a baby. And if you happen to be a woman in your thirties navigating a career and motherhood—timing be damned. This is exactly where I found myself five years ago. With a one-year-old, a new commute, and two years under my belt at an ad tech start-up, I was busy and antsy to make a move. With the encouragement of a former boss, I started networking and interviewing. Within a few months I'd gone through several rounds of interviews across big tech and found myself pregnant with my second baby.

I had a decision to make. I could move forward—now with a growing belly to show off during interviews and presentations— or put my career advancement on hold due to poor timing. I chose the former and continued my next rounds at Google and Facebook. After a long process these roles did not pan out, and just as I was about to call it quits until post-baby, I was up for a role at Pinterest. After a year of interviewing, and at almost eight months pregnant I landed on the Pinterest Retail Team. At thirty-five weeks, I flew to San Francisco for new-hire training and started maternity leave with full pay shortly after. Now nearly four years later, I'm still loving Pinterest and am expecting my third (and last) child. That year was a wild ride. The highs and lows took a toll, but the upside gave me the confidence to take control of my career. It also made me a better mom. Working makes me a better mom and being happy at work allows me to be present when home— which is truly the greatest gift.

Kathleen reflected on her experience with the important self-trust you read about in chapter 5. "My advice to someone who is considering making a career change while expecting would be to trust yourself. Interviewing for my entire pregnancy, at several high-profile companies, took an enormous amount of energy. I was also facing a ton of rejection during a stressful and vulnerable time. And even so, with each step forward I felt as though I was honing my interview skills and moving toward something bigger. Had I gone back to a job I was no longer passionate about, it would have been a very different experience."

PREGNANCY LOSS AND WORK

There is one more topic that I want to ensure I share with you regarding The Hush, one that can unfortunately also be part of your pregnancy, even after you have shared your news at work. Pregnancy loss is technically defined as occurring before twenty weeks, although the majority happen prior to the end of the first trimester prior to twelve weeks, which is when many women feel safe announcing their pregnancies. Pregnancy loss that occurs after twenty weeks is termed stillbirth and happens in 1 percent of pregnancies.

One in four women experience pregnancy loss—through the lens of work, it's likely that it happens to one in four working women, too—and it's affecting their day-to-day. Just because it is more common than you think doesn't mean that if it happens to you it is any easier. If it is the first or third time that it's happening to you, it is hard. Personally I could have used even an ounce of helpful information to navigate pregnancy loss at work versus what I did get, which was gleaned from scrolling message boards from 2002 in a bathroom stall at the office in 2014.

During my research, I found an academic paper, "Miscarriage in the Workplace: An Autoethnography," by two mothers and friends, Emily Benson, PhD, and Professor Elizabeth Siler, PhD, which introduces miscarriage (pregnancy loss) as an important topic in the workplace. They write, "At a fundamental level, miscarriage is a workplace event because it affects a large number of women. It may happen at work and/or cause women to miss time from work. Women and their non-gestational partners may experience significant, even traumatic, grief at the pregnancy loss."

What is so powerful about this paper is that their methodology was autoethnography, meaning that the article began with their own experiences.[3] Much like this book, the vulnerability of personal experiences driving their expert approach and ultimately usable output matters, because this topic, despite its frequency, is still buried. I had the opportunity to speak with Elizabeth and Emily regarding their personal experiences and expert insights. Elizabeth shared:

> *Through miscarriage and ultimately the birth of my child I had sixty-five weeks of pregnancy to have one baby—that's a lot of pregnancy where you do not have a lot of control. But there is one part where, through secrecy, you can decide what you want and don't want to say, including about loss. There are reasons for both. It gives you protection, but also it takes a lot of energy to talk about. Energy I didn't have because of what my mind and body were going through, but also because I was busy at work. For the sharing itself, it wasn't about keeping it a secret that I was afraid of, it was about how people were going to see me and how I would have to see myself—as someone who doesn't have kids. My professional identity didn't change, because it was protected, but I might have to take on my whole identity without the part I yearned for. It was a huge giant sadness.*

This heaviness is what so many women feel after the loss of a pregnancy, not just at home, but in all aspects of their lives, including at work—even if they don't want to.

After my first miscarriage, I remember just feeling empty. I had my husband text my boss when it happened, to give me a few days, then I called her in a very quiet, lowered voice. I remember that it was dark, and I felt physically horrible, but nothing was as bad as how my heart felt. When I had another miscarriage, it was easier to have "the flu" for a few days, and then weeks later I shared, when I could get it out in the right moment, privately with my boss, because it was still weighing on my day-to-day.

If you experience a pregnancy loss, consider sharing with someone in your inner circle who can help support you during this time. In their paper, Emily and Elizabeth write that isolation is a consequence of secrecy and grief, a heavy burden when frankly you don't want to share why. Work and the comradery of your environment can help to relieve this without you having to share much more than what you usually would about something private.

Also, take time for what you need. If your company offers paid time off for pregnancy loss, take it. If they don't, take time as you can. Physically you may need recovery time, whether a loss happens naturally or with a procedure. Or you might be okay to go back to work, then weeks pass, and you find you need some time when it hits you like a ton of bricks. You might just need an afternoon to work from home if possible. As Emily said, "Sometimes you can bring your brain to work, but not your body." Take care of yourself by taking care of both. Work can be a distraction in a positive way, or you can be distracted by grief—both things can be true at the same time, or at different times for the same loss.

Seek out resources you may need beyond this book, including within your community, and don't be afraid to ask for what you need in the way that you are comfortable asking. Here is a suggestion, if it feels impossible to even get the words out: "I am dealing with something personal that I need a few days to process. I'll let you know if I need anything else, or if I would like to share more."

"There are different ways of framing things," says Elizabeth. "What may help is to think of it in the medical sense—you don't need to share everything about a medical condition or treatment if you need to share that you must be out of the office or classroom. You know what you need to share, or not, and you don't need your boss's permission to get that treatment."

What if you're on the other side of the conversation, and a colleague or direct report comes to you with news of their pregnancy loss? Follow their lead. The worst thing you can do is make pregnancy loss feel taboo or embarrassing—or enthralling. Elizabeth put it well when she said, "Your pregnancy is not public entertainment."

When this type of news has been shared with me as a boss, mentor, or professor in the past, I always tried to give people the space and options to speak. I know the courage that it takes to get it out, to admit that something you wanted is gone, and I know the vulnerability of letting others know, even (and especially) if there is nothing they want you to do about it. While I personally may have had my own experiences and I share when I can to make others feel less alone, I am now very thoughtful about not relating, just sharing it happened, with my own vulnerability.

Elizabeth adds, "The good news is that when one woman is vulnerable, everyone comes out of the woodwork and the whole room begins speaking—and it's not the same story or the same perspective. It doesn't have to only be a triumph or a tragedy, and we don't need to tell people how to feel, just that it exists." Emily notes, "Recognizing miscarriage as an experience that many working women face eases the burdens of secrecy and grief, opens the door for more research and discussion, not continuing to erase it from the narrative about pregnancy at work."

You are working, you may already be a mother, you are a partner, a friend, a family member, and an individual with interests beyond all those responsibilities that drive you. Introducing pregnancy into the mix, and subsequently babies and young children, is major, and it can evoke a wide range of emotions, from the lows of pursuing something that seems unattainable to the highs of possibility. Before your pregnancy becomes public, the Hush phase can allow you a private moment to reflect, but it also comes with a lot of weight in terms of what this means for pregnancy and work.

As we wrap up this chapter, remember to enjoy your huge news *and* your precious secret. Do what you need for you. Find your checkpoints, but don't put so much pressure on them if you need to flex for your health or because your future work experience would benefit from an earlier or later disclosure.

If you have sailed through this phase, that's fantastic! In the private Hush phase, you are in control of your information. Now you are about to go over another big threshold—the transition from the private to the public pregnancy. How you want to manage communication is important and requires you to revisit your style and the style of those you are communicating to, to create and maintain your confidence and comfort.

QUESTIONS FOR REFLECTION

What are some of the things that have surprised you in this phase? How are you going to celebrate little moments during this time?

When are you ready to share your news? What are the reasons you might change this moment and who would you want to communicate with? What are you most excited about in sharing your news and what are you most afraid of?

How can you ensure that you are the type of teammate, boss, or friend that if someone around you is suffering with a difficult Hush or with a pregnancy loss, they can count on you?

JULIE THIBAULT, LUXURY RETAIL STRATEGIST AND FOUNDER OF MARTINGALE ADVISORS

My husband and I had just recently started trying. I was thirty years old, healthy, no family history of pregnancy or fertility complications. I got pregnant the second month. I was working full time for a luxury firm and my boss and peers were all female, many who had young families of their own. When you are surrounded by women in the workplace in an industry where travel and socializing are common, it is hard to conceal pregnancy. Women have a sixth sense, especially those in the process of starting a family, and can pick up on the signs very early on.

Luckily, I was feeling great, I had no nausea, and I was able to pretend to drink my glass of wine during the business trips with no one the wiser. Despite it being an easy pregnancy, I followed the unspoken guidelines about telling the workplace. I waited until I was past the first trimester, in case something went wrong. At week thirteen, I got the results of the anatomy scan and nuchal. I was carrying a healthy baby with no signs of any genetic mutations. I went on vacation with my family and decided I'd tell my boss and coworkers when I returned. At week fifteen, I told my boss. She was thrilled and supportive. A few days later, I shared the news with my team and colleagues. When are you due? Late fall. Will you find out the sex? Yes! How do you want to decorate a nursery? Is your husband thrilled? Over the moon.

The next week, I woke up feeling sick, like I was coming down with the flu. I had a low-grade fever and general malaise. I stayed home from work. I did feel achy in my belly, but at that point, my uterus was stretching so it didn't seem unusual. But soon I noticed that I was spotting in my underwear. I called my doctor and she told me to go to the ER. By the time I was admitted, I had a fever of 103. They tried to bring it down, but it wouldn't budge. Twelve hours later my uterus started to contract, and I was in excruciating pain. I felt a rush of fluid between my legs and the next thing I knew I was being rushed into surgery. At that point, I already knew my baby was gone and I just wanted it all to be over. That was my last thought before I went under. When I woke up, my doctor and husband were there. She explained that I had an infection in my uterus and my body expelled the baby. I had lost so much blood that they kept me in the hospital for a few more days. Thankfully, she put me in surgical recovery and not the maternity ward as protocol normally dictated.

I took another week off at home. I wanted to return to work for the distraction, but I dreaded the explanation. Everyone except my boss thought I had been on vacation. I had to explain repeatedly that I had "lost" the baby. I hated that term, it made me feel like I had misplaced my child and that it was my fault. The doctors did not know how or where I had gotten the infection, and I was facing a multitude of tests to figure out the cause. I felt like I had failed as a woman.

A year later, I did get pregnant again and had a healthy baby girl. That pregnancy was filled with anxiety, but I did a few things differently. I told close work friends and my boss very early because I knew that if something did go wrong, I would want their support. But I didn't say anything to everyone else until it was so obvious that people just said congratulations. There are no rules for sharing your pregnancy. Do what's right to you.

CLAUDIA REUTER, AUTHOR OF *YES, YOU CAN DO THIS!*, AND HOST OF *THE 43 PERCENT* PODCAST

I vomited nearly every day of my first trimester, only to encounter severe heartburn during my second trimester, but I knew I was fortunate that my pregnancy had been labeled an uncomplicated one. For weeks I commuted by train and always carried a plastic bag with me, fully prepared to unleash the contents of my stomach into it, knowing that the small bathroom on the train was not always easily accessible. It went on like this for weeks—with a dash to the restroom upon arrival to brush my teeth and prepare for the day ahead—when I realized I needed to work from home until this phase of my pregnancy was over.

I worked in the technology division of an investment bank where I was one of only a few women. I had built a career by working hard to learn new skills, and I enjoyed joking around with my colleagues, always eager to fit in with the group of primarily young men I worked with—to be "one of the boys." However, my morning sickness made it impossible to focus on anything other than the task at hand and simply getting through the day. I spoke to my boss about taking some time to work from home and was relieved by how understanding and supportive he was. My coworkers and employer were incredibly kind, and the company I worked for was very progressive for the time—they had a nursing room and offered a generous maternity leave. But none of that made up for the fact that I found the experience of pregnancy isolating in the workforce.

As I entered my second trimester, I felt ready to tackle the commute again, eager to be back. While I was excited about my future and happy to be with colleagues again, dealing with the reality of a body that still felt out of control, and was so messily distinct from the orderly world of work in which I was used to participating, was not easy. One simply did not discuss personal issues in the office. We discussed technical issues and joked about many things, but I never would have talked about the most intimate aspects of my relationship with my husband.

So when I finally stepped back into the office, I remember feeling uncomfortable as I noticed eyes on my bulging belly. One co-worker commented, "Oh, given how long you were out sick, I assumed you would be much thinner." And with that small, innocuous comment, I realized that my body offered a clear view into my personal life. One could easily make a guess as to when I had had sex to end up in this situation. The size of my belly could help someone figure out when I would be likely to push a small human out of my body. For all the excitement of my growing new family, I somehow felt embarrassed by what was happening to me, and sensed that others took me less seriously as a result.

I didn't know then about research on the "motherhood penalty"—the findings that women are more likely to be perceived as less responsible while men are perceived as more responsible when starting families. But there I was, the "out-of-control pregnant woman" in an office of mainly male tech workers. All my previous attempts to fit in and be one of the boys were suddenly futile, and I wasn't sure how I would ever fit in again.

JILL KARGMAN, AUTHOR, WRITER, AND ACTRESS

I was a writer at MTV when I was pregnant. I was a "permalancer"—I didn't get the benefits, but I was often full-time writing in a series of sprints months apart. So while for the team it seemed like I was just in the office, it had been a few months. When you're pregnant, going from month to month feels like forever. I had gone from not wanting to announce it too early at three months, trying to hide it, to showing up with my seven-month stomach and was just going to seize it. I wore a tight black T-shirt and a jean skirt that basically looked like arrows. At MTV it was all about the youth culture, and the type of people I was with were rock and roll rejuveniles—and I was ten years younger than them, and I was married . . . and pregnant. The second I revealed it, there were jaws on the floor. It wasn't a normal corporate culture, you're supposed to be cool and young and skinny—I joked, tried to make it less of a big deal, I talked about being "knocked up." They never called me again. I had been there consistently for years and felt a lot of pressure to be one of the guys, and I was, in the best way—I would be the only girl at the team lunch. It was cool to be the cool girl until suddenly, in one second, I wasn't.

Years later I had restored my cool, including seeing Nine Inch Nails, my favorite band, only because I sprinted down the street with my daughter in the stroller to get the tickets, shocking the guy who I got the tickets from that I was "full of surprises," not having lost my edge on the delivery table. I ran into one of my former bosses. I was back to myself, in a well-rested place, and he was taking stock of me with my tattoos. I said, 'That was so lame you never called me again." He said something like he didn't want to bother me—and I assured him the best thing to do was to just ask. In fact, I had finished a book three weeks after having my baby. Now I make sure I bring myself back when I need it—to the balsamic reduction of myself, including through concerts, and to never discredit people for the other parts of their lives, including their families—or myself.

NATALIE SUAREZ

I think motherhood is something that comes naturally to a woman, and at the right time for her and her partner. I always see myself *becoming a woman who is balancing a career, motherhood, and family life all at once. For me, family is everything and something I truly value, being a woman who has built a career working with my sister and coming from parents who always worked together as entrepreneurs while raising us. I can't wait for all the fun in reliving my childhood with my own kids and having the strength and focus to juggle it all successfully when the time comes.*

DYLANA SUAREZ

The idea of motherhood has come to mean something much different for me as I've gotten older. I'm newly thirty-three, over two years married, and although I see motherhood in my future, I've come to a place of really being in tune with my sense of self, where I feel like I don't need to be rushed into it despite societal pressures about the "right" age to become a mother. Coming into motherhood in my own time is important to me and a representation of my freedom as a woman to pursue the life I want to lead on my own clock. It is a representation of my strength against the judgments that society has against women my age who aren't already mothers. I think the vision of a working mother is beautiful, a way of life that I see myself pursuing down the road eventually. But it is not only beautiful but also a challenge that I feel is worth experiencing. Being female in general comes with so many challenges, from the toll pregnancy can take on the body to the inequalities in the workplace. Societal judgments and stereotypes don't help the realities of personal decision making, especially when it comes to the decision of motherhood, and I hope that in time these judgments will be eliminated. That to me is a true step in the direction of freedom and equality, one that not just every mother and future mother deserves to have, but every woman.

CHAPTER 9

Phase IV

The Push

UP UNTIL THIS point, you may have kept your pregnancy under wraps, hopefully with a few awesome confidantes to help you navigate and feel supported. In this next phase and through it, it's all out there, often literally. But while that can feel intense, so many women in my research shared that it also felt like a relief and often aligned with a burst of energy to "Push" through your public pregnancy with a self-assured plan.

"I remember the moment vividly when I let work know I was pregnant," shares Nadejda Savcova, model, actress, and mother:

> *It wasn't as easy for me to follow the tips of what to wear to hide your belly. I had a lingerie photo shoot and kept trying to position my body to hide my belly and asking to see the photos. Then someone on the set, said, "It's okay, we know, and you look great." I exhaled. After that I felt so relieved to ask for what I needed—breaks, products without allergens....*

One of the funniest moments was when I switched to mod-
eling maternity swimwear and they said, can you eat a big
bowl of pasta tonight, so your belly is extra big? . . . I was for-
tunate to have support around me, energy for the most part,
and work to keep me busy, but I also remember another posi-
tive moment later when my body and my brain felt back to
"that's me."

In this chapter, after sharing your news in the way you want to, you will recognize The Push and how to make the most of it—and celebrate it.

THE BIG TELL

Oversimplified, The Big Tell is the moment you tell your boss, and others at work, that you're pregnant. I often describe it as one of the "hinge" moments for pregnancy and work, one that can leave the door open or closed, depending on how it is experienced. And there is quite a range. In my first study, I found that 49 percent of women were very to extremely comfortable sharing their news, 36 percent somewhat comfortable, and 16 percent uncomfortable. It is important to highlight that there are significant differences of even more comfort for women forty-five to fifty, entry-level employees, and women in specific industries, and significantly less comfort for women of color.[1]

This moment carries a lot of weight for women. There is the fear of perception, which is incredibly valid, as you read in part I, as well as the exposure of your private life, which forces a reconciliation of your identity, and the simple fact that you need to communicate clearly. Announcing your pregnancy feels as if it can set a tone for the rest of your now public pregnancy at work. It could be met with "jumping-up-and-down-hugging-joy" reactions, as one contributor shared; or with a very neutral response, which might be a relief or feel strange; or it might be handled poorly.

Lindsay Atha, a senior finance executive at a large company, said it incredibly well to me one day when reflecting on her own experience: "The best-case scenario is that your boss says, 'If you put half the effort into parenting that you put into your job, that is going to be one incredibly lucky kid.'" Imagine if that was the outcome for every one of us and how it could play into ultimately retaining women versus reinforcing this moment as a trigger for attrition. Think about that next time someone wants to tell you something personal and important at work.

While some women I spoke to after all the buildup to this moment of sharing said, "That's it?" it's clear that this is an opportunity (among many) to communicate deliberately in order to mitigate stress and navigate your journey to working motherhood successfully. You're not just talking about work, you're talking about your life including work, and communicating effectively can help to create some of your "gravitas that lasts" in this moment and beyond, which we will discuss next, including as you offboard into maternity leave and anticipate your great return (or not).

Let's take The Big Tell step by step. To start, I use the term "boss" to loosely mean whomever you need to talk to about your pregnancy. We'll also revisit the three communication styles we learned about in chapter 4, inspired by the CSI: the conserver, the pragmatist, and the originator.[2] Identifying which styles suit both you and your boss can help you to have the conversation you want to have and ask for what you need.

Conserver. The conserver prefers the known to the unknown, likes structure and to know the rules of the game. If this is you, you like gradual change, and by the time you're ready to announce your pregnancy you have likely already done the research and have your questions ready, but only for what you need right now—versus, for example, when you will start offboarding at the end of your pregnancy.

If this is the person you are communicating with, offer concrete and organized points to give security in the unknown and minimize uncertainty. For example: "I have some personal news I'd like to share. I'm pregnant. Right now, I wanted to let you know that I may need to book a few appointments, but otherwise it's status quo for me. I'm really enjoying my project/case/students and am looking forward to the next few months. I'll check in with you as needed during these regular meetings and set up time for us in X months to talk about my transition for leave."

Pragmatist. If this is you, you prefer an objective approach, meaning you can take yourself out of a situation and can see multiple sides. Remember that this pregnancy *is* about you, not about anyone else. While it's helpful for you to consider yourself as part of the options, make sure that you don't downplay what you would ultimately like to happen in the next few months of your pregnancy at work. And if you don't know, that's okay to express too.

If you are communicating with a pragmatist, ensure that you share your perspective for them to have top of mind, versus how it may have worked with others in the past, and be ready to bring up anything that's weighing on you (or your mind too). For example: "I know that my colleague asked not to go on that trip when she was pregnant, but for me, I'd like to keep it for now and play it by ear until it would affect the project or team, if that's okay for you?" You're acknowledging that accommodations have been made for pregnant people in the past, but you're also making clear that you're not sure when or how you'd like them.

It goes the other way around too. Just because a colleague worked until her water broke in dramatic fashion at forty weeks, accomplishing more than anyone on the entire team did for the past three years, doesn't mean you have to—good for her, but that's not a justified expectation.

Communicating pragmatically also works when clearing the air and putting things on the table: "I'll be due on [insert date], which I know is when we typically do our year-end reviews. I have been tracking my promotion closely and working hard with you toward my goals to make it happen. Please let me know if I'm not, as it's top of mind for me." This way, you make clear that the same things that were true before you shared the news of your pregnancy are true now.

If you have doubts about staying on track at work once your pregnancy becomes public, you can also have a quick check-in with your boss before you share your news, not as a formal evaluation, but so you know where you stand and to invest in goals together. It takes pressure off even having to think about it, and frankly, then you can have something to refer to in future evaluations. This could sound like, "I was thrilled to hear that I'm tracking towards my promotion in my Q3 review, and it made me feel good that I can make it happen this year." Or "I understand that there was a lot for me to continue to work on from my Q3 review to reach my goal of a promotion. I'm still focused on it and very motivated to make it happen. Right now, I'd like to get on track before my maternity leave." Of course, remember to be realistic that the timing is concurrent, and instead of being the be-all and end-all, you still can get promoted after maternity leave (or even during it!).

If you are a conserver or a pragmatist or are communicating with them, you may want to set up The Big Tell as *a* conversation versus *the* conversation. Share the facts for now that are important to you— for example, "I'm telling you this news and it's just for you," or "I'm telling you this first and then I will share with the team." It also could be as simple as, "Here's what it means—I will have a few appointments, or I am not feeling great and may need to work from home," or "There is nothing you need to do now, and I'll look forward to talking through some logistics later together."

Originator. The originator is ready for faster and more dramatic change. If this is you, you may have high expectations for how your boss might respond to the news of your pregnancy. Remember that it's possible they may be in the same mindset, or they might have their mind on other things. If they meet your major news with a neutral or questionable response, it's okay, you have your joy in sharing it and this is the first of a lot of big things to come from your public pregnancy at work. It is also okay to state how important this news is to you: "I have been waiting to share this news for years. I've been thinking about it for a very long time and would like to do so in the following way."

To imagine the full spectrum, The Big Tell from originator to another originator might sound like both of you sharing: "This is the biggest news ever, and what do you want to do right now to set you up for success at work and as a mom?" But if you're not an originator and your boss is, it's also okay to set the tone off the bat: "I'm thrilled you are so happy for me. While this is a big moment for me personally, professionally I'd like to share with just a few of my colleagues for now and focus on the excitement we have going on here. Thank you again for sharing in my joy."

Your communication style might change depending on the situation, but use awareness of their differences to think about the best approach.

There are three more considerations you might think about as you make your pregnancy public. First, I always like to use a "what this means for me" and "what this means for you" framework. Essentially it dilutes why you care and why those you are communicating to should care too. You don't exactly have to say, "I'm pregnant, so what this means for you is . . . ," but by framing your news in these terms, you ensure that your teammates understand the expectations you have for them and that you have thought through how your pregnancy may affect them, those around you, or your work. As my former executive coach Cortney Cahill explained to me, "For highly successful people, their first response will be to think about how this will impact me/us/work. They will go directly to the timing, the projects, and the deliverables. Right now, you just want them to know your exciting news and to share your joy. Framing it this way helps to allow people to be present with you and your news."

Second, the most important communication point to get across in The Big Tell, and any moment you are sharing something personal, is that those around you should follow your lead. I can't say it enough. If you want to lean in more to your work, great! People must respect that. If you are feeling like garbage and need a teammate to support you, then you need to share that so that your colleagues can follow your lead. While there are going to be moments where your community may jump in, keep top of mind that you're the one driving what's right for you and your baby through your words and your actions, and used together for your work this empowered feeling can be freeing.

This is essential, including whether what you are sharing is met with less-than-ideal responses. You can simply say, "Thank you for taking the time to talk to me. This is an important moment for me personally and professionally and I appreciate your support." Even if that is counterintuitive, I can tell you that those words have weight. Pregnancy is personal, which means that it comes with us to our places of work. The support you receive needs to suit you as an individual, not just be convenient for those who are offering it.

With this in mind, remember to recognize moments of benevolent discrimination in this phase. As you read in chapter 4, this is when someone assumes that something like taking you off a project or recommending someone else for a trip is helping you, lowering the expectations, or eliminating stress, often not because they don't think you can do it but because they think that is what you would want or is what's "best for you." Encourage your colleagues to follow your lead here too. It's your responsibility to decide what you can take on and what you can let go of, and being included in the decision making gives you recognition and control. As one anonymous contributor to my research shared, "I just wanted to be told that it was happening, ideally included in making the recommendation and onboarding the person who was going to have my spot. Even though the choice was obvious, I felt like it was weirdly done secretly to protect my feelings, and in addition, the person selected also felt weird about not getting

to enjoy their moment. It was then up to me to go to her and say that
she was my choice—even though no one asked." Of course, when the
actions go beyond benevolent, ensure that you keep track and to elevate any instances of discrimination addressed in part I and revis-
ited in the next chapter.

Finally, if reading this makes your stomach hurt or feel like you're
going to burst into tears (happy or sad), one of the best pieces of advice I can give you is to do a practice run. Get out some of the emotions and chest tightness on someone you trust. You may say exactly
the same thing in the same way, feeling the same emotions, but give
yourself a chance to do it in a run-through. See how you feel. Remember, you're pregnant, there's a lot of blood pumping even in the cool-
est, most confident cucumber. Give yourself a buffer. Cortney always
told me to "calibrate my emotions," and I still appreciate that phrase
when I have that tight stress feeling.

ENTERING THE PUSH

Katherine Schwarzenegger Pratt is a *New York Times* bestselling author, wife, mother, and animal advocate. She is also the creator of
BDA Baby™ (Before, During & After Baby), an Instagram Live series
of candid conversations with experts and friends alike on all things
baby. Through her own experience during the pandemic, she began
cultivating a community on social media. Now she helps others to feel
less alone in their unique journey to motherhood, with no subject off
limits. Her efforts, inspired by her followers' anonymous inquiries,
have created over fifty episodes that create a community of support.

Katherine's story is truly an accelerated and emphasized intersection of The Big Tell and The Push:

> *When I was almost four months pregnant, I went on my book
> tour. I had been working on my most recent book,* The Gift of
> Forgiveness, *for two and a half years. I was also very excited
> about being pregnant. I was both carrying this human baby*

*and delivering my "book baby" to the world at the same time.
With the book, I had been nurturing it thoughtfully. It is filled
with other people's vulnerable and life-altering stories, and I
wanted to make them proud and make the book proud—the
plan was to deliver it into the world and keep my pregnancy
private, and not have that be the focus of the launch.*

*I remember being on tour—mindful to take care of myself,
having only told one person with me, and then only two days
in, COVID became a major factor. I was in New York to do the
Today show. We were going back and forth on scheduling, and
I knew we would have to postpone my book tour immediately.
There was a moment with my confidante that I remember de-
scribing my two babies, including my secret one, and was
overwhelmed by the first time, of many to come, when you
have to choose between your work and this new role—the one
of mom. It was a monumental moment of canceling, hopping
on a plane, and going home. There was no doubt in my mind
as a mom about making health and safety the priority—for
myself, for others, but most important, for my baby.*

*On the plane, I wasn't disappointed; even as a planner, I
was numb to this unplanned moment. It caused me to rethink
everything. The book couldn't not be delivered, just like I
couldn't not protect myself and my baby. My focus shifted to
selling copies virtually, driven by the purpose of the book. It
needed to reach people, and I had put in so much work to get
it to those who needed it. A week later, the book was on the New
York Times bestseller list.*

Katherine further reflected on that moment; she was the oldest
child of her family, and always knew she wanted to be a mother and
was inspired by her own mother and grandmother:

*I remember my mom telling me, this is a great moment for
you, both for the book and in my role as a mother—you'll have
to pivot and so it's also a moment to realize that when you*

become a parent you can never have a plan, they always change. You have to be flexible and go with the flow more and enjoy it.

My mother was and is today as a grandparent—amazing. As her daughter, I saw grace and ease even though now she tells me there was so much chaos. All I remember is that she was always fun and happy to be with us. She made us feel 100 percent solid and loved. She worked throughout my childhood, but as long as I can remember she was there for us and never missed anything. I never doubted my ability to work and be a mother, we were raised to work hard, follow our passion, pave our own way, and that there would always be love and support no matter what.

Once the news of your pregnancy is out in the (work) universe, you're in The Push, the time of "modern nesting," from when you announce your pregnancy at work until you go on maternity leave or have your baby. This is a very special window of time. For many women, it's an opportunity to a "get your shit in order." For others, it's a "holy crap" window or even a "ticking timebomb" slot. Regardless, it's a door of opportunity, often one fueled by energy and clarity that comes with clear priorities, your competence, and ultimately your strength. The Push can be an opportunity to make a career pivot, it can give you confidence to take a leap, it can help you prioritize what's important in life, and it is certainly a moment of pride.

Joanna Coles, whom we met in chapter 1, describes how her pregnancy was a source of relief, giving her the courage to change jobs both times she was pregnant. She shares, "I found it a time about real excitement, real transformation, and I loved being pregnant. I hadn't expected that I would. There was such an existential relief I felt when I was pregnant. With work you can push through, but when I was pregnant, the 'Will I have children?' question was answered."

Joanna is not alone in this sentiment. Many women talked about their career as the given, and motherhood as the big question that was ever-present as they chipped away or zoomed along in their jobs and education. She continues, "Because I changed jobs during my pregnancy, I felt like an anomaly. What I looked out onto was a landscape where women tended to stop working permanently or stop working for three or four years, which wasn't an option for me. But in some instances I did see that for the women who worked, there was a unique energy. Pregnancy was an accelerator for their ambition."

Throughout my research, I discovered the supercharge that comes in the Push phase. This was something I experienced, and you can too. In the rest of this chapter, we will assess some key themes to be aware of, including managing expectations of yourself and of others, as well as some tangible work-checklist items for this phase, including birth-plan basics, travel, and wardrobe, so that you can free yourself up to be the best version of you throughout your pregnancy at work.

A BALANCED DRIVE

Dr. Margaret (Molly) McNairy is one of those women who inspires you with her warm energy, intelligence, and depth of fortitude at the first moment you meet her. A Harvard-trained clinician-scientist, she is an associate professor, Bonnie Johnson Sacerdote Clinical Scholar in Women's Health, director of the Global Health Research Fellowship at Weill Cornell Medical College of Cornell University in New York City, and a mother of three. She shares her story of The Push, with a concurrent lens of ambition, driven by an incredible purpose and sense of self:

> Global health was my first child. In college, I spent time working in the slums of Brazil bearing witness to solvable health disparities where simple clean water and antibiotics could change someone's life. This propelled me to medical school and

decades of training to become an expert in epidemics, infectious diseases, and health systems that affect the six billion people who live in poverty around the world. Global health is certainly not a desk job, and planning pregnancy, being pregnant, and having children were complicated both logistically and emotionally by keeping my job on the rails and meeting the needs of my patients, my family, and frankly my own mental health.

I was pregnant with my youngest child, Leighton, during the Zika pandemic, and I couldn't travel to Haiti for a whole year. Zika at the time was associated with severe birth defects, and the hot zone was the Latin America and Caribbean region. At the time I was devastated and thought this pregnancy was dooming my career. I had just been awarded a large and prestigious project to jump-start a new area of work on cardiovascular disease in the slums of Port-au-Prince, and I felt that being on the ground was nonnegotiable for the project's success. I kept pushing for options to travel and be on the ground, and for many months I did not have a solution. There is a part of me that found success early in my career by never giving up and doing the seemingly impossible in logistically complex situations. This time I felt trapped. If I chose to go, my pregnancy and child was at risk. If I decided not to go, the project could fail and patients living in untenable poverty and dying from preventable chronic diseases would suffer.

The emotional tension of being pregnant and its seeming conflict with my work ambition and passion for patients was uncomfortable and anxiety provoking. What helped is speaking to peer women scientists. One told me about an innovative grant that was specifically for female working-mother scientists. I was able to hire a research assistant to be my boots on the ground. I share this story to affirm that pregnancy in some workplaces is going to be tense, but that there

*is usually a solution if you share your situation with others
to find a way forward and be relentless until you find it. Pregnancy is not a zero-sum game.*

The recognition of pregnancy with this perspective is crucial.
While as a society we need to make the options more visible, your
intrinsic drive and recognition of when you need help or what you
want to do in that moment is powerful. It is way more likely that raising your hand for a promotion, a project, or anything else at work during your pregnancy is not a risk and that you can "make it work." You
just might have to make some adjustments in the short term that support you in the long term. It's also possible to parallel huge career
milestones and success throughout your pregnancy or even on your
maternity leave. Remember this time is concurrent and just needs to
be kept in balance.

In The Push, you may feel a tension of drive and a squeeze of time,
but you need to be aware of alternative ways to make things happen
for you and for work, versus how in the past you may have just taken
more on yourself. In addition, in this phase there are other limiting
physical considerations to be aware of beyond what was shared in
The Hush. Women cited the impact of gestational diabetes, often
identified in a test at around twenty-four weeks, preeclampsia, varicose veins resulting in bed rest or limited time on your feet, or other
conditions that necessitate weekly monitoring toward the end of
pregnancy. This was the case for me. Above all, your health is your
priority, but since so many women spoke of clouded judgment while
in The Push (myself included), keep in mind you can be a warrior, but
don't be a superhero.

Erin Weibel works at Meta in communications and was sixteen
weeks pregnant at the very start of the pandemic when she felt a
tickle in her throat. As she powered through with COVID-19, isolated
from her work teams and her family in her crowded apartment, she
hit her max of overwhelm and it gave her a perspective for her future,

then and now. "You don't always have to be a hero. I wish I would have known that if I took the break and rest me and my baby needed, there would be plenty more projects like those I was tackling at the time when I was ready to take them. Slow down. Take the help that is offered to you. Don't focus on how taking help or your pregnancy might hinder your progress at work. If you're in a supportive work environment, the opportunities and growth will still be there when you're ready." Take the time now to get ready for what's next for you and both your work and your baby.

THE PUSH CHECKLIST

Let's go over some simple but important checklist items. First, re-member your work BFF and/or office ally? Guess what, you also need to make sure they know how to take care of you now that you're get-ting "super pregnant," or will be soon. It's never a bad idea to have this person in the office regardless of your pregnancy status. This indi-vidual needs to know where you keep your purse and have your part-ner and a secondary emergency contact in their phone. If you are in a traditional place of work, there may be an emergency contact list, but this person would also be able to support you in stealth mode if needed too. Of course, this person can also be nominated to know if you would like any kind of celebration at your place of work and if you would like to know about it or not (or know and pretend that you don't).

This is also a good time from a tangible perspective to have a one-page birth plan. While it should include some of your key decisions regarding your birth and newborn care (epidurals, circumcisions, oh my!), I am going to focus on the key work points. First, while your document should include the names of your doctors, it should also include the steps you need to take to communicate your leave, which sometimes must be done immediately. Frankly, I have never met someone in the headspace after giving birth who can sort through a corporate website. Scan your insurance card, driver's license, or passport, and save them to your birth page document. I cannot tell you how handy it can be when you are in a rush of urgency for your health and safety to just say, "It's all here." Keep your personal information safe and use copies versus originals, which can get lost in a shuffle. Print this document and store it in your go bag, email it to your home email, and send it to your partner, who may go to the birthing location with you.

Speaking of a go bag, keep one at work if possible. It should contain an extra pair of underwear, an easy outfit like black leggings and a top, plus some snacks, a water bottle, your favorite on-the-go electrolyte drink powder, a travel-size sanitizer/hand wipes package, and some feminine care pads. In fact, these are some things you may need in your place of work before you head off to have your baby (and then replace again in your go bag). Don't underestimate hydration and snacks during your pregnancy at work. This go bag isn't your full hospital bag that you put next to the car seat in your home, but could go inside it. Make sure that you do the full kit long before you need it. Bottom line—be prepared. One physician in my research shared that she wore a diaper on her rounds toward the end of her pregnancy— not the worst idea, but also ridiculous that her role demanded it that late in her pregnancy.

Up next, work travel was listed as a common stressor for women in my research, either because of FOMO or COMO (reminder: "certainty of missing out"), but also because there aren't hard-and-fast rules. Depending on the size of your belly, you may be uncomfortable early on, or you may feel totally fine and confident on a long-haul flight traveling for work throughout your pregnancy—it may be your whole job too. As a pilot in my research shared, "I remember the look on the passengers faces as I climbed out of the cockpit with my captain's hat and the buttons on my shirt popping. I felt fantastic at work and was thoughtful about when it didn't make sense and grateful for guidelines to follow."

Generally, physicians recommend that you stop international flight travel between twenty-eight and thirty-five weeks and domestic travel after thirty-six weeks; with higher-risk pregnancies, including multiples, the timeline gets closer to thirty-two weeks. When you consider that some international flights may be shorter than a cross-country domestic one, please remember that these are guidelines. Any significant travel should be discussed with your health care provider, especially in recent years, regarding much more than cabin pressure. Viruses and their resulting restrictions, including testing, protocols, and timelines, require review and guidance. There is a risk/reward evaluation of each trip, and many women in my research cited that work travel helped prepare them mentally and physically for the birth of their babies, and their reframing of work with a bit of distance.

For example, Christy Turlington Burns, who we met in chapter 2, recalls the last time she traveled before having her baby:

I was pregnant with my second child and had to travel to London for a presentation. It was December and my son was born in February—it was definitely the last time that I could fly. I remember being on the plane and the flight attendant said, "You're not going to have the baby on this plane, right? It's been a long time since I had that particular training."

There are so many things to consider with pregnant work travel, some true and some myths—susceptibility to blood clots, altitude's impact, the recommendation to wear compression socks and to move around when you can, even what citizenship your child would be if born in the air over international waters. It is a lot to think about. But I remember that trip so clearly, and because my first child was not a great sleeper, and although she had traveled almost everywhere with me until that point, I remember wanting to take this business trip alone—going across the ocean for a hotel bed for

myself, preparing myself for the inevitable. It was just one
night away—and the trip, and the work, was a reset, a re-
prieve.

Along with those gorgeous compression socks when you travel,
what are you supposed to wear to work during this phase? For many
women, it's common to fluctuate between trying to look like "the
pregnant professional" and, as one contributor put it, "basically feeling like I was wearing a sign that said, 'Yes, I'm pregnant.'"

Clea O'Hana is a fashion-tech entrepreneur and the cofounder
and CEO of the online personal styling service WISHI, as in "Wish I
knew what to wear," founded with celebrity stylist Karla Welch in
2019. The WISHI stylists incorporate what you already own to build
your perfect wardrobe. For your maternity dressing at work, her recommendations followed their guiding principles at WISHI, starting
with what you have and evolving. "There's the dressing for before you
announce your pregnancy and then there is when you are sharing it,"
Clea explains. "But still some people want to make their belly the star
and others want to keep it understated. I have found that there are
moments for both." As for how to make it work, she suggests, "Start
with what you love as part of your look at work and make adjustments, wearing a shirt untucked, layering a jacket, sorting your closet
as you become more pregnant."

I found this to be very true in my own pregnancy, but really could
have used the advice to do it proactively with sorting. Instead, essentially every morning went from "Can you see my belly (or really my
bloating that I was concerned looked like a belly)?" to "Does my belly
look cute?" to "Will I be comfortable all day in this?" with a few very
proud new dresses in between (that I would promptly remove when
I got home and put on my low-rise pj pants). Later in my pregnancy, a
friend recommended wearing tank tops under everything. They were
breastfeeding ones for my newfound chest that would be worn into
the ground over the next several months, including when I returned

to work and didn't want to be fully undressed in the nursing space. Tanks made my pregnancy more comfortable, tucked in at work as my buttons popped and pants struggled to stay where they were supposed to.

My other personal favorite item of clothing during this time was maternity opaque tights. I know this is for those of you who have a place of work where tights are even a consideration, but for me they were a game changer. Supportive and chic, they let me have nonmaternity wear go a little longer and were okay with flat shoes—plus they were a relatively inexpensive investment that I could wear several days a week. In fact, when writing this book I sent a love letter to Sara Blakely of Spanx, an entrepreneur, literal supporter of women, and a mother.

Many women also shared that they did not want to buy maternity clothes, and certainly you don't need to, but investing in a few pieces that you build into your budget or borrowing a friend's might help give you a boost for key moments at work—even if you're not physically going anywhere except down the hall in your home to a computer. And while I have always personally subscribed to the idea of dressing for the job you want, when you're pregnant, above all you must be comfortable and safe. As Clea shared, "You stay who you are while your body evolves. Don't force yourself into a new look just because you are pregnant, but you do want to make sure that you make your style adapt to your body."

If you feel powerful in your heels until the end, great, but please be careful to walk gingerly, aware that your center of gravity, offset by your belly, is not being helped by an additional incline. Other women cited their favorite jewelry and new underwear as confidence bolsters. If you have a uniform but there aren't the right maternity options, ask for them or provide alternative solutions. And pass it all on. Those dresses and full belly pants that got me through with poise and polish but never were to be worn again? I passed them along with good vibes.

As you have read, confidence as a theme carries throughout this book, but from what we wear to how we act, it can be made more resolute or waver during pregnancy, including at work.

Clea herself was pregnant with her first child, and as an entrepreneur, she revealed some of the unique challenges of the concurrent timelines of baby and company launch. As the business was in accelerated launch mode, demanding and exciting, her pregnancy progress was flying along as she kept her head down in her work, building her team and setting up the business, which would soon partner with luxury online retailer Farfetch. She shared, "I was concerned about what would happen when I needed to stop, because it's really hard when it's your company to do that—you can't offboard creativity—but I knew I could figure it out for what needed to happen in that moment at the company." But also, as someone who is always the go-to for fashion recommendations for her friends as her second nature, all the other decisions were overwhelming. "How will I find the time to sort through all of the advice, items to buy, things to do before the baby comes?"

As you read in chapter 8, break it down. Ask yourself, what are the must-dos now? What's important to me to manage myself, including what to buy, put on the registry, or ask someone else to recommend? If you cannot "offboard your creativity," as Clea so eloquently stated, what can you delegate now to free up what only you can do? This in fact is how you ultimately create gravitas that lasts by leveraging your strengths.

CREATING LASTING GRAVITAS

Many working women I interviewed in my research do not yet have children, but aspire to, when they see the successful pregnant executive, expert, or icon. They use phrases like "*and* she is pregnant" to emphasize the inspiring impact, instead of the alternative "*but* she is pregnant." While I personally feel pulled to share with them the amount of effort that goes into what they see *and* to normalize the triumph narrative that "of course she can," it is beautiful to hear it in this way without all the caveats. Have this in your mindset, not just the uncomfortable awkwardness in how you walk or what you wear, or regardless of whether you are physically pregnant at all. Pregnancy when visible at work can symbolize owning your femininity with grace, power, and confidence. You *can* "own it," and these attributes, in combination with presence and trust, define gravitas.

Gravitas is about creating or augmenting the type of influence that lasts even while you're on maternity leave, and certainly when you return. Gravitas is a key characteristic for dynamic leadership. Leveraging your strengths is one of the ways to create gravitas in The Push, allowing you to deliver for yourself and those around you. In addition, organization, including delegation and clear communication, build trust and community. Together these skills create momentum that propels you in this phase and beyond to create a supercharged, self-aware moment for you and those around you.

Windsor Hanger Western recounted a time when she felt gravitas. "Especially in the later months it can be a total boss move to do public speaking engagements with a large pregnant belly. I spoke at the Cannes Lions festival when seven months pregnant and spoke at the White House and got to meet Michelle Obama while eight months pregnant. I loved being there and celebrating what the female body is capable of."

In addition, a mentor and contributor to my research, Sarah François-Poncet, writer, speaker, and former global general counsel at a major organization, shared her formative memory, and the importance of capturing its power for the future.

I was a thirty-year-old American lawyer, practicing law and living in Paris. I was a salaried employee at that time, and therefore benefited from the more generous French maternity leave. However, I felt fine and kept working until what I thought would be my last week of pregnancy—which turned out to be my last day!

I still had some work to do. Before I left work for home, I drafted, printed, and signed an important letter that would be ready to go out the next day. My contractions started the next morning, and, lo and behold, I had my daughter that afternoon. Back at the office, my assistant ensured that the letter went out under my signature on the day my daughter was born. I kept a copy of it in my daughter's baby book as a memory that her mother could—and did—do it all.

Leveraging Your Strengths

While there are many stories in this book of women who pivoted or tried something new during their pregnancy, in this changing time, they also used their best abilities and experiences to stand firm before reaching for something new. Leveraging your strengths is how you can feel good about what you are doing, set up those around you for success, including in your absence, and show your value in a natural way. Realizing that you are the ultimate teammate for ideation, the one who best connects others, or whose attention to detail is unparalleled, is a gift. Unsure of what your strengths are? Ask those around you today. Ask your friends or partner. Recognizing and utilizing your unique skills in this time is incredibly appreciated by the teammates of working mothers I spoke to, along with their "crazy efficiency."

Leveraging your strengths can also help you recognize when you are overcompensating during the Push phase. Throughout the research for this book, I found this was an ongoing challenge for many women who were trying to fight against a change in the perception of their abilities during pregnancy. But the problem isn't just the implicit demand on you in the moment. It is the potential for burnout.

This can happen in two ways. One, you could be pushing so hard during your pregnancy that once the baby arrives you might feel it isn't worth it to be away from your children and work this hard, especially when after the childcare, commute, and lunch you might be "making forty-five dollars a week." Two, you could have such high demands of yourself and your employer when you come back post-baby ("I accomplished more than any other human in my role ever, *and* I was pregnant") that you are left unsatisfied and with unrealistic expectations of promotion or change in responsibility.

Lastly, keep in mind that this Push is yours, and you must be aware that those around you aren't pregnant (well, technically sometimes they are, but that requires its own set of advice), and they don't have the same finite window, yet are implicated. Remember, you do not owe anyone anything by being pregnant at work. Sure, you shouldn't slack off and say to your diligent teammates that now you have new priorities and they just went down a rung (even if they did). But you can recognize that this is a moment for them too in a way, that they will surely appreciate, and likely miss, your strengths.

Organization and Delegation

Time, as we have discussed, is finite. Honing your efficiency and reliability through organization and delegation skills including during pregnancy is invaluable. Right about now you might be thinking, "No shit. How possible is it to be organized in these few months of The Push, on top of your usual work and being very pregnant?"

Organization is primarily about lists. I have a strange system, but one that works for me. I have to-do lists in my phone that are longer-term items or things that I don't want to forget on the go. Then I have lists in a notebook that I revisit on a weekly basis. Finally, I have Post-its. These sticky notes are the intention-setting, get-this-done-now, day-of notices. Sorting to-do items among sticky notes or the long-term lists clears my mind and allows me to focus my time where it needs to be in the moment.

You may have your own ways of being prepared. Do what makes you feel comfortable but ensure you find a clear method and time to set you up for success. How can you carve out the time for organization that will ultimately benefit you later? Can you find an hour a week to revisit these checklists and cross a few items off? Every Sunday, I revisit the prior week, review the week ahead, check in with my husband and childcare to see if there's anything out of the ordinary that isn't on my master calendar, and then share it with everyone. My husband doesn't like to be handed a list (surprise!), or a shared Google Doc, but does like invites on the calendar with details in the body, emails, and texts—which he also sends to me, and then I sort into my own system.

At work, I try not to give people to-dos outside of our regular meetings if they are not urgent. Instead, I keep lists in a running document on my computer that I use for me to share verbally and allow for clarifications, and use the communication that they generally prefer to keep boundaries in place, if more urgent. I encourage the same from my team. You don't have to have this list obsession, but you do have to find what works for you—and what works for them.

However, keep in mind that handing a list to someone isn't generally effective unless this is the process you have established together, and you've been clear about what you are delegating. Are you giving your direct report free rein on a project that previously you would have handled start to finish? Or are handing it off as a work in progress that you need to be completed in a certain way? Or is it for them to reach a goal however they see fit? Additionally, what are the timelines or other parameters that maybe you know but aren't obvious to them? Think about how you can power others around you with gravitas—so that you also will be elevated, stretched, and grow like your belly.

Delivering

The last part about creating gravitas that lasts while you're pregnant is about follow-through. I call it delivering. What have you committed to for yourself, and what will happen if you don't deliver on these commitments? As time passes in The Push, realistically revaluate that list. What is going to give you energy and not feel like a drag on the energy that you need for work, but more importantly, for your health?

With that in mind, ensure that you uphold what you have dedicated to completing, even as you get further into your pregnancy. Gravitas is about reliability and about trust, and something that is earned with a bit more difficulty as you are pregnant because of the perception. Remember, you're not delivering on responsibilities or communicating to overcompensate, you're doing both because it's responsible. You are competent and are going to deliver what you said you were going to do even if that has been pivoted to properly ensure that someone knows the last status of your work before the birth of your baby is imminent. Emergencies and exceptions happen, but often there is a way to be more open and transparent on the status of work as you head toward the biological finish line.

If you can't carry through on a commitment, then communicate that and why, and your recommendation on how to see it through. Is this a task someone else can do? What do they need to succeed? Or is it something that just isn't going to happen, and you are sorry, and then everyone moves on? It doesn't have to be a dissertation, just an acknowledgment that creates gravitas and manages expectations for the future.

If something drops, it's okay, but it's also okay to be super proud and pumped that you completed a milestone while creating your personal milestone. Normalizing pregnancy at work is about sharing your day-to-day triumphs and failures with vulnerability, appreciation, and recognition. It is also about honoring our limits and knowing what we need for ourselves, especially during the Push phase.

Robin Arzón is a bestselling author, ultramarathoner, vice president of fitness programming and head instructor at Peloton, and mother. She fearlessly left behind a successful law career to embark on new adventures in the health and wellness space and has since reinvented herself into an avid ultramarathon runner and global fitness leader. Her life's mission is to "redefine, reform, and rethink possibility through movement." Robin's first children's book celebrates this mission for her daughter, Athena. She told me, "*Strong Mama* was written as a love letter about the journey they took on together as training partners, and teaches kids that self-care is not selfish, and movement is medicine."

Personally, this deeply resonates with me. When I go for a run, I tell my sons, "I'm going to get strong for me—and for you." You're going on a run; this fact doesn't need to be framed negatively or with an apology. It's a way to establish for our children that it's important we take care of ourselves without guilt.

This goes for work too. Many women spoke about leaving for work, even when working from home, as a tough pull. You are providing for your child or future child, and being fulfilled as a person by your job is a positive driving force—an opportunity to model your relationship to work that can and should be ongoing when you return to work.

Robin shares a moment of delivering through The Push by trusting yourself:

> My pregnancy at work was public with millions of people in my live classes along for the journey. Together with my husband, we decided to announce our pregnancy during a Peloton ride, early in my second trimester. I was teaching five days a week, developing programming, and my schedule did not slow down. I have a super supportive team, but I had no idea how my body would react. I felt pressure not only to create the programs I was already doing but to be a very visible pregnant athlete. Our first at Peloton.
>
> I was fortunate that I had an easy pregnancy, which allowed me to continue to do rides and strength training. With our wellness council including an OB, I created the first pregnancy and postpartum content beyond yoga, and I was very

authentic about how I was feeling. It was important for me to show it was possible, from a place of strength, with thoughtful modifications. It was very intentional. While I encourage "modify, modify, modify" for pregnant athletes, I also don't want to talk down to them. I want birthing folk to have enough confidence and body awareness both for their workouts but also for their doctors or their care providers, for those around them they need in support. You are in these intensely personal moments, and you have to trust yourself. You know what's up.

Motherhood to me feels intuitive. I was thirty-nine when I had Athena, I know who I am. I have an inner knowing that I'm supposed to be her mother. I have a curated scope of influence. That scope of influence, those whom you have around for advice and support when you need them, is just that—curated. You need to know when to shut it off. Some of the best advice I received from my friend Eva Longoria Bastón, when I asked her what she wished she would have known before becoming a mother. She said, "I wish I knew less, I wish people told me less." What you need to know you will educate yourself, you will ask for, and you will receive advice from those you trust. Again, trust yourself.

The idea to Carry Strong for Meghan Duggan, the Olympic athlete whose reflections were shared in chapter 5, with the lens of her inspiring athletic career, took on two meanings. "On the physical side, I worked out and trained as a professional athlete until the day I delivered—it was important to me, I loved that my body was able to do that for me—of course with some modifications, but I was really energized for myself and my son. Pregnancy was a time of real assessment to think about both my health and my son's.

"Mentally, when I think of Carry Strong, the word is truly 'empowering.' Every single day you are creating an amazing environment to guide you in your decisions, which is important, including creating the best, safest environment for the child you are growing and assessing what world you want to be part of. This hyperconscious and aware feeling is that of being deliberate, which I embraced then and do now."

Being a "professional pregnant person" is not ironic. It is normal. Leverage your strengths, get organized, and deliver through managing expectations and delegating to create lasting gravitas. Throughout The Push phase, remember that pregnancy is temporary. Enjoy the drive if you feel it and push when you want to push and enjoy the feelings of gratitude for what your body and mind are doing without guilt. Reflect and take a break when you need a break; reset the best ways you know how. It is likely that no one else is putting the kind of pressure on you that you are on yourself. Most importantly, know your limits—trust and take care of yourself. Cherish this moment to celebrate where you are.

QUESTIONS FOR REFLECTION

What are the important things to do in this phase to set yourself up for success as you head toward having your baby?

When have you felt the highest high in this phase? Lowest low? How can you capture the energy of that high to propel you through the lows?

Take a moment to reflect on where you are right now. That belly and you have been through a lot, you spend a lot of time together, you are pregnant at work—both creating your child and working on your career concurrently. Talk about impressive!

Carry Strong Stories

LAUREN GORES IRELAND, DIGITAL CREATOR AND COFOUNDER OF SUMMER FRIDAYS

I was seven months pregnant, at 1:33 in the morning, and the weight of my career fears crumbled: how will I do both? *I was in the midst of beginning a business and wondered if it was the worst idea I'd ever had. Why now? Why start something so new as I begin a chapter of my personal life I waited so long for? Will my child be proud of the work I do someday?*

The questions were infinite, and my mind was exhausted. It was 2017, by the way, and there seemed to be this movement around becoming a multihyphenate: mother, career woman, philanthropist, and whatever else you could fit into a bio. It all sounded good, but the reality seemed nearly impossible, and I felt a lot of self-doubt.

That night—or early morning, I should say—I texted my own mother and asked her how I would do it. How would I keep up with career goals I had spent the last decade working toward, while also being the present mom I had always wanted to be? And she said, "You won't be both every day, but you can *be both some days, and your success in either role will never be defined by a single day. Remember that, and so the hard days won't feel so permanent."*

She was right, even though it has taken me four-plus years to believe her. Some days I miss something at work because my son needs me at preschool pickup. Some days I miss preschool pickup because of work. But I know for a fact I am better at both of my roles because of the other, and I feel most at home with myself as a working mom.

TANYA PRIVE, ENTREPRENEUR, FOUNDER LEPRIVÉ

I walked into my doctor's office for what I thought would be a regular twenty-six-week prenatal checkup. I was pregnant with identical twins, which meant that my pregnancy was high risk, but everything had been going smoothly so far, other than the discomfort of carrying two babies in my slender frame. So when my husband, Alejandro Cremades, offered to accompany me, I insisted he stay at work and deal with all the pressing matters at Onevest—a company we had founded together close to eight years earlier, which we had decided to sell. Before taking off, I told Alejandro that I'd meet him at the office later, unaware that our lives were about to be turned upside down and forever changed.

That was the day our in-utero twins, Liv and Alya, were diagnosed with twin-to-twin transfusion syndrome, a rare condition affecting the placenta in identical twin pregnancies, where blood is transfused disproportionately from one twin (donor) to the other (recipient), causing the donor to have decreased blood volume and the recipient to be overloaded with blood, which often results in the death of one or both babies. This pivotal moment unleashed a series of events in the following three hundred days that would plunge us into the depths of uncertainty and pain, reshape our priorities, drive us to experience life-altering learnings, find power in facing adversity, and discover the true meaning and extraordinary healing power of love.

How did we cope with having our twin daughters' lives swaying on the tightrope between life and death? How did we manage to charge ahead with the acquisition of our company and handle the elephant-load of pressure that came with knowing that if the sale did not go through we would lose everything: our incomes, the endless hours of work and deep personal investment throughout the last eight years, and our investors' money, which in part included close friends and family?... The same principles in self-development training that led us to launch and grow our exponentially successful company were now the ones that would help us triumph over adversity and overcome the most difficult experience of our lives.

KARA MCEACHERN, OPTOMETRIST

I was living the dream life of a mom in her early thirties. I was working part time while also staying at home with my five- and two-year-olds, with one on the way. My life forever changed at a follow-up appointment at the perinatologist for our twenty-week ultrasound, when I heard the words that no mother ever wants to hear. "We think there is something wrong with the baby's heart."

I knew with my medical background that this was not just a simple hole in his heart, and this was going to be the beginning of an unimaginable ride. The shock, the grief, the worry, the fear of the unknown took my breath away, but I knew I had to stay as levelheaded as possible to fight for my unborn baby.

From the ultrasound, my husband and I rushed straight to the cardiology department at the children's hospital. After a three-hour echocardiogram on my pregnant belly, our fetal cardiologist was able to diagnose my baby with complex congenital heart disease (CHD), with four heart defects. The next part of the visit I wouldn't wish on anyone.... We discussed the need for an amniocentesis, the surgical repair options and their predicted survival rates, life expectancy, and the option for a medically necessary late-term termination. These things can be hard to hear, but it is important that parents are aware of all parts of the journey they are about to embark on.

The next step for us was to find the right heart center that would give our baby the best chance for a full heart repair and the best quality of life. With the help of our amazing fetal cardiologist, Dr. Nita Doshi, we researched different heart centers and their published survival and complication rates. Ultimately we decided the best place for our baby was at Lucile Packard Children's Hospital at Stanford, four hundred miles from my home in Southern California.

Now came the hard part. I would have to move to Palo Alto at thirty-six weeks pregnant to birth my baby at the Children's Hospital, where they would have the heart team in place to care for him. We knew that most likely our baby would need at least two surgeries, one to limit blood flow to the lungs to let him grow, and then one for a full heart repair. Not knowing how long I would be living in Northern California, I let my boss know when my last days would be working for him. I told him I didn't know if I would be on leave for four months or eighteen months, and that I knew he couldn't hold the position for me with such uncertainty. The next day, to my surprise he told me, "Your job will be waiting for you whenever your baby is healthy enough for your return."

Max was born and was rushed straight to the NICU. At ten days old he had his first major heart surgery. After twenty-eight days and many complications we were allowed to go home. The next few months were filled with countless appointments and therapy sessions. At eight months old Max was stable enough that I returned to work with an office full of staff and patients that had been following Max's heart journey and rooting for our family!

My son's diagnosis forever changed how I look at life. I truly view every day with him as a gift, because without medical intervention he would not have made it to his first birthday. Through the worst day in my life, my son's CHD diagnosis, I have found the best in people and the most joy in the mundane. Work allowed my mind to shift away from the what-ifs while I was pregnant and focus on the right now. It was the only time of the day when I was able to think about things other than CHD.

CHITRA POURANA, HEALTH AND WELLNESS COACH

I had worked at the same company with the same boss for several years. Continuing my work in accounting was part of a long-term career plan. I felt secure in my role, yet when I got pregnant, the typical workplace fears crept through me. I had worked hard early on in my career, got an MBA, a CPA, and was progressing well at work and on the path to an upcoming promotion to VP.

During my maternity leave, my fears came true. I got a phone call from my boss that he was moving on to a different role and the organizational structure had changed. I was upset that I would return to a new team and role, but I wasn't ready to rock my work world and look for another job during this sensitive time as a new mom. I returned with a positive attitude after fourteen weeks of maternity leave. Little did I know what I was walking into. I was very different. It would have been challenging even without being a new mom.

I stopped breastfeeding earlier than planned to cope with the pressures. It was a hostile environment. I pulled through it for a while until my bonus in the following year was cut in half, and the reason given to me was that my role had changed. I felt like I was being pushed around and pushed out of my job. That was the day I decided that this was not my calling. I had to make a change. I have always had a keen interest in health and nutrition. Both during pregnancy and after, from nurturing my own body to feeding my family, I was unknowingly moving toward a new direction. During the last year at my work, I enrolled in nutrition school and became a health and wellness coach with advanced nutrition studies in hormone health. I am also a meditation guide and sound bowl practitioner. It brings me great joy in helping other women incorporate wellness into their busy lifestyles.

CHAPTER 10

Phase V

Anticipating the Great Return (or Not)

I N THIS FINAL chapter, we *anticipate* your great return to work post-baby (or not). This phase is defined more broadly than the other four phases, which are delineated by specific threshold points. Instead, this phase may occur concurrent to The Push, or you may experience this mindset shift closer to your due date, or even after your baby's birth. In this phase, you will both prepare for and project what that return to work after baby could look like, whether it is a few days, weeks, or months (or longer) down the road.

Remember, this could all change, and while it's not worth over-thinking everything, there are some things that are good to know for navigating this phase with comfort and confidence. There are three key topics in this chapter with that in mind—the walk-through, on-boarding and offboarding, and knowing your value.

Before going further, I want to acknowledge that the number one thing that makes women comfortable in preparing for work post-baby is job protection with paid leave. Legally, job protection, as you read in part I, is part of the Pregnancy Discrimination Act (PDA), which "forbids discrimination based on pregnancy when it comes to any aspect of employment, including hiring, firing, pay, job assignments, promotions, layoff, training, fringe benefits, such as leave and health insurance, and any other term or condition of employment."[1] Maternity leave in the United States is regulated by U.S. labor law and the Family and Medical Leave Act of 1993 (FMLA), and requires unpaid, job-protected leave for eligible mothers of newborn or newly adopted children. It also requires that their group health benefits be maintained during the leave.[2] There are requirements for eligibility, including the size of the organization and the amount of time you have been there.

While statistics vary greatly regarding the percentage of public and private companies that provide some portion of paid leave, and there are supplemental policies at the state level, the fact remains that the United States at the time of this writing is the only industrialized country in the world not to have a federal policy in place.[3] It is certain that policy changes are needed to address the spread of benefits to future mothers like you. Today it is incredibly variable. Some women are returning to work mere days after giving birth, while others, mostly at large companies, have a four- to six-month combination of paid, partial-paid, and unpaid leave to heal and care for their children, normalizing that they will return to the workplace, retained and not at a physical, mental, or financial deficit due to their leave requirements, because of choice or need.

In fact, there are mothers who have had very different maternity leaves across their pregnancies even if they worked at the same employer throughout, due to the consistent evolution of policies across the United States. Kate Gold, whose advice we read in chapter 2, had four children over the course of nine years and was employed by the same company. Her story gives us hope for a positive evolution:

For my first baby, I was given six weeks paid leave and I remember saving my annual bonus that year so that I could "pay myself" during the remaining six weeks of maternity leave. For the second baby, the policy changed while I was on leave to cover full pay for the twelve weeks, and I was able to get retroactive pay for that time. But for my fourth baby, not only was I paid for the full amount of leave, but I was able to take six months to bond with my baby! I know I am incredibly lucky to have any paid maternity leave at all, but I hope this trajectory advances leave for all families welcoming children into their lives.

In addition, I want to acknowledge why the second part of this chapter's name, the "or Not," is important. It's because choosing not to return to work after your baby is born is okay! And it's in parentheses because this book's objective is to rethink pregnancy and work with the goal of curbing pipeline attrition for working women who today may feel as if their desire to become a mother restricts their potential at work, and that sentiment can be influenced during pregnancy. One of the book's ambitions is to bring light to the fact that one out of two women in my study said their treatment during the pregnancy had an impact on their decision to return to work (35 percent positive, 13 percent negative).

That doesn't mean that it's a bad thing to not return to work if that's what you chose. You can return to work at any point after having children, from months to years later, not just only if you take a temporary leave. You can come back to a totally different type of work with a new schedule, or none of the above. There are many reasons why what you thought you would do may change—including the needs of your child, as was the case for many women whose stories are in this book.

Katherine Schwarzenegger Pratt shared this sentiment with a poignant insight from her mother, Maria Shriver. "Both routes are incredibly admirable. I will never forget when my brother was young, that my mom was talking to one of his friend's mothers, who said, 'I'm just a mom' in response to her talking about a recent work trip. She said, 'Take that sentence out of your vocabulary. You are not just a mom. Be proud of that role. If you are doing seventy-five other ones or if you are doing one with your sole focus, it is a really tough, fun, rewarding, and some days impossible role, so just get rid of the 'just.'"

Contributor to my research, actor Sara Sohn, who is now the co-host of the refreshing *Being Bumo* podcast (*bumo* means "parent" in Korean), recounted her decision to step away from work with reflective insights:

> When my second child was months old I booked my first little role in a studio film. I was still nursing exclusively, and once my booking was confirmed I had ten days to wean her so I could spend four nights in Atlanta. My daughter wouldn't take a bottle, but I left anyway, because my lactation consultant assured me all babies take the bottle at some desperate point. And she did. And she was fine. I felt excited, grateful, and deserving to be on set surrounded by some of the most successful people in my industry. But something changed. What I desired for myself became less important to me. I finished shooting my scenes and flew back home.
>
> I stopped auditioning for a few years and felt empowered in that decision. I choose to stay home. I choose to live simply. I choose to use my time and talents to build a happy, peaceful, and healthy home.... There were moments of doubt, but I wish I had the assurance I have now—to know that I can't lose when I focus on others, especially family. I wish I had known that by focusing on my babies I would find inner healing, and ironically use that to become a better actor. There is no right answer. Your worth is not tied to your job. There is so much more than your job. A healthy and peaceful family that you nurture is something to be proud of.

YOUR WALK-THROUGH

One thing I recommend before you start thinking about career moves or lifestyle changes post-pregnancy is quite simple—do a walk-through of your day-to-day. This concept can be helpful to imagine what life could be like, in order to set expectations and educate yourself for what you may need to change. The walk-through can also give you peace of mind as you anticipate obstacles, reducing stress and points of friction. While nothing can prepare you for the curveballs of life post-pregnancy, doing a walk-through can be a helpful learning exercise. Professional athletes often use visualization techniques to get their mind set for a big game. You can do the same thing for your life with baby.

First, do a walk-through at home. Literally, walk into your front door. Where will you go with the baby? If it's to their room, imagine you come in the door and you need to change a diaper—which side is easier for you to use while the other hand is holding a wiggly belly? Where are you going to breastfeed and/or pump if you choose to do so? How are you going to store and clean parts? You get the idea. For me, this was especially helpful to prepare for the arrival of my second baby. I needed to think through the basics so that I could remove stress and enjoy the last moments with my first son.

Second, while you're still at work with your big belly, walk through what it could be like when the baby is on the "other side." Start at home. What does the commute look like? Do you need to add additional time for childcare handoff or drop-off? Do you have a backup in mind? Do you have everything you need to pack up for baby and for you? If you have a partner, what is their role in your work/baby morning routine? What is your ideal timeline? When you get to your place of work, do still want to go to your favorite place to get a coffee or get to work on the early side a few days and leave a little earlier than you used to? If you're working from home, what does getting ready for work look like? When you're at work, will you have your phone or your smartwatch ping you if the caregiver or day care calls? And so on. This will change as "seasons" change for you and your little one, but it's worth thinking about and imagining the best (and not the best) case scenarios.

With regard to breastfeeding, should you decide that is the plan for you and your baby, this is one part of the walk-through that I think is incredibly helpful. Setting yourself up for success and thinking through this part of your return to work isn't just about the ability to pump/breastfeed, it is about reducing the strain and time at each checkpoint. Identify what you will need logistically to feel comfortable. Find the space, determine how it is reserved if relevant, and figure out where the refrigerator is and where can you store supplies—like backup valves (ugh) for the pumps, depending on your style and manufacturer.

When I was very pregnant with my son William, I brought up to my HR partner that the pumping situation—women were using a bathroom stall where the terrible noise reverberated—was less than ideal. It made me nervous and uncomfortable. Even if I wasn't going to be able to breastfeed, I wanted the option, and that was my sticking point in being able to imagine my life at work post-baby—not the travel or challenging projects, the fact that someone could hear the pump. Quite a lot of women agreed. I am so grateful to her today, because before I ever needed it, a new door with an appropriate lock and comfy chairs were in place.

Amy VanHaren is the founder and CEO of Pumpspotting, a community-driven breastfeeding and baby-feeding support app that creates a nurturing environment and includes places to pump and how-to content, and mother of two. She shares her story with expert advice for mothers-to-be and insights on how companies can foster breastfeeding-friendly cultures: "I was in the corporate world for an organic food company, helping to feed people for a very long time, then I had to commute and pump in a closet with a broken chair to feed my first child. With my second I was an entrepreneur running my own agency, yet when I went back to work, again I felt it incredibly difficult to make breastfeeding and pumping work [at work]."

But Amy became invested in finding a solution:

When I brought my daughter home from the hospital, I hadn't taken the pump out of the box and milk was pouring out, my father and my husband trying to help me by attaching whatever piece they could to another. But then I was flying across the country every other week, nursing, pumping, thinking about it when I wasn't doing it—where to do it, physically pumping in Ubers, hotels, everywhere, plus how to ship, store, and keep it going. . . .

Exhausted and overwhelmed, on a very dirty bathroom floor with the line of women waiting for the stall, my pump sounded like Darth Vader. I was beside myself wanting to quit all of it, but instead I texted my sister, and she said, "You've got this."

Through technology like the Pumpspotting app, you are immediately not the only woman who is navigating how to feed your family and pursue your career for what has been estimated as an additional full-time job at eighteen hundred hours a year.[4] This also highlights another important point. As Amy says, "Breastfeeding is invisible work. It's something unseen, especially at the workplace."

Amy explains, "There is a federal law in place called Break Time for Nursing Mothers that requires employers with fifty or more employees to provide reasonable break time for an employee to express breast milk, and a private place to do so other than a bathroom, for up to one year. There are also varying workplace breastfeeding laws in over thirty states. Awareness of the laws and protections can be confusing and lacking, and it can be uncomfortable even to ask, so it is important to give breastfeeding at work visibility." That's why Amy also bought a twenty-five-year-old RV and turned it into the "breast express"—a nursing and pumping suite to bring to moms' front doors, workplaces, birthing centers. She shares that during her travels it "became really clear through talking to women that workplace support was needed to remove barriers for parents and remove them for employers—creating an ease between the two."

Amy's advice for both mothers-to-be and employers is to remove logistical, physical, and cultural barriers for pumping in the workplace, not just create a "wellness room." Number one, have a conversation with your employer about what returning to work post-baby is going to look like for you. Not just the policy, but how is this experience going to play out? Humanize with your direct manager your intentions around this and get your support before you need it. Prepare *with* your employer—saying ahead of time with your team this is what you need.

Number two, prepare your mindset that whatever your feeding journey looks like is great for you and your family, as with everything, expectations are going to change, and every day looks different, just like your baby looks different at every stage. Amy shares, "Remember it is about supply and demand which means it is ever changing. Be gentle to yourself. If it is helpful for your mindset you can even do an intention for each pump—a mantra that keeps you going and gives a pause from the chaos of the day."

Think about who you will call if you need a boost to get this mindset right. You also need to prepare your gear, and this includes food and water to fuel you in a way that makes you happy. Get organized, including having extra supplies, and have your partner or someone who is supporting you take part of the responsibility of prep.

Lastly, and most importantly, be protective of your breastfeeding/ pumping. Don't compromise on your decision and be proud to have that time—it matters for your milk supply. Be proud, not pressured. Create a system that works for you. Make your schedule and stick to it. Reassess if it is not working or as you switch your amount or frequency of breastfeeding if applicable.

Amy also shared advice for employers, which I think is a very helpful and refreshing perspective for you to have in mind:

Remember that this is a human journey, and everyone is an individual; it's not just about checking a list, not only about a policy or a place to do it, but needs to be done by looking holistically, collectively removing the barriers all around. Instead of reinforcing barriers, help your employees to feel proud, and to never feel seen as less. There is a big difference between being a breastfeeding-tolerant environment and a breastfeeding-supportive environment. Pull it out of the closet, talk about it at the senior levels—but don't superhumanize it. There is nothing wrong with that pump or feed if that's important to you and your family. If she misses one session it can derail her plan to feed her child, a health ramification, but in setting her up for success you are building deep loyalty.

DOUBLE DOWN ON YOUR BOUNDARIES

As you anticipate the return to work after baby, take a moment again to revisit the boundaries you want to have, or may need, for your return before you go. What boundaries do you need now or do you want to have on your leave? Can you start putting any of those in play, or try them out? For example, where you may have previously been very responsive at night or on the weekends, can you try limiting it more, or better communicating when you will be working outside of what your place of work and role demands? Or what control do you have of your schedule, of your partner's schedule, of your childcare, of travel?

Recently I gave advice to a dear friend who was preparing to return to work. She was stressed because she would miss the playful and awake time with her new son when she went back to work, plus she was most productive in late afternoons and evenings at work. I suggested she approach her employer with the suggestion that she temporarily start work later in the day two days a week, so that she could have the mornings with her happy baby and could power through her evenings like she used to, without the guilt and COMO. Her husband would ensure he was home one of those later days and her nanny would shift her schedule one of the days. Notably, she could have those evenings for later work, but also if she wanted to use them to see friends or just not have to rush home. Sometimes just a few hours are what we need to refill our batteries.

Like everything, this could be a temporary shift, just like kids' naps, that for a short time really matters to you, even if it is more of a minor, if any, disruption to work. If you are on a set schedule based on your place of work, do you have other things that you want to tack on to the start or end of your day based on childcare? Or do you need a few evenings a week so that the usual tasks you do when you come in the door you can do later at night while your child sleeps, and you can play when you come home instead?

As you read in chapter 2, those margins become even more valuable in The Great Return, to allow you to adjust to your new normal and manage your priorities. Calling these pockets of time "margins" doesn't discredit (or marginalize) them, it just means that you need to allow for them and count them out, squeezing a little space between those big responsibilities—including time for yourself—without guilt.

This time is still important to me, every darn day. It's where this book was written—a magical "unicorn time" that you'll hear about in the conclusion. As you prepare for leave, during it, and when you return, that time for you is important.

YOUR OFFBOARDING PLAN

In my first study, only about half of women felt comfortable transitioning for maternity leave, while 19 percent were uncomfortable.[5] One common reason was that there is a sense of urgency. One contributor said, "I felt as if I was waving my hands saying, 'I'm not going to be here, people!'" In addition, many women shared that they "could use some reassurance" during this time both that everything is going to continue without them and that they would not be forgotten as that happens.

Contributor Michele Ganeless went on maternity leave when she adopted her daughter. Although she was further into her career, she expressed worry that her absence would jeopardize her role:

> *I was already president of a [television] network at the time. I worried when to tell the company that I was trying to adopt a child and how I would handle my job responsibilities once my daughter was born. However, the real struggle for me was more about my time on maternity leave. I had a great team and a great boss, and I knew the company was in good hands. I kept tabs on what was going on, but not on a day-to-day basis (I had a newborn, after all), but as it got further into my maternity leave and closer to the time I was due to return to work, I started to have incredible self-doubt. Would they decide they didn't need me if my team could handle the work? Even if they couldn't legally fire me, would people treat me differently, would I be perceived in a different way by my peers, staff, or my superiors?*
>
> *I wish I could go back and tell myself how valuable I was to the company—but it felt like another version of impostor syndrome, and in the moment it was hard to see clearly. The lack of sleep didn't help.*

As you get closer and closer to your delivery date, use the gravitas that lasts to delegate, elevate, and thoughtfully communicate, but not overcompensate at work, so that you prepare your colleagues for your departure and smooth return. Easier said than done. Offboarding, that is, handing over your work responsibilities or work in progress when you are preparing for maternity leave (or leaving a job altogether) can feel very awkward. Without alignment about what's theoretically supposed to happen, even when you have a direct supervisor who is on it, it can feel like a game of favors, perceived grabbing for power, and/or falling through the cracks. But this is a game you can play where everyone can win (or let's just go for not lose).

Dr. Amy Wechsler, one of only a small handful of physicians in the country who is board certified in both dermatology and psychiatry, an author and mother of two, captured this important awareness. Amy shared with me, "I think it's normal to feel guilty about leaving work for maternity leave, because kind, hardworking women never want to burden others with more work." Reframe this as normal, shared positive responsibility, and collectively, not just "on" others. She adds, "Apologizing for being pregnant and having a baby does not feel good. We must stop apologizing, but the environment around women needs to make the idea never cross her mind."

Deciding who can do what, what resources are needed, and when transitions should happen can't all be on you, but you may need to drive the plan. For example, from a timing perspective, generally it is better for you to have your responsibilities and tasks already off your plate a few weeks before maternity leave. At this point, you should just be adding consulting value instead of trying to tie everything in a bow while you're going into labor.

Here are a few scenarios to have in mind to make the offboarding process as smooth as possible. First, if someone is doing a maternity cover for you—i.e., they come in, you go out, you come back, they go out—then the goal is to get them up to speed as soon as possible, transitioning so they are following you, then you're their backup, and the reverse upon your return.

Then there is the spread coverage situation—that is, if you are spreading your responsibilities among your team, you need to ensure clear handoffs, simple next steps for each person to follow, and then re-collection upon your return. I recommend you make a grid or document outlining "who's on first" in this situation if it's not entirely obvious whom someone can go to for each responsibility. Have a point person listed on your email auto-response who also can filter requests.

In some cases, direct reports or more junior peers will step up to cover for you while you're on leave. To them (and often managers who need them and ask them to), this is as an opportunity for a "stretch project" on top of their current responsibilities. This can later mean leverage for a promotion or compensation. Many women also shared that it can come with tension with these teammates upon your return, especially as their boss. They shared a natural response to feel weird about it, but instead we should look at it as an opportunity to lift them up and return the favor. Their success can be your success. Contributor Julie Kaplan, a marketing executive, told me, "If it weren't for my boss who went on maternity leave, I wouldn't have had the opportunity to grow as fast as I have in my career."

So let's look at it differently. One of your team members steps up for you when you are on your leave. In fact, you recommended them for this job because they have shown great initiative and interest. You set them up for success with sufficient offboarding. You come back and they don't want to give back this responsibility. They want acknowledgment of what they did, and that they took it to the next level. It's not something that you shared was a critical part of your retention and drive to return to work. It added value to you, but they are doing a good job, and in fact it has shown you something you would love to stretch on yourself to complement the work. You acknowledge them, create a plan, and share this with your manager, demonstrating ambition and your engaged energy. You both have stepped up.

Asking a direct report or team members to cover for you while you're on leave can also mean you come back to relief and respect. Your teammates may thank you for the things they didn't even know you did for the organization, or that them doing it with partial capacity on top of their own work just wasn't the same.

For all three scenarios or a combination of them, organization is key. Who do they need to know or work with to be successful? Where are the resources necessary to do your job found? Are there emails that can be sent while you're still at work to help loop in on key topics so that you can share what the cover person needs to do next? To ensure that your top priorities don't fall through the cracks, can you create a system of checks and balances—that is, someone who is primarily responsible and someone whose work is already involved and who will ensure that it happens for all of you together?

Lastly, one more reminder that no one is doing you any favors. Covering for a colleague who's having a baby is part of being a good teammate. However, the relationships you have built and the gratitude you express for their effort way beyond the time that you are offboarding or even publicly pregnant at work go a long way when offboarding and ramping back up.

Another thing that you need to do as part of the offboarding process is to ensure that you are up to date on your review processes prior to your leave, including things like offboarding itself and stretch assignments as part of your goals. If you do not have a formal review process, then do a check-in anyway. This is a great direct way to put it all on the table with your manager—how you're feeling, what your expectations are, and where you want to go—so you feel confident and so that upon your return you can use it as a jumping-off point.

Having a check-in with your manager and teammates can also create reassurance prior to your leave. Share your accomplishments and what you are proud of during this time, thank them for their continued support if you received it, and use it as a moment to take stock of how you feel about the scaffolding you have—or don't have.

One thing I always tell students is that if they never get feedback from their manager, or don't have a formal process but wish they had one, say that your professor is making you—or feel free to blame this book. Some starter language: "One of the pieces of advice that I would love to put into action before I leave is to check in with you regarding my performance in the past six months and to share with you some of my thoughts regarding my future ambitions."

It's also incredibly important that you share your development feedback and current assessment of those who work for you if your direct manager will now be responsible for them. This can include identifying their strengths and opportunities, how you work best together, and their current goals and workload. This is something you can do after you have a review with your team members so that you're transparent about what you're sharing with their new/temporary boss. You will want to do this for direct reports if you have them, but also if you have very close cross-functional team members or members who would appreciate your feedback—it doesn't have to be as formal as a review, but it would be helpful to take a moment as part of your transition.

Finally, communicating to your boss and teammates whether you want to be connected or contacted at all during your leave should be part of your offboarding. Having that point person who can be asked for your information if it's absolutely necessary is helpful, but no one should bother you unless you invite it. And even if you invite it, don't be afraid to take it back. Women I spoke to in my research had a range from full disconnect to updates to working significantly, but I encourage you with enthusiasm to navigate this on your own terms, and with the understanding that you need to recover, and you need time with your baby—or more so that they need you very much, especially at the beginning. Maternity leave is not a vacation. The number of times I heard this in interviewing women was staggering. Second- or third-time (or more) parents wanted to shout it as they left their places of work or upon their return.

If you're worried about being disconnected from work for weeks or even months, contributors' suggestions included putting news alerts on for your company or industry to read, scanning the company website weekly, or simply checking in with a friend at work every few weeks. Personally, I enjoyed seeing friend-colleagues in limited amounts, going for walks with the stroller and hearing bits and pieces about the office, but remained truly grateful I could just ignore most of it. I did both times ask those close to me what I needed to know so that I didn't feel out of sorts, like an alien with a breast pump, walking back in after my maternity leaves. I also had a check-in with my boss, the second time over a very nice lunch that made me feel seen, celebrated, and welcome, just prior to returning to work. If this is something you would like, I recommend you make the first move so that they can follow your lead. Otherwise, they should give you the space you deserve—if not, it can have major ramifications for how you feel about coming back.

Ruth was an accessories editor, running all over New York often unnecessarily for a highly demanding and discerning boss, even when she was pregnant with her first child. After a complicated and traumatic birth and challenging recovery, this boss called Ruth continually throughout her leave. As she was nearing the end, she asked her to immediately travel for work, to Switzerland no less, telling her that it was essential. Ruth quit. She shares, "Looking back on it now, I feel that if my boss would have given me the time that I needed, I would have been able to come back to work healthier. All I was asking for was the standard eight weeks of maternity leave when you have a C-section—especially since mine was so complicated. I had preeclampsia, which can be life threatening. I still think about the last phone call we had and how she said, 'I worked freelance and didn't even get a maternity leave. You girls have no idea how lucky you are.' It was a trip that another editor could have taken in my absence. But she just wanted me at her beck and call. I wasn't ready to leave my baby and I needed to heal."

Here are a few examples for your tactical checklist for offboarding. Make sure to adjust for your place of work. You can even have another walk-through of your day-to-day "what people need to know":

- A shared file with key resources, saved in an easy-to-find location and emailed to your team and bookmarked by your point person
- Delegations in systems

- Passwords (within security guidelines)
- Clear your queue with your personal passwords and info stored on your computer (you probably shouldn't have them there anyway).
- Do your expenses if relevant
- Pre-leave review

What if there is no one at work who will cover for you while you're gone? Perhaps you're an entrepreneur or a business owner. Let's hear again from Arianna Taboada, who we heard from in chapter 6. She says, "Think about the system you have in place or that you need to put in place, what do you want to be doing when you return to work or just simply differently when you become a mother (or a mother again)."

With regard to the leave itself, Arianna shares a unique perspective for business owners who have more control over their own leave but also more demands on them as the one to make those plans:

> *Time for that leave is so personalized, dependent on business model, personal needs, and financial reality. For entrepreneurship versus in a corporate lens, the leave including onboarding and offboarding can be much more gradual and uniquely tailored to your needs. Treat this as a silver lining, much more flexibility in shaping how you are on leave versus at work. Do what you need for you and for your business. Remember, you are an asset, you are a big part of your business, and therefore so is your individual health.*

THE GREAT RETURN

Congratulations! The baby is here, maternity leave is over, and it's time to reenter work as a working mother. (Let's hope you're reading this before it's true, but a positive headspace about this time even in the future is important!) After your leave, onboarding is just as important as offboarding. While slightly less than half of women were comfortable for leave, the numbers are similar upon return, with a slightly more positive correlation to comfort upon return. So there is lots of room for improvement (on both).[6]

Women I spoke to shared that you may feel uncomfortable to come back to the job you knew so well before you left, even for just a few short weeks, or maybe it's changed significantly in your absence. They also shared that it might be more of an excited uncomfortable, not necessarily bad, just a little nerve-racking, and that they hope to be met with enthusiasm. You just went through a major life change and an intense physical one, and while this is "normal," it can feel strange, like the first day of school. In fact, similarly, after the first few hours (leaving your child at home or at day care for perhaps the first time isn't everyone's favorite moment), many women shared that the first week back is kind of fun. It's like the day after a break—people want to hear about your baby and ideally give you lots of good energy. You may want to think about how you want to answer the question "How are you?" and how much you want to share about you and the baby broadly. Then week two and three feel "like a landslide." Preplanned outfits and packed bags slip, caregivers or day care have issues, work gets piled back on, and you're not sleeping great. This is where you need to build in a pause and a support system, and anticipate that you may need them after that first push back. At work, you need to be met with clarity and empathy; you want to feel valued.

One of the ways that employees often assess their value—all the time, not just during pregnancy—is to reflect on their résumé. From a timing perspective, you don't need to do this before you go on your leave, which could feel like another thing on your to-do list, but you may want to add it to your list of to-dos in a few months, when perhaps post-baby and a bit of distance to work you have a fresh perspective. Is it up to date? Notably no one is going to say, "And which job was it that you took a maternity leave?" or "Were these things accomplished in the other four years and three months?" And on the rare chance they do ... you might want to think about that job a little more. Even if you don't *need* your résumé or your LinkedIn profile to be updated for future job prospects, by reviewing your résumé as you prepare for your return to work post-baby, you have a moment to reflect and feel solid in your return, or maybe even consider whether you want to push, pause or pivot.

As you read in chapter 2, the pause or pivot are just as important to consider as a push, depending on what you need for you and your family. As you assess with that résumé and these options, revisit the three columns from chapter 2. What am I good at? What do I want to learn? What do I need for my life right now? And for each, where do I get my energy? You will need to keep your reservoir full, especially when physical energy is drained, including from sleep deprivation. This is what contributor Brianna Chan, brand management associate director, did in anticipation of her return to work post-baby:

> *During maternity leave with my second child, I was informed of my performance rewards. As a result of working with HR to converting my team members to full-time employees, I was aware my rewards were below market. I was encouraged to "follow the process" and trust the "formal review cycle" to make things right. However, the rewards shared with me that fall were not commensurate with my level and responsibilities. I took back control and with a twenty-one-month-old and a five-month-old at home and a working husband, I networked, I interviewed, and I landed a job offer to show my value in the marketplace. I presented this on my first day back—showing I can do it all. In hindsight this story feels totally empowering, "like a boss," and sends a message that being a mom doesn't make me any less ambitious/driven.*

Another way to evaluate how you are valued? A clear plan upon your return. Let's look at it from the other side. If you're the manager in this situation with a returning employee, imagine you're hiring a brand-new one. You want them to feel welcome, you want them to be engaged, clear, and up to speed as fast as possible, but you are realistic that they are "new" (or in this case returning from leave). Just before or within the first few days, invite and answer any weird questions they may have—think about releasing a knot in their stomach (one that I always had as a new employee and as a pregnant returning one). Have a welcome-back coffee, tell them that there is a new printer or new type of badge you need for some door, or a weird protocol you are all now following, and do it with sensitivity but not with discrimination, benevolent or otherwise, or microaggressions that will hit especially hard. Workwise—within the first few days share the plan for their first weeks back along with goals for the first month, three months, and six months. This provides tangible and achievable guidance on expectations with time to review them together at each of those checkpoints as you dovetail back into the regular goal setting and review processes that hopefully exist in your workplace.

If you take this approach at the onset of onboarding, you can work through the expectations for when you should be fully up to speed and how to transition your work back (or to something new), then there is less pressure to awkwardly maneuver through it in the next few weeks when you have those life-adjustment moments. Otherwise, I have found that women switch right back to that need to overcompensate, and in fact it can turn off your team members. Remember, they were here covering for you, not on maternity leave. You know how hard that was, and that your body needed the time off work (for the perpetuation of society), but the fact remains that you need to avoid microaggressions too. Someone might not have been as good as you at executing in the way you saw fit, but maybe it was on top of their workload. Instead of saying, "I guess this is in about the same place as when I left it/nothing happened when I was gone," give yourself, and everyone around you, some grace. Then later, a few months in, you're in the groove, using those work and mom skills interchangeably, and possibly even assessing what you want to do in this current role, place of work or not.

AWARENESS OF POSTPARTUM DEPRESSION

There is one more topic that you need to be aware of for you and those in your community while Anticipating the Great Return (or Not): the potential for postpartum depression (PPD) and symptoms that need to be shared with your care provider if you experience them. Keep in mind symptoms can occur at home, at work, and anywhere in between.

PPD is one of the most common medical complications during and after pregnancy.[7] "Approximately 70% to 80% of women will experience, at a minimum, the 'baby blues'—temporary emotional changes which include sadness, sensitivity, and mood swings, and feeling overwhelmed or anxious. When these symptoms persist and evolve further to feelings like isolation including withdrawal, anger, and incapacitating doubt or fear, often also including physical symptoms, it is PPD, which occurs in 10–20% of mothers over-indexing in many non-white ethnicities. In addition, keep in mind that PPD does not need to be postpartum, may occur with pregnancy loss, and can also affect men."[8]

Contributor Hina Choudhary, PharmD, shares that the most common barriers to obtaining professional help include fear of being judged, stigma, lack of information on where to seek help, and time constraints.[9] Dr. Choudhary is associate director at Sage Therapeutics, Inc., which sponsored a survey conducted by HealthyWomen, a nonprofit organization, to highlight this often-overlooked postpartum period, the fourth trimester or the first twelve weeks after a baby is born. She explains, "We saw that of the 261 pregnant women surveyed, 76 percent created a birth plan, and only 21 percent put together a plan of action for the postpartum period. This is why we created and recently launched a new maternal mental health support

program called Check on Mom. The program provides new and expectant moms with information and resources to help them prepare
for and get the support they need during the fourth trimester, including a tool to help put together a maternal mental wellness plan that
captures the mom's needs and postpartum priorities."[10]

While the program does not replace having discussions with a
health care provider, a mom's best resource for individual medical
advice, the program offers new and expectant moms resources, inspirational content, and community, encouraging women to prioritize
their mental health and identify a group of trusted loved ones who
can be of support through the postpartum period and help recognize
symptoms of postpartum depression.

Maryam Nazemzadeh, MD, whom we met in chapter 5, was an associate oculofacial plastic surgeon and new mother when she was
diagnosed with PPD, and ultimately used it as a launching pad for
radical change:

> Motherhood was never an end to me; it represented the begin-
> ning of a new journey. One that I knew would be difficult to
> incorporate into my other identities, but something I knew I
> would do over time. The process of incorporating this new
> identity into my "old life" was challenging, to say the least. I
> thought that it would simply just fit. Instead, I realized that
> every part of my identity had to be reconstructed. It was in
> those moments that I began to crumble. I tried to do every-
> thing the same, plus add motherhood, plus breastfeeding, plus
> spending time with my daughter, plus plus plus. I didn't listen
> to my body. It kept telling me to slow down. I didn't listen. I
> was diagnosed with postpartum depression. I kept going, told
> myself I could take it. And then one day, I couldn't get out of
> bed. It had happened, finally. I broke.
>
> Looking back, all the signs were there. I was short-tempered,
> lashed out, and just wasn't myself. I looked in the mirror and

simply didn't like the woman who was looking back at me. She was tired. So tired. When I broke, I began to question everything. I questioned my job, the people who I had let into my life, but most importantly, I had to look at myself. I had been holding in years of trauma that was so desperately trying to come out and heal. That's the beauty of motherhood. It gives women a chance to question their own identity, but we're told not to go inward, to keep pushing outward. We're taught to keep doing, keep giving, all the while we are emptying ourselves.

I had to change.... I learned to say no, draw hard boundaries, and do things that aligned with my soul. I surrounded myself with women who didn't judge what kind of mother I was, didn't tell me that my daughter needed to spend more time with me or that I was doing something wrong. I chose to align myself with women who could hear me, see me, and walk next to me on my path to healing. I had to heal, and my outward life had to match that process.

I got to work. One by one, every part of who I was had to be reexamined. I decided that my work environment wasn't conducive to growth, so I quit with no backup plan. Drastic times called for drastic measures. For the first time in my life, I learned how to find comfort in the chaos. I was rebuilding, which meant being uncomfortable. I chose self-care and self-love. I spent time away from my family to be alone. I gave myself space and time. I chose not to feel guilty if I didn't spend every ounce of free time with my daughter. It was my time now and I had to refill to make her full.

Maryam reflected on her story: "Looking back, I wouldn't change a thing. The breaking was my awakening. My God was it painful, but my God, the change that came from it was transformative. Coming out of postpartum depression, coming out of the cage that I had built around myself, has become the most liberating experience of my life."

Above all, throughout this phase and beyond, remember that you are not alone. Seek the resources you need and do not be afraid to ask for help. With all the potential of this phase, keep in mind that prep is positive versus worrying about the what-ifs. Remember it all can change, this phase is hypothetical—but thinking through the possibilities helps to foster your confidence, instead of a looming feeling, going in. Consider a walk-through, revisit your boundaries, and prepare thoughtful offboarding (and encourage thoughtful onboarding). But most of all, enjoy the anticipation as much as you can, a reset and brief respite before another season of change. Carve out a moment, take a picture of you at your place of work for the baby book, and take a deep breath of pride.

QUESTIONS FOR REFLECTION

> What is most important to you in offboarding? Make your checklist for what you must do, what you want to do, and as you do it, with joy not guilt, be sure to think about what you don't need to do too.
>
> Before it even happens, what are you looking most forward to in going back to work?
>
> How will you ensure that you have the mental health support in place for you postpartum?

Carry Strong Stories

CAROLINE, CHIEF OF STAFF

In all honesty, I wasn't ready to go back to work. My mind wasn't 100 percent into the business. I realized that what I was looking forward to was regaining my independence. I wanted to be able to determine what I did with my day and how I chose to spend it. I missed my freedom. That first week back was an enormous mixture of feelings. I was just being caught up on topics so didn't have much to do yet. I took advantage of that and enjoyed doing some Pilates during the day, going for short walks, reading articles online, or simply doing nothing. Objectively it was a wonderful week, yet I experienced it with such stress. I felt the pressure of needing to find my place at work but not wanting to push any harder. I felt guilty about enjoying my new freedom away from baby even though I missed him so much. I pushed myself to do things for me because I wanted to make sure I took full advantage of this moment when there weren't too many external pressures yet . . . but by doing so set myself a bar I had to reach. I couldn't understand why despite all the good things happening I was feeling so consumed, until I realized that the greatest source of pressure in my life was coming from me. . . . People will tell you often not to put too much pressure on yourself, but the problem is that you don't realize you do it. The best way to know is to make sure you are talking to someone (your partner, a friend, a sibling) so they can tell you.

SARAH MARKLE

When my husband and I got pregnant with our first child, Morgan, we had decided that I would become the stay-at-home

parent. For a variety of reasons, this made the most sense mone-
tarily and emotionally. It felt like a chapter I was excited to experience, pushed me and grew my heart and mind as an innate
nurturer, and fulfilled me in a very new, very different capacity than my previous job in pharmaceuticals. We welcomed another little girl to our family, Milly, when Morgan was two and a
half years old. And when Milly was two and a half, we added a
baby boy, Mack, to the brood. Life was full and busy, yet I remember thinking—this is it—this is going to be the chapter we
planned for—in all its messy kids/bedtime routines/toddler
music classes/kiddie park glory. During my pregnancy with
Mack, we had noticed Milly's developmental delays. We did all
the things—early intervention evaluations, developmental pedi-
atrician visits, etc. When Mack was all of three months old, our
Milly was diagnosed with autism. I remember so vividly nursing
my son as the doctor shared with us her diagnosis and the litany
of follow-ups and evaluations and orders charged to us to do for
her. More evaluations, a private school for ABA therapy forty
hours a week, related services in the form of occupational therapy, speech therapy, and so on. And I can remember acutely in
that moment thinking to myself, that timeline we had always
envisioned—carting Mack off to kindergarten and me reaccli-
mating to corporate America—would no longer be an option. I am
now a full-time advocate, coordinator, life CEO for my daughter,
Milly, with no end in sight.

   This story of mine represents a valley. I do not call it a "life
low," although rock bottom is what it felt like at the time. In hindsight it was just level one rock bottom. I wish I had known how
capable I was of handling this diagnosis and what it meant for
my family. I wish I had known that only when life is flipped completely upside down, shaken and stirred, does one realize what
they are truly made of. I wish future me was able to tell myself in
that moment that this isn't the end. There are beautiful parts to

this story you haven't even begun to see or witness that will carry you through.

JENNIFER BARRETT, AUTHOR OF *THINK LIKE A BREADWINNER* AND HEAD OF CONTENT AT FIDELITY INVESTMENTS

After my first pregnancy, I was fortunate to be able to take several months off (mostly unpaid though). I was also working on a book during leave, so I had some additional income coming in, which helped. But by my second pregnancy nearly four years later, I was the primary breadwinner for my family and in a managerial role, running a popular women's health site. I didn't think I could afford to take much maternity leave this time. I ended up taking about eleven weeks, some of it covered by leftover vacation days and (partially) through short-term disability insurance.

As I prepared to go back to work full time, I remember having to speak with the director at the preschool and day care center our oldest son was attending to get a special dispensation for our baby. They typically didn't accept infants younger than three months but agreed to make an exception since our oldest son was also there. I was grateful for that. But I didn't anticipate how difficult it would be to leave Sebastian in a nursery when he was barely eleven weeks old. He weighed just twelve pounds at the time and was less than twenty-four inches long—not much bigger than a rag doll. I could still cradle him in one arm.

I distinctly remember dropping him off that first day before heading back to work. I'd curled my hair, put on makeup and a new dress and low heels. (I was carrying him for thirteen stops on the subway in a BabyBjörn, after all, with his older brother, Zachary, in tow as well.) I had a bag packed with diapers, formula, bottles, wipes, blankets, and burp cloths on one shoulder, and a breast-pumping bag and tote bag for work on the other. I had broken a sweat by the time we arrived at the day care and preschool center, and it was the middle of winter.

When I found Sebastian's room and laid him gently in the crib with his name tag, he immediately started wailing. I remember looking down at him, writhing around in the crib. He seemed so small and vulnerable. I felt a surge of guilt. (How could I leave this tiny baby here with strangers?) I instinctively picked him up, calmed him, and put him back in the crib. And he immediately began wailing again. It was as if he knew I was leaving him. It was gut wrenching.

The lead caregiver for that room kept assuring me that he would stop crying and she would keep a close eye on him. She implored me to leave, reminding me that the longer I stayed, the harder it would be. Eventually, reluctantly I left the room. I could hear Sebastian's wailing all the way down the hall. I held it together while I passed the other rooms and checked in on our oldest son. But when I got to the stairs leading out to the street, I broke down.

I sat down in my brand-new dress on one of the steps and sobbed. I remember another mom coming by on her way out and touching me softly on the shoulder as I tried to pull myself together. "The first day is really hard," she said gently. "But it will get easier." She was right, of course. But I'll never forget that day.

PRIYANKA PATEL, MD

Our ICU was slammed with multiple COVID-19 admissions, back to back all night. I had been on my feet and awake for seventeen hours at this point. We had a patient who needed a central line (basically a big IV in his neck). He was COVID positive. I was twenty-seven weeks pregnant. It would mean I would be standing

by his head as the ventilator was breathing for him, exposing the
virus into the air and into the room, as I would do the procedure.
I walked into the room fully donned in PPE, prepped the area, and
prepared to insert the IV. Never in my life have I cried before
doing a procedure.

In medicine, we learn to compartmentalize, to separate the
strong emotions from the job and task at hand. I have cried over
patients, but this was different. I wasn't crying for the patient. I
was crying for my son. My son, who was just forming his sense of
taste and smell and sight, who had no idea that on the outside of
the warm womb he was comfortably swimming in, there was a
deadly virus that would do anything to get to him. Tears fell
down my face as I wondered, why did I choose this profession?
Why did I choose to help people when the cost was exposing my
son? Would I still be here if I knew it would cost me this?

I snapped out of my own thoughts. My intern saw the tears
quickly rolling down my face and wiped my tears for me, as I was
sterile and about to perform the procedure. It was a clear-as-day
moment of the crux of medicine and motherhood. I went into
medicine to help people, but also to provide a good life for my future children; to show them women can do anything; to show
them hard work, determination, and grit pays off in life. Never
did I think the very thing I went into for my children would possibly expose or cost me their safety.

When I think of issues or things that hold women back from
thriving in their careers, this comes to mind. Women are incredibly smart creatures, especially mothers; we are always evaluating what is the cost of a decision. As mothers we care for our
young. Prior to COVID, I knew medicine would have sacrifices,
but perhaps this brought it into a new light. Something that encouraged me as I encountered sadness, death, grief, and remorse
in the hospital was that medicine needs women. This career
needs women who are strong yet tender toward the job. Medicine

needs mothers who are fearless yet cautious. Medicine needs moms who are courageous yet aware of the costs that lay ahead of them. As crazy and difficult and sobering as this time has been, pregnancy in a pandemic as a doctor has made me more authentic, more truthful, and more understanding of those who have walked before me.

In the moment, the situation made me feel defeated. Now, it empowers me. It reminds me that I am strong; my son is strong. It reminds me that my son was with me every consult—every discussion with a family member, every COVID case, every death—he was there. Growing a life and nourishing it while working and executing the same demands as anybody else who isn't pregnant is wildly empowering. I can perform CPR and save a life, all while growing a life. Miraculous.

Conclusion

B EING A MOTHER has made me better at my job, and my job has made me a better mother. I know I am also more than the sum of these two parts, fueled by purpose. I recognize that I can do it all, not at the same time, and not alone. I know too that it isn't always obvious or easy. That "success" in achieving it all depends on how you define it.

"'Strengthen' is an attested word from Old English: strengþu, strengð, a strong feminine noun in Old English (OED). It had a sense of bodily power, vigor, and fortitude, but also a sense of moral endurance," shared contributor Jennifer Chon, head of marketing at a luxury home retailer and mother of two. Nothing is truer about motherhood, and motherhood has become a strength for all facets of my life.

While my own experience has shaped this perspective, I am grateful and humbled to have seen these sentiments reflected in the data and through the stories of incredible individuals I met in my research. Women like Elana Meyers Taylor who have helped to fuel a collective groundswell of thousands of other incredible women with their stories, proving that capability and vulnerability can be an opportunity to flip the script on working motherhood, encouraging us to Carry Strong.

Elana, who was introduced in chapter 1, is the most decorated Black athlete in Olympic Winter Games history. She is a five-time Olympic medalist, four-time Olympian, four-time World Champion, and if that wasn't enough, she has an MBA in finance, an MA in sports management, a BA, and most importantly, Elana is Nico's proud mother.

In 2020, Elana and her husband and fellow athlete, Nic, welcomed their son, Nico. Nico was born with Down syndrome and severe hearing loss and spent the first week of his life fighting to survive. While she faced a grueling year following his birth navigating the pandemic for both his care and her training, Nico renewed Elana's sense of purpose to return to the Olympics. In Beijing in 2022, despite a last-minute positive COVID-19 test that kept her in isolation from her family, who had traveled to China to be with her (and to breastfeed, which she managed with pumping and thoughtful notes), Elana made her way back to the podium twice, winning silver in the first-ever Mono-bob competition, and bronze in the two-woman competition.

Elana is an inspiration of fortitude and grace. When speaking to her, I felt inspired by every one of the principles—from her perspective to an intrinsic appreciation of balance (and lack thereof), expressed with a wise self-awareness and optimistic humility.

She shared how she makes it work. "I do it day by day. I surround myself with as much positive energy as possible." Elana has also struck a powerful chord to disrupt preconceived notions, like that of work-life balance:

> I don't know if there is any single day that's going to be clearly balanced—33 percent work, 33 percent mom, 33 percent wife—and that's freeing. It's not always a perfect percentage, but I give my most where I am. We have this preconceived notion that work-life balance is giving everything with the same attention. It's unrealistic. There are fluctuations; some days you give overtime, some days not at all, but bring your best to

*where you are. As an athlete I know that every day you can't
give 100 percent to your training, you won't be able to keep it
up physically—in fact you get stronger when you recognize
your limits. This has helped me in motherhood to set boundaries. Things inevitably spill over because we want them to, but
you must make that your decision—not others'.*

Most of all, Elana captures what really matters for all of us—and
how to get there—even when the road is long, or more appropriately,
the track is tough:

*I've been raised to always problem solve, to find a solution—in
fact, I have always gotten fired up and motivated thinking
about challenges as opportunities for solutions and know there
is value in going after our goals. But I also know now whether
you win a race or come in dead last it's part of the journey. . . .*

*Nico changed everything. I always have something on my
to-do list, I always have another goal; I have a hard time stopping to smell the roses. But with Nico, who was born with
Down syndrome and profound hearing loss, we've been forced
to slow down, but more importantly to enjoy every moment—
so much joy in every milestone. It took him a year and a half
to say "Mama" and "Dada," and it's one of my most prized moments. Being his mother has increased my gratitude and
broadened my perspective—I have so much more empathy, including for my teammates, for what we all have going on in
our lives at work and at home.*

I also asked Elana what it means to be a strong mother. She replied, "Doing the best you can to raise a kind, caring child. Doing that
day in and day out is going to require a different skillset for everyone
and for every child. It's not easy, but it's the most rewarding job anyone can ever have."

The intersection of work and life is powerful and personal. In part

I, you were encouraged to rethink the intersection of pregnancy and your career through the five principles: perspective, balance, community, communication, and identity. In part II, you applied those principles to navigate the five phases now or someday: BTTC, TTC, The Hush, The Push, and Anticipating the Great Return (or Not).

This conclusion is your call to action. While this book serves to bring visibility to our places of work and fuel our collective responsibility as a society, most of all it is about what *we* can do. While the need for policy change at the highest levels is evident, together we can continue to approach this current point of workforce pipeline attrition with pragmatic optimism. It is not impossible. Now is the time. We can normalize and celebrate becoming a working mother with an appreciation of all the many paths to get there, including our own. There is power in raising the bar on our expectations. We must change the question "Can you believe this is *still* happening?" into the statement "We can change this." This is where I started and how I was fueled while writing *Carry Strong* late at night or during my younger son's naps on the weekends.

I want you to be confident carrying this book, even if you don't have a visibly pregnant belly, comfortable at twenty-two or forty-two to ask about the maternity leave policy before you take a new role, and unafraid of gossip if you don't order a drink at happy hour, and instead to seek out and create community of support at work. I want you to be encouraged to find your voice, recognize the need to self-advocate, and embrace your strength—for you and the next generation. This is a big ask, but it's important. We are part of the solution to rethink pregnancy and work.

You are not alone in taking this on. There is a powerful momentum you have seen throughout this book: companies, advocates, and resources, created out of the need to galvanize support against being "stuck," are unconstraining women at this pivotal point in their careers to reach their full potential.

In this conclusion, along with a recent personal anecdote, I leave you several more examples of women who are doing just that. While their ambitions and impact exceeded their personal experiences, they share practical applications of the five Carry Strong principles to carry with you and perpetuate positive momentum in our places of work and for ourselves. These are reminders of both our capability and the care and attention we deserve.

PERSPECTIVE

Abbey Donnell is the founder and CEO of Work & Mother, a network of full-service lactation suites, founded and funded while pregnant with her two children. Its mission is to help companies provide a better way to support working moms—a win-win for employers and employees. Work & Mother shares that "94% of working moms at companies with lactation support programs [are retained in the back-to-work transition], compared to the national average of 59%," and reminds us that "when factoring in lost productivity, recruiting, training, and onboarding, it can cost on average more than $150,000 to replace an experienced employee."[1]

Abbey offers simple yet powerful advice that can keep women on the path of permanent change without carrying the burden: "I always encourage people, instead of asking *if* an employer has a mother's room, ask *where* it is. The burden isn't on the mom. Don't ask *if* they have benefits, ask them to explain what they are. This simple change of wording takes it from something women carry to something that is required of the employer to own it, shift the fear to expectation. This is something that anyone can do—future moms, dads, coworkers; it's a nuance, but it has an impact."

This is an example of both perspective and normalization at its best, a starting point to change expectations for ourselves and others through using our collective voices in the workplace, with the purview including understanding and exceeding the caregiving expectations of our future workforce.

BALANCE

In the past year, I have been fortunate to experience a shift to permanently working from home up to two days a week. This means I am much more likely to have drop-offs for school, dinner, bath time, and just be physically present when my sons come home and say hello. With the ultimate work-life fluidity I can go straight from the bus stop into a meeting ten minutes later. It is a gift.

One week last fall, for the first time in two years, I was in the office for a full week when we had international visitors. Monday morning, I distinctly remember driving toward my office building on the West Side Highway, passing the New York skyline with my well-prepared meeting notes in my hands. I had our presentation created by an amazing high-performance team on my laptop and I was wearing a new dress. I was bursting with pride and ready to embrace giving my work my full focus on the sliding scale of work to life—and to enjoy it. I had dreamed of this feeling. I knew how lucky I was, that it was rare and to be savored—the opportunity and the privilege of having the feeling of effort realized and the system in place do it while being the mother of two small children.

That week there were endorphins pumping from great work (and results), an engaged team, a buzz of in-person connection, but later that week I missed my kids more than I do when I'm on a long business trip. They were long days, and so despite being in the same city I missed my boys waking up and going to sleep every night for four days in a row. By Thursday, I was toast and had a silent meltdown at my desk.

When I'm away for work, I mentally know I'm away—I acknowledge with my family that I'm going away, that I'm going to both miss them and enjoy that my work allows me the opportunity to meet people and experience cultures other than ours. It fills up my adventure and independence reservoirs too. I also promise treats. But this time, I was home, I was just not there, and when I finally was, I would be exhausted but would need to shift gears to embrace my shared family responsibilities and, in fact, relieve the strains on my husband compounded by my time away. One team member could see I was hitting a wall and asked why. I told them that the breaking point was that William had left a note on my toothbrush the night before "so I would be sure to see it." It said, "I miss you. Come back."

But as I said it out loud to her, something clicked. I stopped what I was doing, I FaceTimed the boys and walked them briefly around the office, showing them the big windows and all my teammates, who waved. How proud I was, but how much I missed them, and I wanted to them to know they were on my mind when the sun came through those same windows. They were amazed at how many computers were in one room and at the stacks of paper. They asked me to bring some home to color. With a big smile I hung up and I released the tears (I have them in my eyes now while writing this); so did my colleagues.

People at work know I have kids. I talk about the good and the hard, not all the time, but I hope enough for anyone who has them or who may want to have children someday to feel comfortable. I didn't always feel comfortable myself, but now from the combination of getting used to being a working mom, my environment, and my role in it, I do. In fact, I feel a responsibility to overindex this openness while also respecting the reality that so many people have their own private struggles on the road to motherhood and have many other major commitments and interests beyond work and family. But for me, it's also been important to "work out loud" with my kids. They know I have a job that I love with people I respect. They know it provides for us, but also that it makes me feel good. It's another way of thinking about balance, turning the tables.

Callan Blount Fleming, who we met in chapter 5, shares, "It would be transformational if we could create workplace cultures where caregiving is valued, and people feel comfortable parenting 'out loud.' If you are comfortable, be a parent who parents out loud at work. If you aren't, support those who are. Be affirming. Encourage your

places of work to engage and empower—to give space. It's about creating space for you as an individual, for communities, and it's about
communication. In the workplace we can change the conversation,
including for pregnancy and work, when we find our voice and when
we listen."

That moment on the highway and that moment in the office both
carry so much weight in my recent memory. The world of work has
been disrupted dramatically, and we have an opportunity to seize
this moment to redefine it, including for working mothers. You can do
it all, not at the same time, and not alone.

COMMUNITY

Lauren A. Tetenbaum is an advocate and therapist certified in perinatal mental health who was introduced in chapter 5. Lauren, a first-
generation Cuban American, pursued her MSW and JD simultaneously
and spent a decade in the legal industry. Today she facilitates support
groups for working, new, and aspiring parents, and provides consulting
and mental health coaching to support parents in corporate settings.

Lauren says, "When I had my first child, I was working in big
law, working well past midnight at the office even with an infant at
home. It wasn't sustainable. I shifted into a new role, which included
coaching expecting and new parent lawyers. I was living it while supporting others. Shortly before I got pregnant with my second child, I
led an initiative to change the staff parental leave policy at the firm.
Then the pandemic erased our village. We were alone without childcare or school or support, but the workplace, though remote, seemed
unchanged. I knew I wasn't the only one feeling like this, and I was
inspired to make a difference. I had my license as a social worker, so
I decided to do additional training in perinatal mental health to best
work as a therapist for vulnerable moms."

Lauren now offers coaching and therapy to young women beginning to navigate the workplace and to new and aspiring working parents. She continues, "Personally and professionally, I'm living the ins

and outs of being a young, ambitious woman, of being a mother of young kids who wants to have a thriving career and a fulfilling personal life. I went from feeling lost to recognizing my strengths, and with my effort, education, and drive, I found a path that I knew could help others. I know that not everyone is comfortable speaking up, but I also know that I hold a lot of privileges and in turn have a responsibility to use my voice. If those of us who do have that voice don't use it, we will all suffer in silence. It starts with sharing. We are not alone. We can do so much together as a community to create positive change."

What women want at work is so visible in this window that it creates a moment of impact. Flexibility that includes time protection and respect with autonomy are critical, not optional. Resources and benefits gain extra focus, activated and utilized. What else? They want clear expectations and recognition of their efforts, and they want open, responsible, and engaged colleagues and leaders who model flexibility, expectations, and recognition as well, and who foster a culture of empathy and do not tolerate discriminatory behavior. You are current and future leaders of your places of work and can impact change in a way that sticks and attracts employees who will align with these values to continue their momentum during their pregnancy and beyond. It is a shared responsibility to create the future in big ways and in small.

I was inspired in writing this conclusion by the following words of Kim Buisson, cofounder of Whooden/Studios, executive coach, and mother of two under three. Kim shares, "My hope is that we can all feel that every time we support a mother, we are supporting the well-being of our entire community. Clearly, the idea of survival of the fittest is a dangerous patriarchal concept that is pitting us against one another and robbing us of the magic that comes when we honor our interdependence. Let's all lean in to the survival of the collaborative: one's healing journey heals all of us. When given the chance, give what you wish you had received, and pay forward everything you were given."

Christy Turlington Burns reflected, "When I was pregnant, I had my own business, I could bring my child to work whenever I needed to, for feedings or just to visit. I could do that openly and freely. Now, as a leader of a nonprofit that centers on mothers, I recognize how important that is to model and to support others to do the same. After ten years with Every Mother Counts, we are advocating for all the things that will improve the experience of the mother, from pregnancy through postpartum. Postpartum is forever for a woman health- and well-being-wise."

Each action in our many places of work and each story told represents both the power of the collective community and the unique responsibility of us all as individuals. However, in turn, especially during pregnancy, our well-being is critical. Hyperaware, we know that everything we do we are doing times two (or more). We literally can't take care of anyone (and we certainly can't start a movement) if we don't take care of ourselves first. Your health and the health of your baby is priority number one. At work, this includes freeing ourselves from judgment and recognizing the importance of self-care and advocacy through communication.

COMMUNICATION

While baby bumps have become proud fashion celebrations, public figures often embracing their bold statements of ultimate femininity, Jourdan Dunn, mother, model, actress, and philanthropist whose community-building advice you read about in chapter 3, was one of the brave and inspiring first.

"When it was announced that I was pregnant," she recounts, "I remember reading the 'fashion forum' and seeing the thread title, 'Jourdan Dunn is Done.' People were saying I was over, that 'another one bites the dust.' Even my peers and casting directors were part of it—the same ones who would later say how much they missed me and that I was 'better than ever' after Riley was born. This was tough. Especially at eighteen years old. But again, I was resolute. I knew what I wanted and that I would make it work."

Eight months pregnant, Jourdan got a call to walk the Jean Paul Gaultier runway. She recognized the gravity was bigger than fashion. "I was shocked," she said. "I went from not feeling that the industry was behind me to knowing I was going to be in front of it. I knew it was going to be a moment. That I was going to feel exposed. Jean Paul Gaultier made me feel safe and celebrated, confident. The reception when I stepped onto the runway was amazing, and I didn't care what was going to be said after. I owned that moment. I knew I could show my son. No one could ever take that away from me. I felt so vulnerable but so powerful."

I said to Jourdan, "You were taking on the responsibility for others to have pride no matter the circumstances of their pregnancies." She responded, "I was carrying it."

Jourdan added, "Pregnancy changed my need to be validated by others. Even after having my son, I still feel those moments of judgment, but I don't sweat them—I don't worry about people who don't know me; they need to worry about loving themselves."

The unburdening of the judgment of others is something so many women reflected on overcoming during pregnancy, especially at work. While in the first part of this conclusion I encouraged you to be part of the solution, the other blocker that can get in the way is often intrinsic. Guilt creeps in, both in expectations of how we want to show up to others and in truly doing what we want to do for us, or what we need. This is your reminder that self-care is not selfish. Pregnancy is an obvious example, because each decision is not just about you, but it's always true. Self-care is selfless.

IDENTITY

While I have sought to flip the script on a cultural constant with pregnancy and work throughout this book to shift your perspective, Eve Rodsky is turning on all the lights to shine brightly on another key point of attrition in the pipeline, invisible labor, and to give us all the space we need to be who we are—as we both change and stay very much who we are.

Eve is the author of the bestselling books *Fair Play* and *Find Your Unicorn Space*, runs the Philanthropy Advisory Group to advise high-net-worth families and charitable foundations, and is a mother of three. Eve often shares a story about how one of her inspirations for writing her first book, *Fair Play*, was the moment when despite "killing it in business and in life together," her husband texted her "I'm surprised you didn't get blueberries." She pulled over to the side of the road with the overwhelming weight of being the default for her household's needs and letting something drop, even as small as blueberries for a smoothie. She knew something had to change, not just for her, but in the greater context of omnipresent unpaid labor, an invisible tether holding women back.

"There is a narrative that we have been told when we are younger, educated and aspiring to greatness, that we can shoot for the moon," Eve shared with me. "I thought I could be in the White House by day and a Knicks City Dancer by night. I would jet between the two because of my capability. This is a time before the impending doom of unpaid labor, $10.9 trillion globally, $1.5 trillion in the U.S. alone, a dirty secret that's good for society and terrible to the people that have to do it.[2] Then it hits you—the impact of both unfair expectations and a loss of self."

Eve further reflected about the moment of the "blueberry debacle." She told me there was something else that happened to her right around this time. "I was at an event for my son's nursery school. Our name tags had the names of our children, so mine said, 'Zach's mom.' The teacher said, 'Look around, these women will become your best friends.' And I thought, but they don't even know my name."

This intersection of time and identity is illustrative during pregnancy, including at work, and comes full circle back to chapter 1. It is so important that through this final contributor's advice you recognize your capacity because of your capability, the top of the pyramid you read about in chapter 3, by unconstraining yourself while you find yourself. Eve has three big lessons for us: 1) time is finite; 2) there's power in being unavailable; and 3) protect your unicorn space.

First, Eve highlights time as a key message in *Fair Play*: "Redefine time. All time is equal. With this ensure you keep in mind that there are no studies supporting the notion that women are inherently better multitaskers or have better executive brain function, and yet this message is pervasive." For pre-pregnancy, during, and of course post-pregnancy, you must realize that right now, you have finite time, just like any other phase of your life. Eve says, "During pregnancy and with a newborn, at the end of the day my biggest regret was filling my brain with unnecessary information and time in that precious moment. Recognize your seasons."

As you read throughout part II, the gear shift—down or up—is not bad. It is reality, and the recognition is a good thing. Eve adds, "The power of motherhood is that it allows you—if you let it—to bring so much more clarity to your life, because if you're going to be away from your children, or from any other priority in your life in that moment, then it better be important to you." And I will add, and you will make it count.

Second, in making every moment count, you need time to be unavailable. Eve has reframed this to claim it for all of us:

> The permission to be unavailable is the secret formula—switching yourself from your roles to your values. In addition, if I name myself as an author, activist, and attorney it's easier for me to carve my time out to write. . . . Eve is a holistic person, and then it didn't feel so bad to carve that time out to be unavailable. If it was just mom on a name tag, then Zach's mom isn't with her family on the weekend. It is how I got unstuck; it's the power of naming.

Third, something else that Eve has given a name to in her two books is Unicorn Space. Women throughout this project have shared a common fear of deprioritizing themselves by force with the addition of their new role as mother. "I define Unicorn Space as creative, magical space necessary to develop and pursue your passions," says Eve, "but, like the mythical equine, it doesn't f*cking exist—until you discover or reclaim it. And at its core, it's about the magic and joy of being you and sharing it with the world. Being a mother or father is extremely meaningful and yet there can be more."

These concepts don't have to be giant uphill battles as you take on this exciting life change. I remember the best advice I had from a friend on my maternity leave was to do one thing a day. This could be a walk with the stroller or having a friend visit, not because you need to do more but because just doing one thing helps you to do less while reminding you of your sense of self. For whatever phase of the journey to working motherhood you are in when you are reading this particular page, you need time and space—including real "unicorn space." My "third shift" (or maybe fourth some days) became a fuel for other parts of my life—creativity, purpose, joy, all fueling my capacity and recognizing my capability—and who I am today.

Eve adds, "Motherhood for me is a heroine's journey. The idea of being only defined as Zach's mother for a period of time was the pinnacle. Then I became the phoenix from the ashes. The beauty of watching myself die a death and be reborn in a way that I will forever be connected with women all over the world in a role that is defining but doesn't define me. It is a redemptive arch, a challenge far different than that of the hero's, one where you realize that you were where you needed to be and that you wouldn't be able to go where you want to go without it. A hero's journey is one where they leave for a conquest. The heroine is connected to others, but in that finds herself."

Women I spoke with throughout my research felt the pull of being very much the same person and different at the same time, mourning the shift in the moment, but then celebrating a rebirth. Eve put it perfectly when she said, "I always liked the remix of popular songs better anyway." Consider this the potential for you, wherever you are in the timeline. An opportunity for a remix, one that maybe you couldn't even have imagined before it happens.

Perspective, balance, community, communication, and identity—apply these principles in and beyond the five phases, and most of all pass them on. Flipping the script on a cultural constant is recognition of the challenges, but also the benefits, of working motherhood, which have made it possible for me to share this book with you.

Personally, motherhood has brought me the combination of increased capabilities, including efficiency and empathy. I better maximize my time and prioritize because I have to, but also because I want to even more than I did before children. I have more focus and I remain calmer under pressure, grounded when it comes to what matters for myself and for my teammates regardless of whether they have children. This means I can promote a better work-life fluidity, although I recognize that it's something I can work on. They daily cycle of what I do during the day, at work and at home, is fueled by my own drive, which includes how I show up for my kids and how I provide for them. I now recognize that burning myself out to do it all for them (or for myself) isn't good for anyone. Motherhood has redefined who I am, while I have very much stayed the same.

Unburden your confidence, broaden your perspective, and unlock potential for your journey to working motherhood and through it. Experience your capability and your vulnerability in this moment as an opportunity to Carry Strong. Remember, pregnancy is work, but as a working mother-to-be it isn't your only job. As you build your career, you're considering so much more than "how to tell your boss you're pregnant." Pregnancy at work is not just a milestone, it is monumental. This importance is something to recognize, to normalize, and to celebrate—for you and for all of us.

Acknowledgments

I CANNOT LIST all the incredible people who have made this book a reality. All the people who, when I asked for help, time, energy, and very personal stories and hard-earned expertise shared it without a question. People who I have known nearly my entire life, and others who I have just met or only have admired from afar, whom I sent a note to, and they simply said yes. United by the ambition to make a positive impact for working mothers and mothers-to-be they motivated me to continue with this living project when I wasn't sure I could *and* celebrated with me when I did. I vividly remember running around the house cheering after some conversations and tears streaming down my face with others because of profound respect and gratitude.

There are women in this book who truly went above and beyond. Sarah, who inspired me to conduct the quantitative studies concurrent to the interviews and is a treasured mentor. Caitlin, Kimberly, Sarah, Aya, Annie, Abigail, Windsor, Lauren, and Claudia, who over three years shared their powerful expertise and friendship. My sister, Melissa, who has always inspired me to be the best big sister I can be, for her, but often even more for others. Dasha (and her daughter Boden Mae), Kate, Katie, Laura, Caroline, LaShãda, Julie, Stephanie, Alison, Chitra, Jenn, Amy, Joan, and Molly, who are friends first but have been incredible resources for this book and throughout my life, particularly as a working mother. While their names grace the pages, often more than once, others were powerful forces behind the scenes. It takes a village to be a working mother, which for me has lovingly included caregivers, Marie, Hannah, and Wilene. This also includes the team at ECI (Evaluative Criteria, Inc.), including Jason, Rachel, and Lauren, who conducted and analyzed my four studies; and my earliest readers, including Samantha, Zoe, and several incredible women who privately read this book in the BTTC, TTC, and The Hush of their pregnancies while so much more was on their minds. Thank you to my own physician, Dr. Kelly Greening, and her incredible team of nurses and office staff, who cared for me throughout my journey to motherhood and the birth of my sons. Thank you to members of my own board of directors, including Ann, Stephen, Adina, Amy, Stephane, and Colin (and my nieces Ginny and Sadie), and the amazing leaders and team members I have worked with at Chanel and L'Oréal, where I am so grateful to work today.

Duvall Osteen, thank you for taking my FaceTime while you were breastfeeding Wilds and championing this book while pregnant with Shields; I am so grateful that you became my agent and so much more. I can't capture how much you mean to me. To my incredible and tireless editor, Nina Rodríguez-Marty, who guided me with fortitude and grace, and to Meg Leder, whom I trust implicitly, and the entire Penguin Life team, thank you for your vision and partnership because you believed in this book, and humbly, in me. Lydia Hirt, Shelby Meizlik, Kate Stark, Alex Cruz-Jimenez, Sabrina Bowers, Elizabeth Yaffe, and Jane Cavolina, thank you. You have brought this book to life, with the energy that I dreamed would vibrate through those who touched it.

Most of all thank you to my husband, Cooper, and my two sons, William and James, whose experience with me in becoming and being a working mother would have been impossible without, and who have proudly supported my writing, mostly during naps and after bedtime, but sometimes at a sacrifice to all three of them. Finally, thank you to my own mother, Sue, who is not only a working mom and now a working Nana, but an incredible selfless force for good. Without her this book would not have been possible.

I believe, with my whole head, heart, and gut, that you truly can do it all, not at the same time, and absolutely not alone.

Notes

INTRODUCTION

1. Carry Strong® Evaluative Criteria, Inc. (ECI) study of 400 U.S. noncon-forming/women 18–50 who worked as full-time employees while pregnant, in non-primarily-manual-labor-intensive positions, informed employer/ place of work about pregnancy, conducted 8/2020–9/2020.
2. Elena Lytkina Botelho, Kim Rosenkoetter Powell, Stephen Kincaid, and Dina Wang, "What Sets Successful CEOs Apart," *Harvard Business Review*, July 18, 2017, https://hbr.org/2017/05/what-sets-successful-ceos -apart.
3. Tara Law, "Women Are Now the Majority of the U.S. Workforce—But Working Women Still Face Serious Challenges," *Time*, January 16, 2020, https://time.com/5766787/women-workforce/.
4. Bourree Lam, "Yes, There Really Are More Pregnant Women at the Of-fice," *The Atlantic*, April 8, 2015, https://www.theatlantic.com/business/ar chive/2015/04/yes-there-really-are-more-pregnant-women-at-the-office /389763/.
5. George Gao and Gretchen Livingston, "Working While Pregnant Is Much More Common Than It Used to Be," Pew Research Center, March 31, 2015, https://www.pewresearch.org/fact-tank/2015/03/31/working-while -pregnant-is-much-more-common-than-it-used-to-be/.
6. Jonathan Maze, "Millennials Are Becoming Parents, and That Has Big Im-plications for Restaurants," *Restaurant Business*, June 27, 2018, https:// www.restaurantbusinessonline.com/financing/millennials-are-becoming -parents-has-big-implications-restaurants.
7. Claire Ewing-Nelson and Jasmine Tucker, "A Year into the Pandemic, Women Are Still Short Nearly 5.1 Million Jobs," National Women's Law Cen-ter, Fact Sheet, March 5, 2021, https://nwlc.org/resources/feb-jobs-2021/.
8. Morgan Smith, "More Than 200,000 Women Joined the Labor Force in March: 'We're Heading in the Right Direction,'" CNBC, April 1, 2022,

https://www.cnbc.com/2022/04/01/more-than-200000-women-joined-the-labor-force-in-march-2022.html.

9. Gretchen Livingston and Deja Thomas, "Among 41 Countries, Only U.S. Lacks Paid Parental Leave," Pew Research Center, December 16, 2019, https://www.pewresearch.org/fact-tank/2019/12/16/u-s-lacks-mandated-paid-parental-leave/.

10. Lam, "Yes, There Really Are More Pregnant Women at the Office."

11. Matthias Krapf, Heinrich W. Ursprung, and Christian Zimmermann, "Parenthood and Productivity of Highly Skilled Labor: Evidence from the Groves of Academe," Federal Reserve Bank of St. Louis Working Paper 2014-001, https://doi.org/10.20955/wp.2014.001.

12. Carry Strong® 2021 Evaluative Criteria, Inc. (ECI) study of 150 U.S. current college-age non-conforming/women without children.

13. Carry Strong® Evaluative Criteria, Inc. (ECI) study of four hundred U.S. nonconforming/women 18-50.

CHAPTER 1. Perspective: Reframing Your Reality with a Paradigm Shift

1. Alexandra Sacks, "Reframing 'Mommy Brain,'" *New York Times*, May 11, 2018, https://www.nytimes.com/2018/05/11/well/family/reframing-mommy-brain.html.

2. Carry Strong® 2021 Evaluative Criteria, Inc. (ECI) study of 150 U.S. current college-age non-conforming/women without children.

3. Madison Marriage, "'Pregnancy Is Still a Career Killer,'" *Financial Times*, November 29, 2014, https://www.ft.com/content/59a36f32-7565-11e4-a1a9-00144feabdc0.

4. Carry Strong® 2021 Evaluative Criteria, Inc. (ECI) study of 150 U.S. current college-age non-conforming/women without children.

5. "Employed Persons by Detailed Occupation and Age," U.S. Bureau of Labor Statistics, January 20, 2022, https://www.bls.gov/cps/cpsaat11b.htm.

6. Quoctrung Bui and Claire Cain Miller, "The Age That Women Have Babies: How a Gap Divides America," *New York Times*, August 4, 2018, https://www.nytimes.com/interactive/2018/08/04/upshot/up-birth-age-gap.html.

7. National Center for Education Statistics, "Characteristics of Public School Teachers," Condition of Education, U.S. Department of Education, Institute of Education Sciences, 2022 https://nces.ed.gov/programs/coe/indicator/clr.

8. "Active Physicians by Sex and Specialty, 2017," Association of American Medical Colleges, December 2017, https://www.aamc.org/data-reports/workforce/interactive-data/active-physicians-sex-and-specialty-2017.

9. "Women and Leadership Public Says Women are Equally Qualified, but Barriers Persist," Pew Research Center, January 14, 2015, https://www.pewresearch.org/social-trends/2015/01/14/women-and-leadership/.

10. Shelley J. Correll, Stephen Benard, and In Paik, "Getting a Job: Is There a Motherhood Penalty?" *American Journal of Sociology* 112, no. 5 (March 2007): 1297-1338, https://doi.org/10.1086/511799.

11. Carry Strong® 2021 Evaluative Criteria, Inc. (ECI) study of 150 U.S. current college-age non-conforming/women without children.

12. Claire Cain Miller, "Mounting Evidence of Advantages for Children of Working Mothers," *New York Times*, May 15, 2015, https://www.nytimes.com/2015/05/17/upshot/mounting-evidence-of-some-advantages-for-children-of-working-mothers.html?_r=0.

13. Susan Kelemen Gardin and Gary A. Richwald, "Pregnancy and Employment Leave: Legal Precedents and Future Policy." *Journal of Public Health Policy* 7, no. 4 (Winter 1986): 458-69, https://www.jstor.org/stable/3342235.

14. Courtni E. Molnar, "'Has the Millennium Yet Dawned?': A History of Attitudes Toward Pregnant Workers in America," *Michigan Journal of Gender and Law* 12 (2005): 163, https://repository.law.umich.edu/mjgl/vol12/iss1/4.

15. Chloe Schama, "Ruth Bader Ginsburg: Hero for Pregnant Women," *Elle*, November 5, 2015, https://www.elle.com/culture/career-politics/news/a31721/ruth-bader-ginsburg-hero-for-pregnant-women/.

16. "Pregnancy Discrimination Charges FY 2010—FY 2021," U.S. Equal Employment Opportunity Commission, https://www.eeoc.gov/data/pregnancy-discrimination-charges-fy-2010-fy-2021.

17. "Fighting for Overdue Protections for Pregnant Workers," *CBS Sunday Morning*, January 12, 2020, https://www.cbsnews.com/news/fighting-for-overdue-protections-for-pregnant-workers-pregnant-workers-fairness-act/.

18. Alexander V. Bulgakov et al., "Specific Features of Psycho-Emotional States of Working Women During Pregnancy," *Electronic Journal of General Medicine* 15, no. 6 (2018): em86, https://doi.org/10.29333/ejgm/99829.

19. Carry Strong® Evaluative Criteria, Inc. (ECI) study of 400 U.S. nonconforming/women 18-50 who worked as full-time employees while pregnant, in non-primarily manual-labor-intensive positions, informed employer/place of work about pregnancy, conducted 8/2020-9/2020.

20. Matthias Krapf, Heinrich W. Ursprung, and Christian Zimmermann, "Parenthood and Productivity of Highly Skilled Labor: Evidence from the Groves of Academe," *Journal of Economic Behavior & Organization* 140 (2017): 147-75, https://doi.org/10.1016/j.jebo.2017.05.010.

21. Carry Strong® Evaluative Criteria, Inc. (ECI) study of 400 U.S. nonconforming/women 18-50.

CHAPTER 2. Balance: Deciding to Have It All, Just Not at the Same Time

1. Carry Strong® 2021 Evaluative Criteria, Inc. (ECI) of 150 U.S. current college-age non-conforming/women without children.

CHAPTER 3. Community: Choosing the Company You Keep

1. Carry Strong® 2021 Evaluative Criteria, Inc. (ECI) study of 400 U.S. non-conforming/women 18–50 who worked as full-time employees while pregnant, in non-primarily manual-labor-intensive positions, informed employer/place of work about pregnancy, conducted 8/2020–9/2020.
2. La Leche League International, https://www.llli.org/.

CHAPTER 4. Communication: Creating Confident and Comfortable Conversations

1. Carry Strong® 2021 Evaluative Criteria, Inc. (ECI) study of 400 U.S. non-conforming/women 18–50 who worked as full-time employees while pregnant, in non-primarily manual-labor-intensive positions, informed employer/place of work about pregnancy, conducted 8/2020–9/2020.
2. W. Christopher Musselwhite and Robyn D. Ingram, *Change Style Indicator* (San Francisco: Jossey-Bass/Pfeiffer, 1998).
3. "Fact Sheet: Pregnancy Discrimination," U.S. Equal Employment Opportunity Commission, https://www.eeoc.gov/pregnancy-discrimination.
4. This technical-assistance document was issued upon approval of the chair of the U.S. Equal Employment Opportunity Commission, "Fact Sheet: Pregnancy Discrimination."
5. "Fact Sheet: Pregnancy Discrimination."

CHAPTER 5. Identity

1. Arianna Taboada, *The Expecting Entrepreneur: A Guide to Parental Leave Planning for Self Employed Business Owners* (self-published, 2021).
2. Christie Hunter Arscott, *Begin Boldly: How Women Can Reimagine Risk, Embrace Uncertainty, and Launch a Brilliant Career* (Oakland, CA: Berrett-Koehler Publishers, 2022); www.tendlab.com.

CHAPTER 6. Phase I: BTTC: Before Trying to Conceive

1. "Percentage of Childless Women in the United States in 2018, by Age" Statista, https://www.statista.com/statistics/241535/percentage-of-child less-women-in-the-us-by-age/.

2. Jessica Soffer, XinYi Wang, Jack Ferber, Tak Ishikawa, "Carry Strong® Analysis of Pregnancy & Work at the University Level" BCOM 329: Social Media and the Changing Nature of Business Communication.

3. Carry Strong® 2021 Evaluative Criteria, Inc. (ECI) study of 150 U.S. current college-age non-conforming/women without children (Study 2), Carry Strong® 2021 Evaluative Criteria, Inc. (ECI) study of 150 U.S. current college-age nonconforming/men without children (Study 3).

4. "Planning for Pregnancy," Centers for Disease Control and Prevention, last reviewed September 20, 2022, https://www.cdc.gov/preconception /planning.html.

CHAPTER 7. Phase II: TTC: Trying to Conceive

1. Carry Strong® 2021 Evaluative Criteria, Inc. (ECI) study of 400 U.S. non-conforming/women 18–50 who worked as full-time employees while pregnant, in non-primarily-manual-labor-intensive positions, informed employer/place of work about pregnancy, conducted 8/2020–9/2020.

2. "Infertility: Symptoms, Treatment, Diagnosis," UCLA Health, https://www .uclahealth.org/medical-services/obgyn/conditions-treated/infertility.

CHAPTER 8. Phase III: The Hush

1. Carry Strong® 2021 Evaluative Criteria, Inc. (ECI) study of 400 U.S. non-conforming/women 18–50 who worked as full-time employees while pregnant, in non-primarily-manual-labor-intensive positions, informed employer/place of work about pregnancy, conducted 8/2020–9/2020.

2. Joanna L. Grossman and Gillian L. Thomas, "Making Pregnancy Work: Overcoming the Pregnancy Discrimination Act's Capacity-Based Model," *Yale Journal of Law & Feminism* 15 (2009), https://scholarlycommons .law.hofstra.edu/faculty_scholarship/101.

3. Emily Porschitz and Elizabeth Siler, "Miscarriage in the Workplace: An Autoethnography," *Gender, Work & Organization* 24, no. 6 (2017): 565–78.

CHAPTER 9. Phase IV: The Push

1. Carry Strong® 2021 Evaluative Criteria, Inc. (ECI) study of 400 U.S. non-conforming/women 18–50 who worked as full-time employees while pregnant, in non-primarily-manual-labor-intensive positions, informed employer/place of work about pregnancy, conducted 8/2020–9/2020.

2. W. Christopher Musselwhite and Robyn D. Ingram, *Change Style Indicator* (San Francisco: Jossey-Bass/Pfeiffer, 1998).

CHAPTER 10. **Phase V: Anticipating the Great Return (or Not)**

1. "Pregnancy Discrimination and Pregnancy-Related Disability Discrimination," U.S. Equal Employment Opportunity Commission, https://www.eeoc.gov/pregnancy-discrimination.

2. "Family and Medical Leave (FMLA)," U.S. Department of Labor, https://www.dol.gov/general/topic/benefits-leave/fmla.

3. Alicia Adamczyk, "There's Still No Paid Leave for US Workers—but Advocates Aren't Giving Up," CNBC, November 3, 2021, https://www.cnbc.com/2021/11/03/still-no-paid-leave-for-us-workers.html.

4. Amy Nelson, "The Politics of Breastfeeding (and Why It Must Change)," *Forbes*, October 24, 2018, https://www.forbes.com/sites/amynelson1/2018/10/24/the-politics-of-breastfeeding-and-why-it-must-change/?sh=2b6f99033163.

5. Carry Strong® 2021 Evaluative Criteria, Inc. (ECI) study of 400 U.S. nonconforming/women 18–50 who worked as full-time employees while pregnant, in non-primarily manual-labor-intensive positions, informed employer/place of work about pregnancy conducted 8/2020–9/2020.

6. Carry Strong® 2021 Evaluative Criteria, Inc. (ECI) study of 400 U.S. nonconforming/women 18–50 who worked as full-time employees while pregnant, in non-primarily manual-labor-intensive positions, informed employer/place of work about pregnancy, conducted 8/2020–9/2020.

7. B. L. Bauman et al., "*Vital Signs*: Postpartum Depressive Symptoms and Provider Discussions About Perinatal Depression—United States, 2018," *Morbidity and Mortality Weekly Report* 69, no. 19 (2020): 575–81, https://doi.org/10.15585/mmwr.mm6919a2.

8. Kimberly Langdon, "Statistics on Postpartum Depression," Postpartum Depression.org, March 21, 2022, https://www.postpartumdepression.org/resources/statistics/.

9. University of California, San Francisco Family Health Outcomes Project, https://fhop.ucsf.edu/.

10. "Special Delivery: A Unique Support Program for Expectant and New Moms," Check On Mom https://www.mycheckonmom.com/.

CONCLUSION

1. Work & Mother, https://www.workandmother.com/for-employers/.

2. Gus Wezerek and Kristen R. Ghodsee, "Women's Unpaid Labor Is Worth $10,900,000,000,000," *New York Times*, March 5, 2020, https://www.nytimes.com/interactive/2020/03/04/opinion/women-unpaid-labor.html.